Great Expectations

*To Doug & Becky,
with good expectations
and many thanks,
[signature]*

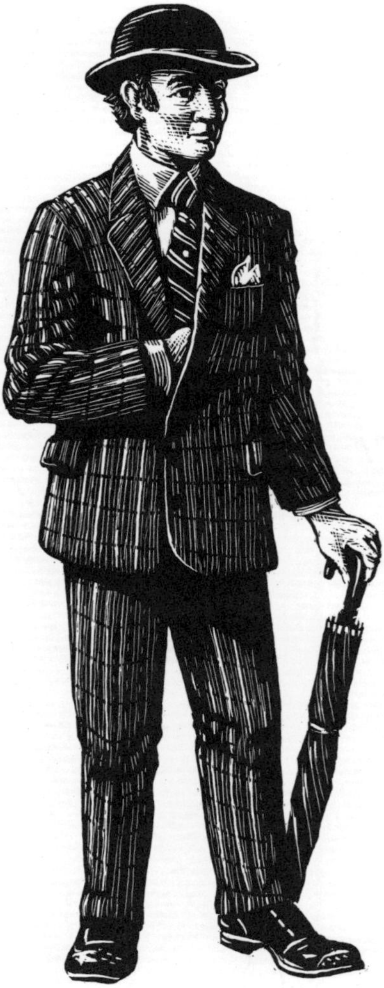

Grant C. Robinson, FCA
Great Expectations

———

A Survival Manual for the Canadian Entrepreneur
at the Dawn of the New Millennium

❁

VOLUME ONE

'The Entrepreneur's Fantasy'

❁

The Porcupine's Quill

CANADIAN CATALOGUING IN PUBLICATION DATA

Robinson, Grant C., 1953 –
Great expectations: a survival manual for the Canadian entrepreneur at the dawn of the new millennium

Contents: v. 1. The entrepreneur's fantasy.
ISBN 0-88984-206-X (v. 1)

1. Title.

PS8585.O351624G73 2000   C813'.6   C00-931100-9
PR9199.3.R5336G73 2000

Copyright © Grant C. Robinson, FCA, CFP, 2000.

Published by The Porcupine's Quill,
68 Main Street, Erin, Ontario N0B 1T0.
Readied for the press by John Metcalf; copy edited by Doris Cowan.
Typeset in Ehrhardt, printed on Zephyr Antique laid,
and bound at The Porcupine's Quill Inc.

This is a work of fiction. Any resemblance of characters to persons, living or dead, is purely coincidental.

The cover image – the Alhambra Palace in Granada, Spain –
is after a photograph by Jennifer Dickson, RA.
Interior illustrations are scratchboards by Wesley W. Bates.

Represented in Canada by the Literary Press Group.
Trade orders are available from General Distribution Services.

We acknowledge the support of the Ontario Arts Council, and the Canada Council for the Arts for our publishing program. The financial support of the Government of Canada through the Book Publishing Industry Development Program is also gratefully acknowledged.

1 2 3 4 · 02 01 00

Canada

Contents

Foreword 7

1. The Enigmatic Mr Bowles 11

2. Galen Nicholas Aldebaan 37

3. Philippe LeBoubon 63

4. Will Duckworth 93

5. Jayne Beauregard & Co. 119

6. The Horseshoe Inn 147

7. Dominion Lumber 179

8. S.M. Eleña de Compostela 209

9. Hessen Atlantic 241

Foreword

June 1977. The summer after I completed my CA, my wife Sheila and I emigrated to Bermuda on the pretext that I would continue my studies under the tutelage of Morris & Kempe.

The tennis was great, the Fuzzy Navels tolerable, but it wasn't long before Sheila and I came to the realization that living on an island could be idyllic – provided one had the wherewithal to get off the island. And provided one had the wit to use the wherewithal, and was disposed to debit the wit and expense the wherewithal at least once each fiscal quarter.

The tennis took a decided turn south towards the end of December when two of the natives were executed by hanging in Hamilton for the assassination of an ex-governor. There were riots in the streets. Breaking glass. And downdraft from Bell 212 helicopters on patrol over the doubles courts.

Sheila and I beat a retreat to the safety of Southwestern Ontario at the first opportunity, but before we left Hamilton I did get to meet the very famous Galen Nicholas Aldebaan – just the once, at a reception at the Royal Bermuda Yacht Club. Aldebaan and his wife were both accomplished sailors who had more than twice loosed their stays in Chignecto Bay and found a slip in Hamilton Harbour. His wife, apparently, had graduated from high school in New Brunswick.

Aldebaan and I talked about Canada.

Investment opportunities.

Aldebaan himself was a striking man. Tall, and tanned, and sartorially resplendent in military khakis, knee socks, tailored shorts and a safari shirt that sported button-down epaulets. The kind of man you would remember if you saw him a second time but I never did see him again in Bermuda, and I never met him once in Canada, though for a time in the mid-eighties Aldebaan's exploits animated the pages of the *Globe and Mail* virtually every second business day.

Safely back in Wellington County the following summer, I rejoined an established accounting practice – somewhat less than earnestly after my brief taste of international intrigue, and certainly very much on the lowermost rung. My first account was a small book-printing company in nearby Glendaele Village called Penmaen Lithography. The proprietors, Thom and Sophie, were in their late twenties and reputed to be both eccentric and penniless. Their fledgling enterprise had little to recommend it to my superiors, which may in part explain how Penmaen Lithography came to be my first professional responsibility.

Accounting firms are hierarchical.

The partners' job is to do lunch.

The employees who do not do lunch are line staff.

The line staff is expected to post the client's self-generated bookkeeping creatively enough to justify the partners' often-overstated elocution fees, added to the more legitimate expenses occasioned by burgers and fries; occasionally cucumber sandwiches and tofu, but this was Guelph, in the late seventies. The Penmaens were the first entrepreneurs I was permitted to advise directly, maybe because their business was deemed to be precarious at the best of times or maybe it was fate. Maybe it had something to do with the coincidence that my father's father had spent a lifetime at the *Beacon Herald* in Stratford. Maybe it was simply that not one of my new employers was willing to undertake any sort of a risk on behalf of Thom, Sophie or little Penmaen Lithography.

I accepted the challenge.

FOREWORD

I didn't, in retrospect, have much of a choice.

In researching this story I was surprised to learn from my grandmother, Lamotta Robinson, that her father at one time owned Weitzels' Bakery in Stratford. And that one of her father's brothers owned the Keystone Bakery shortly after the turn of the century, and yet another brother owned the Stratford Bakery, which was eventually acquired by the Westons. The wealth created by these family businesses and by their eventual sale has not, unfortunately, trickled down to this present generation of Robinsons — which leads me directly back to my story about Thom and Sophie.

Penmaen Lithography, this tiny little printing company in Glendaele Village, became something of a mission for this Robinson — this was my one chance to make a real difference to someone else's financial future — the opportunity to put into practice any number of theories scavenged from thousands of pages of accounting texts — the responsibility to ensure, first and foremost, that Penmaen Lithography, though it may never flourish, at the very least never founders. Each passing year brings new trauma. Sometimes it's cash flow. More often than not it's the lack of cash that does not flow, though I have tried, more than twice, to convince Thom that the management of wealth can often be more onerous than the management of debt.

I don't think Thom believes a word of it.

On one memorable occasion the Penmaens' application for a chattel mortgage, which had been denied with all due diligence by a Canadian chartered bank on a Friday afternoon, was unexpectedly approved the following Monday on the grounds that the manager happened to overhear Thom interviewed on CBC-Radio while the junior banker grilled chicken on his backyard deck.

GREAT EXPECTATIONS

'I hadn't realized you were famous,' the manager explained when he phoned up Monday to reverse his diligent and doubtlessly due decision. At the time Thom hadn't realized that he was famous, either. And I sure as hell hadn't realized that a chance interview on CBC-Radio could elevate a Wellington County printer from poverty to credit-worthiness, even for fifteen minutes. Facts are facts. They're derivative, often overstated, and often not that useful in business. Perception, on the other hand, is almost always the better part of reality.

It would be misleading for me to suggest that Penmaen Lithography is a corporate success. It is no such thing. But ten years have passed. Thom and Sophie still live above the shop in Glendaele Village, Thom still responds to any query as to his personal well-being with the grim retort 'Still in business!' and Thom's improbable understanding of life, business, his employees and his neighbours on the Main Street has provided me with a wealth of stories that help illuminate challenges facing the Canadian entrepreneur on the cusp of the new millennium.

Many of these stories are more or less true, acknowledging in the first place that Thom and Sophie, and of course Galen Nicholas Aldebaan, don't exist, and neither does Glendaele Village, any more or less than the place Stephen Leacock called Mariposa in his *Sunshine Sketches of a Little Town*. And even if Thom and Sophie did exist, as much as Peter Pupkin or Zena Pepperleigh, then Thom would be both a colourful *raconteur* as well as a notoriously unreliable observer of his own situation.

Grant Robinson FCA, CFP,
Guelph, January 2000

Chapter One

The Enigmatic Mr Bowles

Geoffrey Bowles phoned up on a Tuesday afternoon late in June 1988. Just like that, right out of left field.

June 21st. Summer solstice.

The phone rang.

Jayne Beauregard, 'JB' as she fancied herself, was a big fan of the Toronto Blue Jays at the time, which was remarkable in itself because baseball fans who grew up in Sarnia in the 1950s normally followed the fortunes of the Detroit Tigers. The New York Yankees, occasionally. The Cleveland Indians, only rarely, but the Toronto Blue Jays, never! This was the George Bell era. The year Bell hit three consecutive dingers in his first three at-bats off Cy Young award-winning Bret Saberhagen on opening day in Saberhagen's home park, Kansas City. The year Jimy Williams tried to get George Bell to DH. With not much luck. The beginning of the end for Jimy Williams in Toronto.

The phone rang again and there he was at the end of the line, right out in left field. Geoffrey Bowles.

'Could I tell Thom who's calling, please?' asked Jayne.

[11]

'Thom won't recognize the name. We have acquaintances. Mutual acquaintances,' Bowles replied.

Mutual acquaintances sounded a bit too close to mutual funds for Jayne to swallow easily. Her boss had lost a few hundred dollars some years earlier in a penny stock promotion. Oil in Oklahoma had sounded like an OK deal, to Thom, at the time. Only there wasn't any oil in that particular quarter-acre of Oklahoma. Every few months the Macpherson brokerage called again, usually under a different name, often more than once the same week. Thom Penmaen was a man of certain principles. One principle was that Thom did not care to be reminded of his many failings on a regular basis, particularly not by Jayne Beauregard.

'Could I give Mr Penmaen some idea of the purpose for this call?' Jayne tried again.

Jayne's hair was black, slick, and styled androgynously into a pageboy. Her wardrobe included a variety of oversized knit sweaters not unlike the kind of thing Joan Baez would have felt comfortable wearing to a Bob Dylan concert in Washington Square in 1964 – big scoop necks that Jayne habitually wore off the one shoulder or the other. The straps of her brassières were black, ornate, and overly wide as if to suggest the need for full-figured support.

Wishful thinking, perhaps, on her part.

Bowles laughed. Maybe not quite laughed ... he chortled, a throaty little masculine chuckle. 'I don't think I'd want to confuse you, Jayne. Or Thom. It's rather complex, to be truthful, but you *could* tell your boss I am calling on behalf of the Pegaesean Corporation.'

'And how is it that you happen to know *my* name,' Jayne inquired, peevishly. 'I don't recall that we've been introduced?'

Geoffrey Bowles laughed again.

A regular joker, Jayne decided, as she offered the receiver

to Thom. This Bowles character sounded to Jayne not unlike the kind of minor leaguer who might just be capable of walking home a run ... in batting practice.

Thom Penmaen knew something about the Pegaesean Corporation. No more than the next subscriber to the *Globe*'s 'Report on Business', but anyone who read the business pages of the *Globe* daily could scarcely avoid the exploits of the mercurial financier Galen Nicholas Aldebaan and the improbable success of his Pegaesean Corporation.

Thom Penmaen was devoted to both the *Globe* and its business pages. Thom had read about the recent strategic alliance between Aldebaan and Jake Wellcock's Hessen Atlantic, though he didn't understand it. Few investors did, though Thom remembered Wellcock from his days playing defence for the University of Toronto Blues. Thom had even, on occasion, walked by the corporate head office of Pegaesean on Scollard Street, and he remembered a painting displayed against a black fabric backdrop in the window. An original seventeenth-century oil painting by Diego Velázquez, depicting a bucolic scene of pre-Columbian Amerindians panning for gold in a stream high in the Sierra Madre. Thom remembered the painting vividly, and a small bronze statue of a winged horse set on a pedestal beside an imposing glossy lacquered black door.

Thom decided to accept the call.

Jayne's eyeballs rolled back into her skull in search of empathy from some ethereal goddess who might be able to explain Thom's unpredictable telephone manner.

Sometimes he took the calls.

And sometimes he wouldn't.

Sometimes Jayne understood something of why Thom might take this call or decline that call, and sometimes she fervently hoped he wouldn't accept half the calls that he did.

This one off the hook at the moment was right out of left field. It might as well have been George Bell on the phone as Geoffrey Bowles, not that Jayne knew anywhere near as much about Bowles as she did about Bell. The so-called 'Pegaesean Corporation' was a shade beyond Jayne's ken and her appreciation of the Highland culture was limited to an accustomed taste for single malt whiskies.

Glenlivet, in particular.

Geoffrey Bowles came quickly to the point. That he was employed by Nicholas Aldebaan and that he had been given Thom's name by some people in the City and furthermore, straight to business, Bowles was involved in a market-research kind of a project and could Thom possibly spare a minute to answer a few questions?

Bowles was direct.

Thom answered the questions as best he could but he was puzzled. The questions were weird. Distinctly out of left field if not out of the ballpark altogether. Many of them leaned towards print-production capacity. Maximum sheet size. Press speed. Standard impositions. Turnaround time. The questions were odd. They might as well have concerned themselves with batting averages, RBIS, even the recent fortunes of the Detroit Tigers – a subject about which Thom chose to remember very little. Kirk Gibson had been traded to the L.A. Dodgers, Thom knew that. But he couldn't remember when.

Geoffrey Bowles asked if Thom ever came to the City.

'Not a lot. Sometimes. It's been known to happen, but Sophie and I are closing the shop for holidays the last two weeks of July so I'm sorry but I, that is I ... mean I, I really can't....'

'Glendaele?' countered Bowles. 'Could you spare me an hour of your busy week if I met with you in the Village and bought lunch?'

THE ENIGMATIC MR BOWLES
* * *

Geoffrey Bowles arrived at the printing shop in Glendaele Village on a clear, hot, dry late morning in early July.

July 12. Tuesday.

There had been no rain in the Village for weeks. A month, and then some. Nineteen eighty-eight was the summer a transformer by the Cross Street dam malfunctioned and ignited the transmission line to Witherspoon's Dairy. Thom was in the garden with Sophie's dog Kit Carson when he heard the dull thud of what sounded like mortar fire behind him and looked up to blinding flashes as bits of molten copper dropped flaming from the guy wire which then split and laid a live cable across the trunk of Gayle Wicket's parked Volkswagen. Thom drained the contents of three pyrene fire extinguishers trying to keep the sparks away from the lid for the gas tank, and then spent the rest of the summer trying to convince the Glendaele PUC that by rights they owed him forty bucks for the refills.

Thom and Sophie Penmaen had moved to Glendaele Village from the City in the fall of 1970. Late October, Halloween. They were preoccupied, the first few weeks, sorting and unpacking and building bookshelves and adjusting to the daily regimen of Mrs Grundy's oil stove and the unaccustomed rigours of an outhouse, but one Saturday in mid-November Thom decided to take Sophie 'out', as he suggested, enthusiastically, and inquired at the newspaper office of the Glendaele *Gazetteer* as to the schedule of buses.

'Buses?' replied the proprietor, whose grandfather had founded the *Gazetteer* a dozen years after Confederation. Henry Ramesbottom still wore the traditional green visor, a stained apron and metallic tensor armbands to hold his starched cuffs out of the ink. 'Last bus I recall left for Guelph in 1947 and we had rail service too, at one time. Two trains a day to the City either way, morning and night, but the trains got themselves discontinued when all the lads came home after the war or all the lads that was coming home, came home, I should maybe say. There's a list of the others, on the cenotaph at Mill Street,' Henry Ramesbottom paused for effect. 'That would have been the Great War, sonny, the first one.'

'But, sir,' Thom blurted, quite horrified by this latest bit of intelligence. 'How do we ever leave? The Village, I mean.'

'The Village of No Return? You don't,' the editor shrugged.

Glendaele Village in the late eighties was still very much the sort of backwater in which farm widows attended the Presbyterian service religiously on Sundays and planted affordably small numbers of imported Dutch bulbs in single rows the length of tidy white picket fences in the fall. There weren't a lot of places to eat lunch in Glendaele Village in July of 1988. Thom and Geoffrey Bowles had just about passed the front of the five-and-dime and were coming up fast to Witherspoon's Dairy Bar when Liam McTavish unexpectedly stepped out into the heat on the sidewalk.

'Morning.' Thom nodded to McTavish.

Liam McTavish returned the greeting with the practised skill of an elected politician, but then, to Thom's considerable astonishment, added, 'Geoffrey! How very pleasant to see you again,' and brushed by headed south.

'You know Liam McTavish?' Thom inquired, frowning, after they had passed comfortably out of earshot.

'I wouldn't say that I know the man well,' Geoffrey Bowles replied. 'We've met a few times.'

'But I thought ... I mean I don't know *why* I thought, but I guess I just assumed ... maybe someone told me? That's it. Someone must have told me, that you live in the City,' Thom asked for confirmation.

'I work in the City, for the present, that's true enough, but my wife and I bought a place on the tenth line just this past spring. Stephanie desperately wanted to add a solarium, to pull some southern exposure into the stone farmhouse, and we couldn't quite convince the building inspector to cooperate, so I had dealings with the McTavish fellow ... twice anyway, maybe once more.'

Thom found this small revelation amusing. 'You moved to Glendaele Village with your wife in the spring and already by the summer one of you has figured how to work the local politics?'

'The building inspector was a dullard, a regular village buffoon, so I took Stephanie's costly architectural drawings one rung over the dolt's head, to the Reeve. Liam McTavish happened to be the Reeve. There wasn't a great deal of calculation involved.' Bowles apologized for nothing.

'That part sounds simple enough, but then Liam probably recommended you buy the glass for your solarium at Dominion Lumber, did he not?' Thom prodded.

'I wouldn't say McTavish made it a condition for setting the building inspector straight, but yes, in the end the glass turned out to be available. Dominion Lumber had a sale on, and Stephanie did buy a truckload of pressed silicate from McTavish,' Bowles admitted. 'Why do you ask?'

Thom chuckled. 'It's a great racket they've got going. There's the two brothers. Liam does the politics in the village office like his father Dugal did before him and steers the development deals to Derek in the lumber yard who takes the money, loads the two-by-fours on the back of open pickups and makes change. Division of labour, the brothers call it.'

'What, you mean they take bribes?' Bowles raised an eyebrow. The brim of his bowler rose a bit with it.

'No, no, no, not at all. Nothing that complicated. Glendaele is a backwater, but it isn't Thessalon. Have you ever been inside the mill at the back of the lumber yard?' asked Thom.

'No,' Bowles answered. 'A mill? I wasn't aware there was a mill. And I don't think I've heard of a place called Thessalon either.'

'North shore, past Sudbury, not quite so far as the Soo. There's a road sign on Highway 129 just north of Thessalon that says "No Civilization Next 120 Miles". That'll sober you right up. Particularly in winter, with a cloud bank closing in. If you've been drinking, you come out of the bush in a box. If they find the corpse. "Thessalon" is a figure of speech some use to describe the geographic location of the edge of the planet. Very common locally amongst those who still figure the thing is flat,' Thom elaborated.

Bowles looked sceptical. 'And the mill?'

'The mill is the real McCoy. It was built in 1838 by Argus McNaughton, who most folk like to think of as the founder of Glendaele Village, which may or may not actually be gospel truth. Liam's grandfather Dunstan bought the property just before the turn of the century. That part for sure is true. Dominion was a name that was popular then. The lumber mill is still water-powered, for God's sake.'

'Water-powered?' Bowles was genuinely surprised.

'Henry Ramesbottom prints his *Gazetteer* on a flat-bed letterpress and the McTavish mill is water-powered,' Thom confirmed. 'I've never been inside the place myself, when it's running, but I'm told it's quite the show. Derek cranks the sluice-gate open just like his father Dugal did before him, and the waterwheel turns and then the whole building starts to shudder and groan, just slowly at first, with all the belts slapping and pulleys straining to get up to speed. It's quite astonishing, really, that Dunstan could have figured out how to make the thing work at the time he built it, and more incredible that it still works as well as it does, or even that it works at all!'

THE ENIGMATIC MR BOWLES

'And how is it you came to know as much as you do about the genealogy of the McTavish family?' Geoffrey Bowles inquired. 'Were you born in Glendaele Village?'

'Business cards,' Thom responded, negatively. 'Dominion Lumber hired us to design and print up some business cards. This was years ago, when Sophie and I first moved to the Village. The business cards led to discussions about the McTavish family and their history and the lumber yard and the sort of image they wanted to project to their clientele. We hit on the idea of using a nineteenth-century display face for the name – DOMINION LUMBER – and overprinting the type on a steel engraving of a hand-held wood plane. It's a graphic way of suggesting the firm is already three generations old and retains a close connection with its roots even if we admit that milling rough-cut lumber is no longer their core business.'

Geoffrey Bowles was impressed. 'That's a tidy little piece of marketeering you put together for the McTavish clan.'

Thom was pleased by the flattery. 'I know, sir. And they know it too. And I think I charged the niggardly Scots fifty bucks for five hundred cards and I had a hell of a time printing them in register on a beat-up Multi 1250 and I probably lost forty-seven dollars on the deal and now they use that damn wood plane on all their stationery and their trucks and their print advertising and even on the carpenters' aprons they use for in-store promotions and I never got another dime out of them. Not so much as a wooden nickel. This is where we're going for lunch,' Thom pointed across Bowles' lapels to the hotel.

'Maybe you should have quoted sixty dollars?' Bowles stopped on the sidewalk, 'for printing the cards, twenty bucks for the second colour and another sixty for the design concept and the creative.'

'Yeah right,' Thom replied dryly. 'And maybe I wouldn't have won the contract.' It was clear to Thom that Geoffrey

Bowles was less than conversant with the business ethics prevalent in small-town Southwestern Ontario in July of 1988.

'A licensed hotel,' noted Bowles, 'directly across the Main Street from Burns Presbyterian? Is that not considered a trifle modern for a place like Glendaele Village?'

The Holmewood was built in the late nineteenth century, originally as a hospital though it was never used for acute care, but a succession of Drs Martin, Hamilton, McCulloch and Reynolds each did practise medicine on the premises until A.J. Horton renovated it into the Horton Hotel in 1924. The Glendaele Volunteer Fire Brigade maintained quarters in the sample room for a time. In the late twenties, just before the Crash of '29, J.P. Wood bought out Horton and changed the name to the Holmewood, a name that stuck even after Wood himself was forced to sell in the early thirties.

'You printed business cards for the Holmewood too?' Bowles interrupted Thom's history.

'Not business cards, no, not for the Holmewood, but we did print a hokey local history for the Primrose chapter of the Imperial Order of the Daughters of the Empire,' Thom replied.

'Really?' Bowles doubted that he would be interested in a document prepared by the Primrose Chapter of the IODE.

'The chapter on the Holmewood was subtitled "The Perils of Demon Rum".' Thom grinned.

Bowles laughed out loud.

'Rumour in the Village has it that Dirk McTavish,' Thom continued, 'that's Derek's eldest son, Liam's nephew. That Dirk bought the Holmewood in the early eighties as a front for dealing illicit pharmaceuticals. Lots of traffic, coming and going. Could have been true,' Thom speculated. 'Lots of dollar bills in small denominations. Cash that may or may not have been alcohol induced. Hard to say for sure.

'From Dirk's inherently egocentric point of view, he had already, before he was born, lost patience with what Dirk contemptuously dismisses as the McTavish family's "nineteenth-century lumber business". Dirk McTavish is very much of a boomer, but he is also a fourth-generation entrepreneur with just enough genetic talent to orchestrate the extortion ring that got him kicked out of Glendaele Valley Secondary, and also gave Dirk his nickname.' Thom paused.

Geoffrey Bowles looked up expectantly.

'Translate "Dirk McTavish" into English and what do you get?' asked Thom.

Bowles shrugged.

'Mac the Knife.' Thom thought this was amusing.

No one in Glendaele Village who knew the McTavish family at all well could quite figure what crazy old Agnes McTavish had in mind ...'stuffed into a crevice in what was left of a peabrain to begin' ... when at the end she changed her last will and testament and decided to leave the bulk of her deceased husband's shares in Dominion Lumber to Derek's young son, Dirk ... because young Dirk's head of shocking red hair reminded crazy old Agnes of her late husband's father, Dunstan, who had founded the firm in 1896 in spite of the apparent political calamity that the string of five consecutive Conservative prime ministers had been broken in July of that year when Charles Tupper was removed from office after ninety days and the loathsome Liberal Wilfrid Laurier came to power.

Agnes herself wasn't clear any more on just *why* the loathsome liberal Laurier had been so despised, but she took the tawdry reputation as an article of faith, because her father-in-law had assured her that it was so.

'Death evens all Debts,' Dunstan McTavish had scratched

into the margin of his business ledger in his own hand not two weeks before he passed away. Dunstan had been a formidable presence in the Village, even in matters relating to his own mortality.

Dugal McTavish was Dunstan's only son to survive infancy.

Agnes McTavish, Crazy Old Agnes, just thought it felt right, as she rarely failed to remind the executive of the Glendaele Horticultural Society ... young Dirk would have the shares in Dominion Lumber because he looked for all the world like Dugal's father, Dunstan, and because there was no one to dissuade her and because Agnes was sick to death of her own offspring Liam and Derek squabbling about the business of being busy and neither of them could be trusted to visit an elderly lady more than once a month and sometimes not even.

Imagine.

Not like young Dirk, not at all.

Dirk would often make the effort to visit his grandmother. So often that Agnes McTavish herself was called upon personally to bake dozens of chocolate chunk cookies on Sundays in the morning in case young Dirk showed up unexpectedly after lunch, which he did more often than not. For the sake of the cookies. Crazy Old Agnes had made up her mind: young Dirk was to have the shares, 'and have them he would, if Agnes McTavish still had the Power of the Attorney,' so she said, mistakenly confusing a provision in her will that anticipated her own incompetence.

In point of fact, Agnes didn't need either the Power or the Attorney. Agnes McTavish had a notarized will, and some piece of a thing left of a mind of her own. She was, after all, a Grundy by birth. Her father had been a baker. It wasn't as if she lacked credibility in the community, or on the board of the horticultural society.

Young Dirk was still in secondary school when Agnes

passed away suddenly from complications attendant on an unlikely fall in her shower. Dirk's academic career was curtailed shortly thereafter with the public exposure of an 'EXTORTION RING OPERATING WITHIN THE CORRIDORS OF GLENDAELE SECONDARY' as reported under a Resurrection-sized banner headline on page 1 of the Glendaele *Gazetteer*.

'How old did you say Dirk was at the time Agnes died?' asked Geoffrey Bowles.

'Sixteen. He might have been seventeen.'

'There's no way Dirk got control of the Dominion Lumber shares at sixteen,' Bowles interrupted. 'Not a chance.'

'Dirk didn't. You're right,' Thom agreed. 'Not when he was sixteen. There was a trust. And Derek controlled the trust, or Derek assumed he controlled the trust, until he and Liam decided they wanted to buy matching Cadillac Fleetwoods and then it turned out that of course a portion of the dividends to be declared had to be paid into the trust, and young Dirk informed both his father and his uncle that he wasn't in school any more and that he wanted some money.'

'Dirk got the money?' Bowles asked. 'Surely not. Not when he was sixteen.'

'Not all of it, but he got some of it,' Thom replied. 'Probably too much for a teenager who didn't graduate from Glendaele High and wasn't interested in the lumber business and wasn't interested in working with his uncle and particularly wasn't interested in working for his father and didn't have to, because after Agnes passed away, Liam and Derek were both working for Dirk though it took the three of them some time to puzzle it out. Dirk not quite so long as Liam or Derek.'

'I can see maybe Derek thinking at least it's his son, but what did Liam have to say about working for a sixteen-year-old nephew who didn't want to work?' asked Bowles.

'What did Liam say?' Thom replied. 'Or what did he want

to say? What could he say? Agnes was Liam's mother too. Liam was not exactly happy but what could he do? Exhume the body?'

* * *

On the dusty morning in early July of 1988 when Geoffrey Bowles came calling, the Holmewood had recovered from the 'Perils of Demon Rum' and the stinging rebuke of the Primrose Chapter of the IODE. There were flowers on the tables in the dining room, in Coke bottles. Genuine Coca-Cola bottles, some even tinted Atlanta green. Red-checked vinyl tablecloths. And a Wurlitzer jukebox with scratchy vinyl forty-fives from the early sixties.

Elvis Presley.
Bobby Darin.
Del Shannon.

Geoffrey Bowles was obviously not in his accustomed element. His suit was not only pinstriped, and navy, but also double-breasted in the most sophisticated Continental fashion. Thom took note of the jewelled stickpin in Bowles's tie and felt relieved that Sophie had insisted he at least wear his best button-down white Oxford shirt for the occasion. Wearing a tie with a Windsor knot, and blue jeans, publicized what Thom at least considered to be a certain *savoir faire*. A style that was doubtless lost on Geoffrey Bowles.

Lunch at the Holmewood was the regular fare.

HolmeBurger and fries.
Ploughman's pie.
Chicken salad on brown or white, toasted or not.
Halibut and chips.
Grilled cheese.
Tea, coffee or milk.

If Geoffrey Bowles's gustatory expectations were dismayed by the menu at hand, he didn't trouble himself to complain. Bowles took off his suitcoat. 'Do you find it warm?' he asked.

'I'm OK,' Thom answered. 'I prefer the heat, actually, to the snow. I don't sweat easily and I was never that keen on the moors, fog or the novels of the Brontë sisters. Too many characters,' he explained. 'I'm not great with names. I could never keep the characters straight.'

They ordered, the two of them, Thom and Geoffrey, grilled cheese on white with fries, gravy on the side, and Geoffrey Bowles embarked on an extensive and detailed corporate and personal history of the storied Aldebaan family that picked up in the mid-nineteenth century on a tea plantation in Kerala State on the Malabar Coast of India and landed on the docks in Toronto at the foot of Bay Street in 1955 with Galen Nicholas, eldest son, in full charge of the scant remains of what had once been a considerable family fortune, and one younger brother. 'An albatross,' Nicholas would later call him, affectionately.

'The brothers didn't get on that well,' Bowles explained.

It was the Aldebaans' great-grandfather who had created a fortune in tea, his son who managed the money and his grandson who drank the empire to the olive in the bottom of the last glass of Beefeater gin.

'Galen Nicholas,' Bowles continued, 'was enrolled at prep school in Cornwall when the end approached.'

Aldebaan was summoned to the prefect's office. His academic career at Brankesome Hall was finished. His father's last cheque had not cleared Barclay's Bank. This was not the first occasion, or the second, but it was to be the last.

'Very sorry. But, as you can well imagine, sir, we have no alternative other than to insist you withdraw. Now.' The prefect was forthright, and young Nicholas was humiliated. He swore vengeance.

'But I'm getting ahead of my narrative,' Bowles apologized.

Thom tensed his cheek muscles in a feeble attempt at a smile. Thom was not accustomed to smiling.

Galen Nicholas Aldebaan, as Geoffrey Bowles explained between exchanges of salt, pepper, and a recalcitrant bottle of Heinz ketchup that must have been the real thing because it took an age to pour, had prospered in the City. An entry-level commissioned opportunity to peddle advertising by the column inch for the *Financial Post* led to a junior position at Pitcairn, Malden, Rose & Company, and then to a promotion within the brokerage virtually every twelve months. Not even a decade after setting foot off a gangplank at the foot of Bay Street, Aldebaan was already in a position to be able to lend his name to the founding of Howzat, Aldebaan, Mekbuda – an upstart merchant bank noted more for its cocky corporate attitude than for its capitalization.

'More ketchup?' Bowles offered the Heinz.

Thom declined. Tomato ketchup with brown gravy on French fries struck Thom as about as unpalatable as *poutine*. Perhaps it was an acquired taste, perhaps even a British taste. Like fish and chips.

'The centennial year of 1967 was fast approaching. Aldebaan was effusive. He hit on the idea of writing a history of the prime ministers of Canada,' Bowles enthused.

Thom Penmaen was confused, listening to less than twenty minutes of Aldebaan's personal family history.

Business cards, Thom was thinking, surely this serpentine preamble must all meander down to something or other to do with business cards. But what?

Thom tried to recall a few of the more successful designs which he might be able to lay hands on quickly back at the shop by way of an innovative business card portfolio in case

Bowles were to indicate an interest in such a thing – Frank Watt Electric was amusing – a naked lightbulb dangling from a twisted pair of copper wires, and the Witherspoon's Dairy card featured a steel engraving of a kitten, snitched from a shelf copy of Charles Dickens's *Hard Times* illustrated by George Cruikshank.

But this lunch *couldn't* be about business cards. Thom rejected his own speculation. A thousand business cards weren't worth a sixty-minute lunch, ever. Couldn't be business cards. Maybe more like a corporate image sort of print-presentation overhaul. For Pegaesean? Or maybe Springfield or one of the other subsidiaries. Thom read the *Globe*. He had some clue about what might be going on here, but the enigmatic Geoffrey Bowles was certainly not making himself ninety-nine-and-nine-one-hundredths-of-a-percent crystal clear.

Bowles resumed his narrative.

The centennial year was approaching and Nicholas Aldebaan was unaccustomed to any lack of enthusiasm for his business initiatives. But that was on Bay Street. The editorial department at McGibbon and Strong had never heard of the mercurial Galen Nicholas Aldebaan. He had no publication credits, and no track record in either writing or publishing. He wasn't a celebrity, and his proposal – to write a history of senior Canadian politicians – sounded like a risky business. M&S declined. Undaunted, Aldebaan solicited production quotes for a hypothetical 50,000-copy vanity first edition of *The Prime Ministers of Canada*, which he actually had no intention of underwriting himself but the bidding procedure did give Nicholas a keen sense of the competitive nature of the book printing industry in Toronto in the late 1960s. This was not many months before Hunter-Rose, then John Deyell, Alger Press and Ashton-Potter all closed their doors. Like dominoes ...

Thom could restrain himself no longer. 'But why *The Prime Ministers of Canada*? The prime ministers, for God's sake, why not something saleable like, I don't know what. Like *An Encyclopaedia of Canadian Conifers*?'

Bowles laughed. 'You're trying to be clever, are you, Thom?'

'Clever?' Thom certainly hoped not. 'Not clever. No, I definitely wouldn't say clever.'

'Cut us a little slack then, Thom. You know, probably better than I do, that the second book Pegaesean published, the follow up to *The Prime Ministers of Canada*, was *A Compendium of Canadian Gardening*,' Bowles replied.

Thom was horrified at the news. 'I didn't. I swear, believe me. I had no idea....'

'And you expect me to believe you just invented the book title, *An Encyclopaedia of Canadian Conifers*, now. This minute?' Bowles chided. 'I really must insist that I doubt it.'

'Now that you put it like that.' Thom struggled for words. 'I don't, no, expect you to believe me but I did, yes, make it up just this very second and I really wish I hadn't, in retrospect,' Thom tried to remember whether *A Compendium of Canadian Gardening* was a title he should know from somewhere. But where? His hands felt clammy and his bowels unsettled. The gravy for the fries might not have been the best of ideas. The gravy might not have been the best of gravy. The luncheon meeting with Geoffrey Bowles was starting to feel, to Thom, rather more like an employment interview than not, and if so, the prospects for Thom's immediate future had just taken a lurch towards the equator. One further slip and '*Der Rhein*', as Sophie put it succinctly, would likely be '*in Flammen*'.

'If you were a twelve-year-old American schoolboy' – Bowles chose to let the indiscretion pass – 'say, from Hibbing, Minnesota, you would be able to prattle off the names of forty-one American presidents in order, is that not the case?'

Thom nodded agreement, and he did know the name of a famous expatriate from Hibbing, but there was no way Thom could have named more than two dozen American presidents in any kind of an order. Definitely not chronological.

'So what was the name of the second Canadian prime minister?' challenged Bowles.

'Aahh?' Thom hesitated.

'That's just the point. That was Aldebaan's point, exactly,' Bowles gestured with a finger. 'Centennial year of Confederation, and Nicholas Aldebaan realized most Canadians knew very little about their prime ministers, and don't forget that Aldebaan himself grew up in India which didn't have a parliament of any kind before 1947. Democracy is a political system that's always of less interest to those who have it than to those who do not.'

'Who succeeded John A. Macdonald?' Thom rose to the bait. 'Pray tell.'

'Alexander Mackenzie,' Bowles answered. 'I just finished reading Aldebaan's book. I'm up on this stuff. And after Mackenzie?'

'Nope. Still don't know,' Thom was forced to admit.

'John A. Macdonald again, second term. And let me ask you this, knowing that Macdonald was first, and Mackenzie second, how many prime ministers have we had in Canada since 1867?' Bowles pressed his advantage.

'Mulroney, Trudeau. Joe Clark, but not for long,' Thom began with the most recent, the more familiar, and worked his way back. 'Pearson won a Nobel Peace Prize for something to do with Suez, I remember that. Diefenbaker cancelled the Avro Arrow. Louis St Laurent, Mackenzie King ... what am I at now, seven? Plus John A. Macdonald and Alexander Mackenzie, nine? ... Borden? Maybe Robert Borden? I'm not great on the early ones.'

'You're not even halfway, and you forgot John Turner,' Bowles chided.

'Turner? Oh yeah, Turner. I forgot Turner. Does he count? How long was he in office?' Thom could not remember.

'Ten weeks,' Bowles advised.

Penmaen conceded the point. Thom knew very little about the prime ministers of Canada, not much more than he knew about the Detroit Tigers, but he was still confused. It wasn't that Thom was uninterested in Geoffrey Bowles's anecdotes about Nicholas Aldebaan, the Malabar Coast, the Pegaesean Corporation, or even the prime ministers of Canada, but Thom could not for the life of him fathom why he was being showered with such a wealth of utterly useless information.

The thought occurred to Thom that maybe Geoffrey Bowles was already well into the process of making some sort of potentially embarrassing error. Perhaps the enigmatic Geoffrey Bowles had inadvertently switched a cipher and thought Thom Penmaen was someone other than Thom the printer from Glendaele Village? In which case this luncheon of grilled cheese on white was likely to turn awkward, and Thom Penmaen himself might yet be the toast?

Oliver Blakeley was not a name Thom could place, and Thom was quick to admit his ignorance.

'You've heard of Chuck Yeager?' asked Geoffrey Bowles.

'American test pilot. Broke the sound barrier in 1947 in the X-1, then in 1953 set a world speed record of 1,600 mph plus, in the X-1A rocket plane,' Thom answered. 'I read Tom Wolfe's book, *The Right Stuff*. Recently.'

'That's Oliver Blakeley, same sort of fellow,' Bowles nodded in agreement. 'Our number one guy. Canadian fighter pilot. Top gun. Blakeley actually took first prize in a William Tell competition at Pensacola Air Base in Florida in a CF-101

Voodoo. Embarrassed the United States Air Force quite thoroughly when he was younger, but he's a Canadian, which explains why you've never heard of him. *Time* magazine doesn't publish feature stories about the USAF when they get their butts disinfected. Now that he's out of the air force Blakeley pilots hot air balloons in his spare time. He's our operations guy.'

'Hot air balloons?' Thom was even more confused than he had been as recently as five minutes earlier. 'Really? What do you get from the USAF when you win a William Tell fighter-pilot competition – the apple? What about Jake Wellcock and the strategic alliance with Pegaesean? How does Hessen relate to Springfield? Or Blakeley to Wellcock?'

'As a hobby,' Bowles ignored the second question, the third, the fourth and the fifth. 'Blakeley left the air force with a degree in electrical engineering, took an MBA as a mature student at Queen's and was working for General Electric at a derelict wire and cable plant in Cobourg when he first approached Aldebaan with a business proposition....'

The General Electric plant in Cobourg was ancient, tooled for winding transformers and scheduled for demolition. Partly to sidestep the inevitability of his own termination, Oliver Blakeley approached Pegaesean with the notion of buying the Cobourg plant for cheap to spare GE the shutdown, demolition and the severance costs, and then retooling and repositioning the facility to supply plastic components to General Motors in Oshawa, which wasn't all that far away. Pegaesean loaned Blakeley $200,000, more for the retooling than the purchase of the physical plant, which wasn't worth more than petty cash. But Blakeley and Aldebaan did manage to dodge the severance costs, and to keep the labour force employed. That was the birth of Springfield.

Twenty-four months later Pegaesean bought a controlling

stake in Confederate Glass with the proceeds from twenty-four months of Blakeley's plastic auto-parts production. Aldebaan started casting about, looking to diversify.

'It was at this point I was invited on board to explore the prospects for what Nicholas likes to call a "horizontally integrated communications company",' explained Geoffrey Bowles, leaning towards Thom and lowering his voice conspiratorially, as if to include Penmaen in a secret to which he was already privy.

'Which is?' Thom asked, feeling somewhat queasy because despite every expectation to the contrary he did not have the faintest clue what Bowles was talking about. And the gravy did not sit well on his stomach.

'We're not sure yet,' Bowles whispered. 'We haven't got the thing done. A lot of the traditional book publishers are hurting....'

'I can think of one publisher that could stand some help.' Thom was thinking of D&OL, a mid-size Toronto firm with a sterling literary reputation based mostly on the editorial panache of Rebeca Labellarte, niece of the renowned Colombian novelist Gabriel García Márquez. William Duckworth, one of the founding partners, was a clever fellow, and amiable enough, but not as wily with an abacus as Rebeca Labellarte was a seductress of manuscripts. Duckworth & Osborne, Labellarte was regularly, and repeatedly, and publicly, in financial difficulty. Thom had read about their several plights in the *Globe*. More often in the arts section than in the 'Report on Business'.

'There's no shortage of people to talk to, but I can confirm we are thinking about one firm in particular and I do think we're getting close to a deal.' Bowles was evasive.

'We're not both talking about D&OL, are we?' Thom pressed to the chase.

Bowles smiled enigmatically. 'We're not going to answer

that question for you just yet, Mr Penmaen, but you might want to watch the *Globe* closely the first week of August, right after you get back from your holiday. You did tell me you are about to embark on a holiday, didn't you? Cut yourself a little space, get a perspective?'

'Something else?' the waitress interrupted, collecting the scant remains of grilled cheese sandwiches.

'Water,' Thom answered. 'Could I have a glass of ice water, please, Sally Ann?'

Forty-five minutes of non-stop, thrill-a-minute revelations about Nicholas Aldebaan's financial prowess and Oliver Blakeley's engineering skills were just about enough to twist Thom's head away from the task at hand, but Thom's principal squeeze would be back at the driving end of the Sulby AutoMinabinda by one o'clock and there would be a sticky piece of reckoning if Thom wasn't there in person to help with the complexities of the opposing lock nuts that secured the piston under the cover feed plate of the Sulby.

Time was soon to be a concern.

Thom thanked Geoffrey Bowles for his entertaining luncheon conversation and apologized that his afternoon schedule was constrained but explained that Sophie had a problem with the Sulby binder and explained further that he had promised to be back at one to work on the thing and could Geoffrey *please* come to the point?

'The point?' Geoffrey Bowles repeated, rhetorically. 'You didn't get it?'

'Get what?' Thom did not get it.

'About the horizontally integrated communications company,' Bowles expanded.

'Oh yeah, I got that part. You said Aldebaan wants to buy a publisher...'

'... and a newspaper, a magazine, a radio station, a

television station and a printer,' Bowles repeated. 'A printer. You're the printer. How could I possibly be more explicit?'

Thom looked back across the table vacantly.

Bowles continued, 'The Pegaesean Corporation, on behalf of Galen Nicholas Aldebaan, wishes to tender an offer to purchase 100 percent of the voting shares of Penmaen Lithographers. Did I not mention that earlier?' Bowles asked, somewhat less than completely ingenuously.

Time stopped. Space contracted. The room itself seemed to darken. Or maybe not, maybe that part was just Thom's imagination. Thom thought he heard the sound of rushing air, but faintly, and very far away, as if the sound were approaching from the opposite end of a tunnel. Thom slowly became aware that he was still breathing and seized on that, thankfully, as something that needed to be done.

Right away.

The highest priority.

Breathe in, then breathe out, slowly. Just one small breath at a time.

In, and then out.

He ran the sequence through his brain a second time.

In the distance Thom heard what he thought sounded like the rumble of thunder. But then he thought not. He turned in his chair to look out through the lace curtains and was astonished to see that the sky had indeed gone black and that what sounded like thunder was thunder. Thom watched dumbfounded as a bolt of lightning traced across the roof of the Royal Bank and singed an aerial on the roof of the Bank of Montreal on the opposite side of Main Street, and then the rain began in earnest.

The clouds split and it began to pour.

The eaves of the Holmewood sagged with the weight of the

water and the window at Thom's back rattled from the force of the driving rain.

Thom brought his head slowly back into the dining room to face Geoffrey Bowles who was ostensibly engaged in memorizing the list of ingredients printed on the label of the ketchup bottle.

Jeesuz Christ, Thom thought. I'm sitting here eating grilled cheese garnished with tomato-based condiments talking to Beelzebub about selling my immortal soul to Pegaesean and Beelzebub just mentioned a price! And I thought I was looking at an order for a thousand business cards, maybe with a bit of a design premium, maybe two-colour.

Thom continued to breathe.

Had Geoffrey Bowles in fact mentioned a price? What price? Or had Bowles just said something about voting shares? Thom couldn't be certain he remembered it all quite right. What the hell was Sophie going to make of this? The part that Thom remembered, and the other part. Thom's face felt flushed. He looked down at his sneakers.

'I hadn't realized,' Thom said at last, looking up, forcing himself to look Geoffrey Bowles straight in the face, a twitch in his right knee knocking a bit under the table, 'that it's started to rain.'

Chapter Two
Galen Nicholas Aldebaan

Sophie Penmaen was less than taken with the prospect of a formal introduction to a purchase order for a thousand business cards at a quarter past the accustomed starting hour after lunch. And Sophie was distinctly less than enchanted when Thom proposed to 'take a moment' to give Mr Bowles a 'quick tour' of the shop before turning his full attention to the funny noise in the drive chain of the Sulby AutoMinabinda, which Thom customarily couldn't hear even when Sophie, 'and anyone else within half a village block' as Sophie insisted, could hear it. Loud and clear.

Sophie Penmaen could name the title of virtually any pop song released in the 1960s on hearing the first two bars, and she knew the name of Stuart Sutcliffe's girlfriend from the Beatles' early days on the Reeperbahn. Sophie's knowledge of the pop culture of the sixties was considerable.

Thom didn't hear as well as he once had.

Sometimes Thom's wilful deafness left Sophie with little choice but to agree with Jayne Beauregard that Thom was bizarre, unfathomable, and possibly even hopelessly male. Not that Sophie and Jayne often saw pupil to iris. Sophie knew less than Thom about the current plight of JB's beloved Toronto Blue Jays baseball team and couldn't be bothered to care less. Jayne antagonized Sophie by accusing her of pandering to Thom, though secretly Jayne admired Sophie's twenty-inch waist, and especially her thirty-two-inch hips.

'Service was slow then, was it? At the Holmewood?' Sophie was not in a mood to pander. She had a thing that she did, with her eyelids, that left little doubt as to her intent.

Thom considered ignoring the question. It was rhetorical, there wasn't much to say to the contrary. Thom was late, again, and he had promised he would not be late. 'Sally Ann wasn't too quick with the change,' Thom agreed, and hoped against faint hope that Sophie would drop the interrogation.

'We gave the waitress a twenty, Sophie,' Geoffrey Bowles offered. 'There was a delay while Thom and I waited for the change.'

The tour of the printing plant was awkward, and as forced as it was abbreviated.

Another time, under less strain from the barometric pressure rising on the ground floor, Thom would likely have been pleased to set up the Baumfolder to fold sixteen-page signatures, perforated and scored, and taken some genuine delight in demonstrating what Thom considered an ingenious piece of Depression-era technology. Many visitors to the shop couldn't help but laugh as they watched large sheets of printed papers get folded three times at two right angles in one pass through a large machine that rattled and whirred and slapped simultaneously before their very eyes. The Baumfolder wasn't as elaborate a whirligig as the McTavish sawmill – nowhere close – but the folding machine was amusing in its own way. You couldn't help but laugh at the thing.

This time, under pressure from the charged atmosphere in the bindery, Thom ushered Geoffrey Bowles quickly down the stairs and out to the back through the pressroom, pointed briefly to the Polar cutter, the Heidelberg, the Baumfolder and the NuArc platemaker and bid Bowles his fare-ye-wells looking out onto the lilacs by the millpond.

'This is an idyllic spot,' noted Geoffrey Bowles as he stepped smartly around the summer screen. 'What do you call the water, beyond the parking?'

'It's a millpond,' answered Thom. 'That's the hydraulic potential that powers Dominion Lumber. The birthright of the very same Dirk McTavish we discussed earlier, not that Dirk has shown much interest in the river, or his destiny in Wellington County.'

'And the name of the river?' Bowles continued.

'The Credit. A minor tributary of the West Credit. That's maybe the reason Sophie and I have been as successful in business as we have,' Thom replied. 'That's maybe why we're still in business, at all.'

'Hello?' Bowles raised an eyebrow.

'Easy access to the Credit!' Thom grinned in spite of himself. The pun was stale, and Thom had not delivered it as effectively as he might have after a beer or two.

'You wouldn't happen to have a business card?' Bowles asked, almost as an afterthought, at the top of the ramp. 'I have some literature at the office I could put in the mail, about Pegaesean. If you think you might be interested?'

'I think I might, actually,' Thom confirmed, reaching for his wallet. 'There's a joke. Not a very funny joke, I'll admit, but still ... about printers who don't have time to print their own business cards. I should maybe explain though, in case anyone asks, that the pressmark we use on these cards is called a *Druckfehlerteufel*.'

'That's a mouthful,' noted Bowles. 'And I think maybe you should explain, because that's not a word I would use frequently. Just in case anyone should happen to ask.'

'*Druck* means printing, in German. The rest of it doesn't translate fluently into English but the idea attempts to rationalize the theoretical possibility of typographical errors, given that printers of course never make mistakes. You can see the *Teufel*,' Thom pointed to an impish-looking creature printed in a warm red on his card, 'is sitting on a roll of paper. He's dipped his quill into an inkpot and he's holding in one hand a freshly printed sheet of paper, getting ready to insert the errors.'

Bowles tipped his bowler and unfurled his umbrella. 'You'll call me, then, will you, Thom?'

The pressman on the Heidelberg, Philippe LeBoubon, was not happy. Something about deadlines, stress, holidays, poor management scheduling and a hypothetical low spot on the upper water form roller that was causing scumming in the dark shadows of 150-line halftones, which were 'Hard enough to hold open on the press at the best of times on clay-coated stock' and 'Not that I'd want to trouble senior management when you're so busy obviously giving see-sight tours to prospects for client peoples,' but 'Really must have been replaced, weeks ago.'

'You do have a new roller on order from Heidelberg?' Thom inquired, as pleasantly as he could. A game but futile attempt to instil a superior level of responsibility into his pressman's mantra of the day. Wishful thinking, on Thom's part.

Thom did not get on well with people, as a rule.

Employees, less so.

Thom retraced his steps to the bindery on the ground floor. He was not expecting a Hallelujah chorus, or trumpets and fanfare to announce his arrival, and he was not mistaken in his speculation. Little Lorelei Wright and her trainee Yvette Charbeau stood at the back by the Smythe sewing machine, talking about adjusting the speed of the delivery-chain advance, talking about faster or not faster, clockwise or counterclockwise, basically doing nothing but getting nothing done with panache. Sophie was irritated that Lorrie and Yvette were watching her spine, neither of them doing much of anything that might be construed, in any sort of a way, as useful, but Sophie could not think of a likely thing for either of the pair to be doing while Sophie herself tried to focus on the most persnickety of adjustments to the opposing lock nuts controlling the operating height of the piston below the feed plate on the Sulby.

Yvette Charbeau was new, she had an excuse.

Lorrie Wright claimed to be incapable of using a screwdriver, because she also claimed to be left-handed. Sophie wasn't completely convinced that Ms Wright was, in fact, left-handed.

The AutoMinabinda was a British machine that had not been engineered to exacting German standards when it was new, and the Penmaens' Sulby was a generation or more removed from mint.

Jayne Beauregard sat at the front, at her desk by the window, on the telephone. 'What about the other Friday night in Detroit?' asked Jayne. 'Jack Morris against Mike Flanagan and Tony Fernandez homers on a bunt off the first pitch in the first inning?'

'...?'

'I'm not kidding,' Jayne bubbled into the receiver, '... off Morris, the first pitch! The third baseman scaffolled the bunt in-bounds of the foul line but throws high to first and Fernandez already has an infield hit, but then the right fielder boots it and Fernandez has a double and a half, and then Chet Lemon overthrows third and Fernandez is waved home with a run and the Tigers take three errors on the first pitch ...' Jayne's excitement tailed off like a mighty George Bell cut fouled high to an upper deck at Tiger Stadium as Sophie Penmaen started pitching a few high fastballs of her own.

Inside.

Thom took one throw that grazed his whiskers, and then Sophie started in with the breaking stuff.

'And *what*? Precisely, Mr Penmaen, do you think you're doing giving tours and pointing out the see-sights when we are *supposed* to be binding this damn book for Beaver Books which I *promised* is going to be finished and you agreed yourself is *going* to be finished *before* the holidays?' Sophie asked, with an edge to her thesis that could easily have slivered glass. 'Understanding, of course, that the holidays are three days away and you were already fifteen minutes late coming back from lunch *before* you took it on yourself to masquerade as a tour guide for that Jerk!' Sophie's voice rose on the last syllable.

'Jerk?' Thom replied. 'Jerk, did you say?'

'Jerk,' Sophie confirmed, pointing in the direction of the staircase to the pressroom. 'That jerk. The one that just left.'

'... I *know* the Jays are in sixth place, but they're only nine games out,' Jayne Beauregard babbled on in the background. 'What about Baltimore? With Frank Robinson for Christ's sake, managing, if that's what you'd call whatever it is Robinson thinks he's doing to the ball club! So the Orioles start the season 0 and 21 and now they're twenty-three games back ...' Jayne's voice tailed off again like yet another mighty George Bell foul tip.

Thom Penmaen hated holidays. He hated the accelerated deadlines that led up to vacation and he hated the heightened expectations and he detested the bitterness of the inevitable disappointments that followed inevitably from the heightened expectations and July was annual employment review time as well ... Philippe LeBoubon's one grand opportunity to funnel twelve months' worth of pent-up vitriol into a vicious attack on Thom, his wife, Penmaen Lithographers, Thom's limited management skills and his sanity – all with a view to enhancing Philippe LeBoubon's personal self-esteem and, supposedly, his hourly wages for the coming year.

Nuts, in Thom's personal estimation. Big nuts. Whole, uncracked Brazil nuts. Thom held out his left hand palm down in front of Sophie's nose and brought his right hand vertically up underneath the left, fingers extended – *time out*, he mimed.

Sophie had played a little basketball in high school. 'So?' she asked, impatiently, as Thom wrestled with the clamour that was loose inside his skull.

'Mr Bowles wants to buy the company,' Thom answered as evenly as he could, unsure in his own mind if the words his lips were forming were in fact the truth, the whole truth, and nothing but the truth. Trying to avoid overstating the gravity of the revelation.

'Mr Bowles?' Sophie was not easily cowed by gravity, or revelations. 'I thought you told me Bowles wanted to buy business cards! Mr Bowles wants to buy *what?*' Sophie was incredulous. 'What company? What did you just say? Who in the hell is this Geoffrey Bowles character anyway?'

'I never said for sure that Bowles wanted to buy business cards, I told you that I *thought* Bowles wanted to buy a thousand business cards,' Thom clarified. 'So I made a mistake, OK? I was wrong. No big deal.'

'Praise be,' Sophie interjected, 'you're human? And here for twenty years I'd been thinking you were Perfection Incarnate, a regular Second Coming.'

'Bowles doesn't want to buy business cards,' Thom continued evenly. 'What Bowles actually wants is that he wants to buy Penmaen Lithographers, the two buildings on Main Street, the Heidelberg, the Sulby, a management contract ... I dunno, whatever it is you figure we own, Bowles wants to buy it. And he wants to buy me. And he's interested in you too. Package deal.' Thom smiled tentatively.

'And just about how much do you suppose Mr Bowles would be willing to offer, for a used Sulby AutoMinabinda that maybe needs a new bronze strake and an upper slide block and a couple of pins to hold the strake to the block?' Sophie challenged. 'For openers, like.'

'Didn't get that far. What's a strake? I thought actually you might want some input into the purchase price yourself,' Thom lied, because in point of fact Thom could not remember for sure if Geoffrey Bowles had mentioned a price, or had not mentioned a price. '... but Bowles did tell me his employer has forty million dollars parked in a chequing account in Toronto flagged for acquisitions.' Thom paused. 'Speaking strictly for me, I don't think we're gonna need that much. Maybe not even close!'

'Don't be ridiculous. Are you serious?' Sophie prodded. 'You know damn well what a strake is. Don't try to play possum. Who is Bowles working for?'

'Galen Nicholas Aldebaan,' Thom replied, 'himself, personally. I've heard of him. And the Pegaesean Corporation.' Thom shrugged. He didn't know, himself, if he was serious, or ridiculous, or maybe both simultaneously. He wasn't even completely sure at this point that he could differentiate clearly the former from the latter. And he couldn't quite remember what it was that a strake did, though he did have a recollection that he'd heard the word before. Thom slowly became aware that both Little Lorrie Wright and Yvette Charbeau were watching the interchange with increasing disbelief, and also that Jayne Beauregard had completed her telephone report on the Tigers' game and Tony Fernandez's fortuitous spot of aggressive base-running.

There was a moment of quiet, then Sophie added, 'I'm afraid.'

Sophie was like that. Intuitive. She could figure ridiculous to not ridiculous to fear in fourteen syllables, eight words, three sentences, tuck in a disparaging aside aimed at the Sulby binder in the middle and not require an answer to feed off any of her rhetoric. She knew. Somehow or other she just knew. And more often than not she was right about what she knew.

That was the difficult part, for Thom.

'Where's the wrench?' Thom asked, settling on the floor and into the complexities of opposing locknuts underneath the feed plate on the Sulby. '... and what was the name of the guy who delivered the cheques on the television show called *The Millionaire?*'

'*The Millionaire?* What has that got to do with anything?' Sophie asked, by way of an answer. Her husband did have this utterly amazing talent for losing stuff – eleven-millimetre ratchet sockets, for one thing, his train of thought, for another.

'I dunno. I just thought of him and I can't quite remember his name. Michael? Was it? Michael...?'

* * *

The printing office of Penmaen Lithographers closed at five. The rain had stopped, mid-afternoon. Philippe LeBoubon stayed after hours in the pressroom choreographing what Thom considered to be an elaborate burlesque out of cleaning the upper dampening form roller, the one with the hypothetical low spot that really *must* have been replaced weeks ago, for the third or fourth time.

'A la prochaine, Philippe,' Sophie offered, opening the screen door to the garden for her constant companion, the black-and-white Border collie she called Kit Carson 'because when Kit was a puppy she looked, from the back, like a kitty with just the wisp of a curl for a tail, but when she got up she walked bow-legged, like a cowboy,' as Sophie explained it, in considerable detail.

A fifty-cent name for a dog, in Philippe's opinion. Fifty cents too much, which would be better invested in mutual funds. 'Canadian equity mostly, with twenty percent offshore, and a second twenty percent in bonds.'

LeBoubon did not respond to Sophie.

Jackass, Thom thought, you are a complete donkey, M.

[45]

Philippe LeBoubon. You don't even have the brains to figure out who it is who is in your corner, never mind on which side of the *rôtie* to spread *le beurre*. But Thom managed to keep his thoughts to himself, this once.

'Good God, what happened here?' Thom inquired, surveying the devastation of black willow twigs, branches and in some cases whole severed limbs of box elder that were strewn about the lawn by the water's edge.

'It was right after lunch,' Sophie explained. 'I came out about quarter to one to take Kit Carson for a pee and then I noticed the sky had gone black and the air was eerie still and there was a funny green quality to the light, almost like it was thick. The colour of water more than air, but warm water too, like the water in the Caribbean off Nassau. I walked down to the edge of the millpond and then I heard something.'

'A sound? You heard a sound? What kind of a sound?' Thom asked, dubiously.

'Couldn't place it at first,' Sophie replied. 'First I thought it might be a whistling sound, like a kettle on a stove, but it wasn't. Then I thought maybe it was a compressor on the fritz behind Witherspoon's but it wasn't really a mechanical kind of a sound at all and then I noticed there were twigs and bits of branches falling out of the trees and splashing into the water and then the sound swelled into something much larger and I looked upstream and that's when I saw the thing coming.'

'Coming?' Thom asked.

'A whirlwind. I think,' Sophie answered.

'Like a cyclone?' Thom was sceptical.

'No, no, not a cyclone, not at all, not that big. Like a tornado, you know, it looked like a tornado, but it wasn't. It was little. Not very big at all. A whirlwind, I think. About as high as the roof of Witherspoon's at the back and spinning and bearing down the middle of the millpond churning the surface almost like the blades of a propeller where the base of the funnel cut the water and then the noise was really loud and I couldn't hear anything except Kit Carson barking and barking and the funnel pushed by and smashed into the bridge at the Cross Street dam and then it disappeared, or dissipated, I'm not sure which, and I didn't see it any more.' Sophie looked downstream.

'Wu-hoo! Wu-hoo!' called a voice from a second-storey balcony next door.

'What's that,' asked Thom, 'a screech owl?'

'Don't look up,' Sophie hissed. 'Keep your eyes on the ground and your voice down.'

'Why? Who is it?' Thom whispered.

'That idiot Gayle Wicket,' Sophie sighed. 'Who do you think it is... the Wicked Witch of the East? She died, remember? In 1900. Frank Baum killed her.'

'There's a difference?' asked Thom. 'What's Wicket's problem now? I thought we made it plain enough that we do not want her bloody derelict Volkswagen parked on our part of the blacktop.'

'Not the Volkswagen. That wasn't the issue, not today. She was out there on her porch at noon, after the storm, hooting and yelling and carrying on,' Sophie explained.

'Wu-hoo! Wu-hoo!' called out Gayle Wicket in an entreating voice.

Thom couldn't resist. He half expected to be struck dead or frozen into a block of salt, but he could not resist temptation. Thom looked up.

Gayle Wicket was wearing a broad-brimmed black Mennonite sunbonnet strapped down securely with multi-coloured ribbons, a black petticoat with a hundred buttons down the front of it, and arabesque slippers with little silver bells sewn into the extremity of each toe. Thom couldn't hear the bells, the sound was too faint and high-pitched for his ears, but he could see the glint off the silver in the sunshine. Wicket had dyed her hair, orange.

'*Why* does Wicket have a scarecrow on her balcony?' Thom asked Sophie in amazement.

'I know. I saw it too,' Sophie whispered. 'Keep your voice down. She claims she's got a problem with raccoons in her attic and she's trying to scare them away. With a scarecrow. That's what she was prattling on about at noon....'

'Raccoons? You're kidding! How completely appropriate,' Thom enthused. 'You mean the Wicket witch is finally ready to own up to the fact that she cavorts with familiars?'

'Quiet!' Sophie held up her palm.

'What is it?' Thom asked, impatiently.

'Can't you hear it?'

'Hear what?' Thom could not, in fact, hear it.

'The cardinal. Listen. Now there's two of them, calling to each other. They're in the cedars, above the dogwood somewhere on the other side of the millpond.'

Sophie was something of an amateur birder. Thom could identify the obvious species, the crows and robins and bluejays, even the less common but distinctive cedar waxwing, northern oriole and belted kingfisher, but Sophie specialized in the more subtle distinctions between the house sparrow and the chipping sparrow, between the barn swallow and the bank swallow, between the ring-billed gull and the less common herring gull.

Thom was hard pressed to remember the difference between a common grackle and a European starling, but Sophie had the ears to be able to ferret out secretive Virginia rails, sorra rails and the tiny northern waterthrush in the reeds by the millpond.

The McTavish millpond, and particularly the swamp on the west side away from the Main Street, afforded habitat for dozens of species ... herons, warblers, northern flickers, grey

GALEN NICHOLAS ALDEBAAN

catbirds, sharp-shinned hawks, red-winged blackbirds, spotted sandpipers, mourning doves, American goldfinches, mallard ducks, ruby-throated hummingbirds, red-breasted nuthatches, killdeers, and another half-dozen types of owl from the very smallest to the occasional great horned owl ... Sophie could identify close to a hundred different species native to Glendaele Village, many of them by their song as well as their plumage. Once, in fifteen years, there had been an osprey that dropped like the avenging angel of scripture and took a fish at the foot of the one huge black willow in the Penmaens' garden.

'Wu-hoo! I *see* you. I *see* you two,' Gayle Wicket's voice intruded. 'I *see* you.'

'Come on, Thom. Let's get out of here,' Sophie hissed under her breath.

The recorded history of Glendaele Village begins with an industrious entrepreneur named Argus McNaughton, who emigrated from County Argyle and built a grist mill on a branch of the West Credit River in Wellington County in 1838. There had been settlers in the area previously, one of whom may or may not have been one Henry Pyke, who may or may not have laid an obstruction across the Credit stream at Cross Street in the village as early as 1825. The mill, Pyke's lumber mill, didn't last. If in fact it ever existed as anything more substantial than a business plan.

The alley behind Penmaen Lithographers ended at Cross Street. Thom and Sophie stopped on the bridge to look out over the waterfall for signs of damage from the whirlwind. There were branches down, and more flotsam than normal bobbing in the water against the crest of the dam and pushing against the gate of the raceway that powered Dominion Lumber.

Dunstan McTavish was already dressing lumber on his

own premises some years before the turn of the century, but on the opposite side of Main Street from the site of Pyke's mill and a hundred yards further downstream from the Cross Street dam.

Dunstan's son Dugal was a builder, and a bit of a self-taught architect as well as a local wit. 'Falling Water', a Depression-era fieldstone cottage with a wildly pitched roof, dormers and a wide veranda facing the lumber yard, was one of Dugal's more typical creations. The cottage backed on to the waterfall at Cross Street. Round, weathered fieldstone was the one affordable building material readily available in Wellington County after the Crash of '29. 'Falling Water' was built in the vernacular. It had very little in common with anything that might have been designed by Frank Lloyd Wright.

'D.M.,' Sophie read aloud from a pair of initials carved into a concrete cornice at the top of the dam.

'Derek McTavish,' Thom translated. 'Liam's brother. Haven't you ever noticed those before? There's a photograph on the wall in the mill office of the crew Derek's father Dugal had helping him rebuild the dam in 1935. Right beside the foldout on the wall of Marilyn Monroe. You've never seen it? Derek was the waterboy on the crew.'

'Norma Jean Baker was nine years old in 1935,' Sophie replied, sharply.

'Maybe the foldout in the lumber office is Jayne Mansfield.' Thom skirted the issue.

At Hill Street, very close to the southern edge of the village, the Penmaens, Thom and Sophie and the amazing wonder dog Kit Carson, all turned west off Main Street and started the trek up the gravel road that winds through a jackpine bush planted in the Depression to disguise what had been, up until that time, the village dump.

The trail climbs another sixty yards past a switchback and a grove of sumacs and then continues its ascent on up to the village water works. From the summit the Penmaens turned north and picked their way through an abandoned orchard of Empire apples that opens onto a high grassy meadow aligned with the western extremity of Cross Street at the foot of Milk Snake Hill.

Sophie noticed an eastern kingbird perched on a split-rail fence, not a common sight. She pointed. The distinctive white band across the tip of the tailfeathers made for an easy identification, even without the benefit of Peterson's *Pocket Field Guide* at hand.

Thom threw an unripened apple as far as he could, for Kit Carson to chase. His arm wasn't as fluid as it once had been. He winced, and touched his left hand to his right shoulder.

'Look,' Thom pointed to the east, distantly, at the horizon. 'Oliver Blakeley.'

'Oliver Blakeley?' Sophie pulled a face. 'Who, in God's name, is Oliver Blakeley?'

'Operations. Bowles is acquisitions, Blakeley is operations. Ex-fighter pilot, apparently. He's the go-to guy at Springfield.'

'Springfield?' Sophie inquired, impatiently.

'Part of the Aldebaan empire. A lucrative part, from what Bowles explained. Springfield manufactures auto parts. It's a subsidiary of Pegaesean, Aldebaan's holding company. Springfield, Massachusetts, is the home of Smith & Wesson Small Arms. You know, like Colt .45? I think myself that the name may be someone's twisted idea of an amusement. Springfield is actually just a ploy to extort money from General Motors.'

'Go-to?' Sophie persisted.

'Basketball term. I thought you told me you played a little basketball in high school?' Thom frowned.

'I did. I played small forward. And we had a centre, and a

couple of guards. No "go-to".' Sophie was convinced.

'The forward who dunks, never misses,' Thom explained, 'but Blakeley's really an engineer, and he flies hot air balloons as a hobby.' Thom's voice trailed off as the end of his extended finger found what did, to Sophie's eye, look a lot like a hot air balloon, low to the horizon, maybe five miles to the east.

'I can see the roof of Burns Presbyterian, the steeple of All Saints and the lightning rods on the roof of the lumber mill. I can even see a hot air balloon, maybe, in the distance, but I do not see Oliver Blakeley,' Sophie insisted.

'I'm kidding, OK? I'm kidding,' Thom admitted.

'Where is that?' Sophie asked, looking to the east, towards Cataract Junction. 'Why is the balloon so low to the ground?'

'Look!' Thom pointed to the near distance just across the millpond at the foot of the moraine.

'What *are* you talking about?' Sophie sighed.

'You see our place? And to the right of that, and up a bit. You see Gayle Wicket's balcony?' Thom squinted as he stared.

'I see the stupid witch's balcony, so?'

'The scarecrow isn't in the same place as it was fifteen minutes ago. It moved,' Thom exclaimed. 'Maybe it's alive?'

Sophie shook her head. 'Liam McTavish stopped by the shop at noon,' Sophie changed the subject. 'Just a few minutes after you left for the Holmewood with the Bowles creature.'

'For what? Business cards?' Thom complained. 'Not again, surely? The last time ...'

'Liam didn't say business cards,' Sophie interrupted. 'Liam did say something about his son getting married ...'

'Struan or Sterling? Which one?'

'McTavish didn't say. But I think Struan is a bit on the heavy side to be much of a catch for a girl, so the bethrothed must be Sterling, don't you think?' Sophie speculated.

'So if Sterling is pregnant then I wonder what Liam thinks about Derek's son inheriting the bulk of his mother's shares in

Dominion Lumber?' asked Thom. 'What's young Sterling going to do now, to support a new wife and all that?'

'Maybe that's the reason Liam is steering his son towards politics. Maybe Sterling's future isn't going to be tied so closely with Dominion Lumber,' Sophie speculated.

'Liam's father was reeve for almost two decades. Liam himself has been re-elected once, so sure – it makes sense that Liam would want to encourage Sterling to continue in the family business, but councillor in Glendaele Village is hardly a full-time job,' Thom mused, 'and I'd be very surprised if it paid more than a thousand or two a year. Looks to me like maybe the McTavish clan is heading into some very deep do-do over young Sterling's aspirations and Dirk's inheritance.'

'So? Even supposing that you are half right, which you are probably not, none of that stuff is any of your beeswax anyway,' Sophie insisted. 'None of your damn business, Mr Penmaen.'

The high trail from the waterworks follows the crest of the hills in succession to the northwest, parallel to a branch of the West Credit River. Milk Snake Hill is a glacial moraine – tons of crushed dolomite ploughed to the edge of the last glacier to push through the valley during the late Silurian Age some 25,000 years ago. Thom Penmaen knew something of the geology of the Village from years of printing tourist pamphlets funded by the local chamber of commerce.

'Doesn't look anything like Kansas,' Thom remarked, trying to be amusing, looking out over a patchwork quilt of rolling hills and small fields planted in corn.

To the west the sky was still black with the weight of the receding storm. There were magnificent thunderheads rising thousands of feet above the City of Guelph and long spokes of sunlight radiating through cracks in the cloud, and then there was a single, huge, red-tailed hawk.

GREAT EXPECTATIONS

Sophie spotted it first, wheeling and soaring on the unsettled thermal updrafts, circling, shadowing Kit Carson, or anything else on the ground so bold as to make a move. The shadow of the hawk crossed the landfill and diverted Sophie's attention temporarily to half a dozen turkey vultures picking at carrion in the trash, while Thom and Sophie sat, worrying over bits of what little they could understand of the troublesome Mr Bowles and his unlikely proposal.

'It', the Penmaens called it, as the discussion progressed.

'What in the hell are we supposed to do about "it"?'

* * *

The underlying premise for the proposed 'horizontally integrated communications company' was not that difficult to comprehend.

'Even turkey vultures are attractive,' Thom explained to Sophie, 'to other turkey vultures.'

Sophie looked at Thom as if he had taken suddenly ill. 'You think Bowles knows much about turkey vultures?' she taunted.

'Probably not,' Thom agreed, 'but Bowles is right about the synergies inherent in Aldebaan's "horizontally integrated communications company".'

'Really? You think so?' Sophie tried to sound interested.

It was true that Canadian publishers in the late eighties, and Duckworth & Osborne, Labellarte in particular, were in poor shape. It was also true, as Geoffrey Bowles had underscored, that Canadian publishers were a vain lot, altogether too readily seduced by wily print marketeers ever eager to sing the siren song of lower unit costs, to add a chorus of fictitious margins supposedly attendant on volume, then to layer on the silken credit terms that lead inevitably to publishers' excess and unsaleable, debt-ridden inventory.

'Dead spruce, basically, is what some of these yahoos have taken to calling "inventory" on their balance sheets,' Bowles summarized the quagmire.

'And you don't think dead spruce on a balance sheet is inventory, I take it?' Thom had tried to be agreeable.

'In the logging industry, maybe. Dead spruce is dead spruce whether it's in a forest or on a balance sheet, but it isn't inventory,' Bowles continued. 'Not in the publishing industry. Ever.'

'What's that sound?' Sophie interrupted Thom's extemporaneous précis of Aldebaan's grand vision.

'What sound? I don't hear ...'.

'Quiet!'

...

'I can hear the quiet, yeah, but I still don't hear ...' Thom insisted.

'I don't hear it now either. It stopped. What were you saying, Thom?' Sophie asked brightly. 'About dead spruce?'

'Leave the spruce in the forest. Think about Bowles' situation for a minute,' Thom continued.

Geoffrey Bowles had only recently taken up residence on a century farm outside the village of Glendaele. At the time of the grilled cheese lunch at the Holmewood, Bowles was commuting ninety minutes a day each way to the Pegaesean office on Scollard Street in Yorkville, in the City. The office on Scollard was swish, Thom could attest to that, or at least attest to the fact that the façade was swish, but Bowles was maybe starting to think a substantial Pegaesean investment in a printing plant in the industrial park at the north end of Glendaele Village might provide a plausible enough excuse to cut three hours a day of commuting out of his work week.

'It's a thought,' Sophie allowed. 'You could be on to something there.'

'I know,' Thom continued. 'Location, location and location. The three primary elements in any real estate transaction, and Penmaen Lithography just happens to be long on all three!'

Then there was the matter of Geoffrey Bowles' burgundy MGB, painstakingly restored and polished to within a centimetre of the colour of an aged Madeira.

'I hear it again,' Sophie interrupted Thom's analysis of the strategic plan.

'Hear what?'

'The sound. I hear it again. Listen!' Sophie insisted.

...

'What is it that I'm listening for, exactly?' Thom asked. 'Is this a large sound? A small sound? A round sound? What does it look like, this sound? What colour is it?'

'Rushing air.'

'What, like you hear another whirlwind?' Thom dismissed the possibility as remote.

'Similar, but different. Not a whirlwind, more like a heartbeat, a slow heartbeat. Of rushing air. You don't hear it yet?' Sophie asked, impatiently. 'It's louder.'

'I don't hear it,' confirmed Thom.

'Then clean the wax out of your ears for Christ's sake, man. There!' Sophie added.

'What?'

'The sound stopped.'

Geoffrey Bowles' burgundy MGB was the fruit of a remarkable string of serendipity ferreting out veins of gold ore on the Kimberley Plateau in Western Australia on behalf of Stephen Roman and Denison Mines.

Gogo, Glenroy, Ellendale. Passage by Land Rover to Noonkanbah, places like that.

GALEN NICHOLAS ALDEBAAN

Driving the MGB from his estate in the Caledon Hills to the Pegaesean office on Scollard Street was a costly indulgence. An indulgence at odds with the corporate parsimony practised and ingrained from Bowles' years working for Stephen Roman. Driving the MGB, on the other hand, from a proposed Pegaesean printing works in the industrial park at the north end of Glendaele Village to the Pegaesean corporate head office in Yorkville and stopping by the plant again each evening would render the car, genuine British auto parts and quirky British mechanical labour all tax-deductible, a much more agreeable commute from Bowles' perspective.

For a number of reasons that had largely to do with good fortune and very little to do with business expertise, Thom Penmaen came steadily to the conviction that his diminutive local slice of the market for upscale book printing was, at the *very* least, strategically located.

There were, of course, a few flies in the ointment.

Some of the flies were simply worrisome. These were the houseflies. They irritated. Others were more substantive. Horseflies. They bit. Thom understood the printing, and even a bit of the publishing, parts of the proposed communications empire pretty well, but the machinations of the newspaper, radio, television and magazine divisions were less transparent.

Apart from the acknowledged opacity of large chunks of Aldebaan's vision, Sophie recognized yet another problem, and this one closer to hand than in the bush.

The problem was Thom, who was often his own most formidable adversary.

Penmaen Lithography in 1988 employed six people, two of whom were principals and worked, between them, twice as many hours as the four employees combined, for maybe half the remuneration.

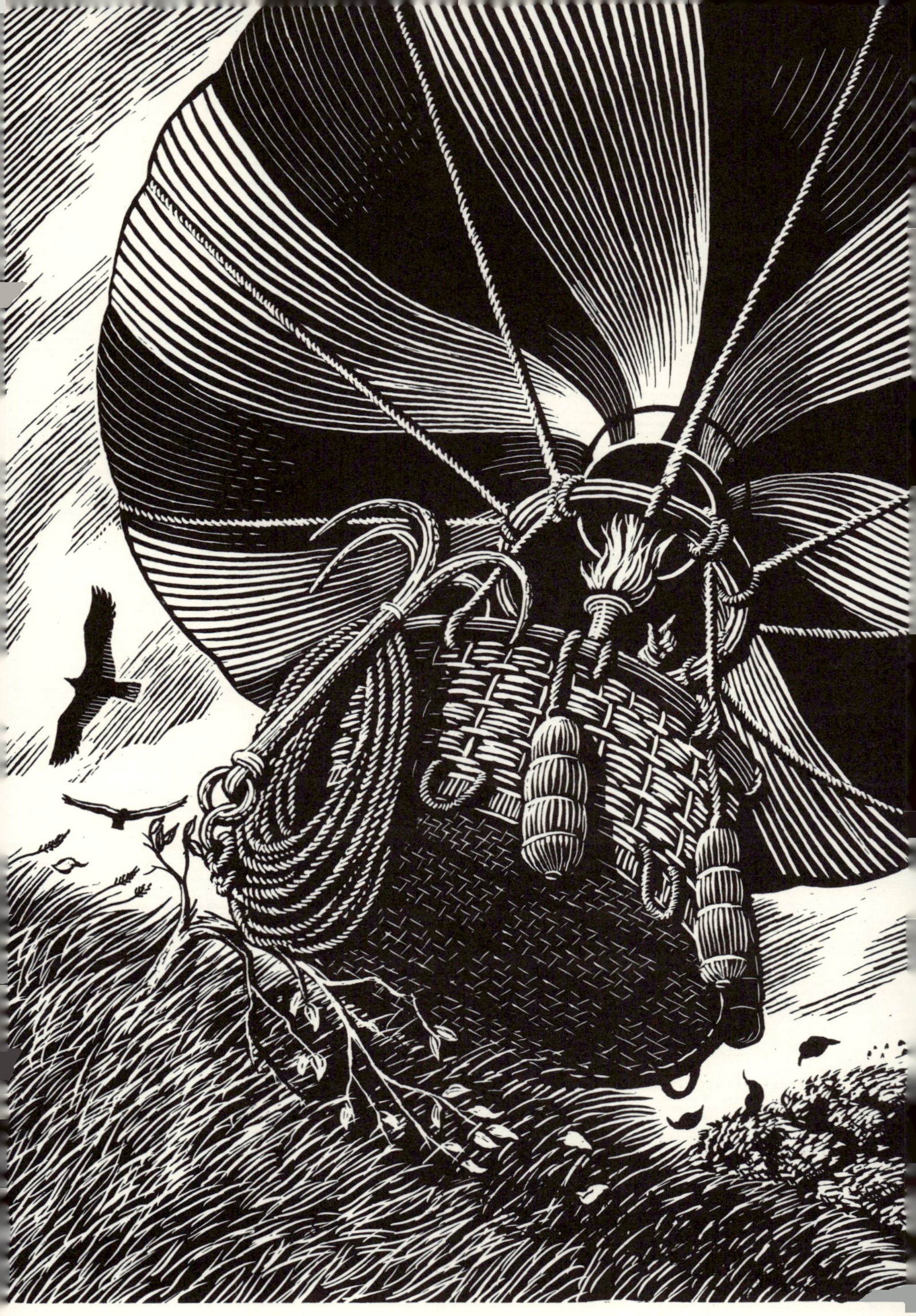

Part of Geoffrey Bowles's proposed implementation of Aldebaan's grand vision was to build a print production facility in Glendaele Village that would employ sixty-five people within three years and have the capacity to print all of D&OL's trade list as well as service the Pegaesean backlist and steady reprints of Aldebaan's own *Prime Ministers of Canada* in addition to the lucrative financial printing side, the corporate annual reports of Pegaesean and Springfield, Confederate Glass and Hessen Atlantic and whatever else the mercurial Galen Nicholas Aldebaan might discover tucked under a feather in the other or the one of his spreading wings.

Sophie bottomed the bolt with a ratchet when she observed, not incorrectly...

'... not that I am trying to dampen anyone's enthusiasm or anything like that. Not at all. But surely someone is going to have to deal with the reality that you have troubles enough with your marriage, Thom. Of getting along with *me*, and I am your one biggest fan, probably your *only* biggest fan, the president and charter member and sole paid-up lifetime member of the Thom Penmaen fan club, but you know yourself that you are *not* good with people, you are a crude judge of character and how in whose name does Geoffrey Bowles or Pegaesean or Nicholas Aldebaan expect you to manage a workforce of sixty-five people when you can't keep Philippe LeBoubon even somewhat pacified just some of the time?'

'Good God, what the hell is that?' Thom leaped to his feet and looked to the sky as the sound of rushing gas jets slammed into both his eardrums then rebounded loud enough to hurt.

'That's! the sound, that you can't hear!' Sophie exclaimed triumphantly, scrambling to her feet as well, pointing up and behind her and to the east as the wicker gondola of a hot air balloon barely cleared the crest of the ridge dragging rope tethers that raked the hillside.

Whooosh! Whooosh!

The gas jets fired again, and then again, as the balloon pilot fought for altitude by the inch when what he really needed pretty quick was metres, at least half a dozen.

Whooosh! Thom could just about have reached up and scratched his initials into the wicker thatching across the bottom of the basket, it was that close. The pilot was laughing and laughing at their sudden fright and the Penmaens, Sophie and Thom, felt all at once as small and insignificant as field mice, dwarfed under the enormous proximity of the balloon that passed four storeys high above them.

Whooosh.

The gas jets fired again and the balloon sailed out majestically over what once had been the Dugal McTavish spread. Fifty yards, a hundred yards, just that quick, as fast as you could say it and then the pilot was waving goodbye and the Penmaens couldn't distinguish his face any more and the sound of the gas jets receded into the west.

'O.V.' Thom read off the side of the balloon, in royal blue lettering stitched onto white fabric almost as tall as the balloon itself.

'O.V.?' inquired Sophie.

'Old Vienna,' Thom replied, '... lager beer. The balloon is a promotion for Old Vienna Lager Beer.'

'I don't get it,' Sophie insisted. 'Why would he want to fly a balloon advertising Old Vienna? I thought you told me Oliver Blakeley worked for Pegaesean?'

'Oliver Blakeley works for Springfield. Oliver Blakeley *owns* a piece of Springfield, mind you, a significant piece, but Pegaesean owns a bigger piece, and I don't actually think the yahoo in the gondola is Oliver Blakeley,' Thom decided.

'Who, then, if not Oliver Blakeley?' asked Sophie.

'Phineas Fogg?'

'Phineas Fogg!' Sophie thought not.

GALEN NICHOLAS ALDEBAAN

'*Around the World in Eighty Days* by Jules Verne. The balloon pilot was called Phineas Fogg,' Thom remembered.
'I think you've lost it,' Sophie replied.

★ ★ ★

The annual report of the Pegaesean Corporation for the fiscal year ended 31 December 1987, when it arrived in the mail the following week, proved itself to be a clever piece of business.

The Pegaesean Corporation was known on Bay Street for the romantic approach it took to fiscal disclosure. Aldebaan had once bankrolled a successful ascent of Mount Logan in return for the favour of a photograph of his 1982 Annual Report, to be taken in the hands of a mountaineer at the peak of the highest mountain in Canada. Aldebaan subsequently offered team leader Borje Niels a directorship on the board of Pegaesean, and made use of the photograph taken by Niels on Mount Logan on the cover of his 1984 Report.

The 1987 Report featured a colour reproduction of an oil painting by the Spanish master Diego Velázquez – of a group of Amerindians in loincloths panning for gold to deliver in homage, supposedly, to their great god Quetzalcóatl. There are no Europeans depicted in the painting but still the image is loaded with a sense of foreboding. The Maya in the mountain stream could in no way have predicted the chaos about to be visited on their civilization by the imminent arrival of the conquistador Hernán Cortés.

Thom remembered seeing the Velázquez in the window of the Pegaesean office on Scollard Street in Yorkville. The image had apparently struck a chord with Aldebaan, though whether the chord struck was plucked from the strings of a lute at court in Córdoba or exhaled slowly through the reeds of a set of pan pipes in the high Sierra Madre was not clear.

The first half-dozen pages of the report were given over to platitudes, not much text. Something about the publishing

GREAT EXPECTATIONS

arm, the art gallery on Scollard, the Springfield and the Confederate Glass acquisitions. The strategic alliance with Hessen Atlantic. A plethora of flattering captions under generous photographs of Aldebaan printed as duotones in warm black and neutral grey. The effect emphasized, but ever so subtly, the quality of the tailoring in Aldebaan's Savile Row suits. The final two pages of the report included bar graphs illustrating Pegaesean's Profit Before Tax from 1967 to date.

In 1967, the year of inception, Pegaesean cleared $13,000.

At the spine of the document, between the years 1977 and 1978, the counter on the graph changed from thousands of dollars to millions. For the most recent fiscal year Pegaesean was reporting a profit before tax of $87 million, absolutely none of it in oil, nothing in major league baseball, and nothing in the American Midwest.

Chapter Three
Philippe LeBoubon

Thom and Sophie's little collection of artwork, such as it was, was modest, Canadian and contemporary — a pair of drawings by Tony Urquhart, two etchings by Paul Fournier including a tiny one of a rat emerging from a drainpipe and another of a huge crow hung like meat from one extended talon. A silkscreen print of a wolf by Alec McCauley from Moosonee, half a dozen lewd engravings cut into the endgrain of boxwood by Wesley Bates, two or three exemplary pieces of ephemera printed letterpress on the Vandercook by Will Rueter at Aliquando. A lithograph by Virgil Burnett of a male swan in earnest pursuit of the wig of a courtesan from an earlier century ... the seventeenth, perhaps, rather than the eighteenth.

Thom and Sophie lived inexpensively but not frugally in a small flat above the printing shop on the Main Street in Glendaele Village. The occasional client would remark on Fournier's disturbing image of a dead crow hung at the base of the stairwell and ask if there might be a gallery on the second floor?

There was no gallery on the second floor of Penmaen Lithography, though there were those in the village, Reeve Liam McTavish among them, who had difficulty understanding that the Penmaens owned a printing shop that did not print wedding invitations, envelopes, business cards, letterhead or even stag tickets on any sort of a regular basis.

'But whatever do they do with their time?' the chins on the counter at Witherspoon's Dairy Bar wagged, and then waned.

Neither of the Penmaens was native to the village. Thom had been raised in the west end of Montreal, Sophie in tobacco country southwest of Delhi.

Social standing in Glendaele Village was customarily awarded on the graduation of your firstborn from Glendaele Valley Secondary, but not likely sooner. Excepting of course dispensation due to preferred status in the Glendaele chapter of the Royal Canadian Legion ... a distant blood relative with a Victoria Cross, for example, had been known to effect wonders and lead not only to advanced social standing but also to gratuitous offers of senior appointments to the board of the Glendaele Horticultural Society, not to mention an open chit at the bar in the Legion Hall.

Such is the stuff that some dreams are made of, but the Penmaens were childless, and neither of them held membership in the Royal Canadian Legion. 'But whatever do they print, these printers?' the chins at Witherspoon's waxed. 'I mean, like. You know?' The local vernacular was expressive, rather than explicit.

'Like. Books?' they asked, the chins.
'I mean, like.'
'Really?'
'You know?' The dialect in currency common at Witherspoon's bore scant kinship to the English employed by Her Majesty in the opening of Parliament at Westminster and there were those, moreover, among the ranks of the local retailers who did attend weekdays at Witherspoon's who had been known to encounter difficulty reading a tabloid newspaper much past the photograph on page 3.

Thom had likely crippled both his wife's prospects of social accreditation and her Border collie's shot at a ribbon in the Glendaele Agricultural Exposition when Penmaen Lithography hit a lull in one of the early years and Thom inadvertently accepted a commission to print up stag tickets for a 'hoot', so styled and to be hosted by none other than the recently endowed Dirk McTavish.

Mr Mac the Knife, himself.

In the absence of a written purchase order to the contrary, Thom and his vivid imagination together took it upon themselves to illustrate the tickets with a half-tone reproduction of a leggy creature in frivolous garters, lace black tights and stiletto heels.

'Incredible, man. I mean. Like,' Dirk paused. Dirk McTavish smoked Players' Navy Cut, plain. Oxygen did not pass easily into his capillaries. 'You know?' Dirk resumed his thesis. 'Like. Whatever gave you the idea, man?'

Young Dirk McTavish was clearly a degree and a half beyond smitten with the tickets for the hoot until Thom the renegade printer and social misfit happened to let slip that the image Dirk was fingering, so fondly...

'... is actually a photograph of Peter Sellers. In drag.'

'In drag?' Dirk was incredulous though Dirk would have been pressed to define the word, let alone spell it. 'A fag? In drag?'

British music hall humour was not, apparently, one of Dirk's favoured tastes. Dirk took another drag on his cigarette.

'A, a fag?' Dirk repeated. 'You printed up two hundred copies of a photograph of a homosexual at my own personal expense?' Dirk was sometimes a bit slow on the uptake, but he did soon grasp the enormity of the transgression that had been visited on his pocketbook. 'What is everyone gonna say?' Dirk demanded, jabbing a finger in the direction of Thom's face. 'Let me jist ask youse that last part once more time,' Dirk lowered his voice and his gaze and nearly dropped his diction. 'What is anyone in at Witherspoon's gonna say? About *me!*'

* * *

GREAT EXPECTATIONS

Philippe LeBoubon was the least content of the four malcontents employed at the printing office of Penmaen Lithography in the summer of 1988.

Little Lorrie Wright was a ready and willing enough accomplice to LeBoubon, but Lorrie held a junior bindery position and pecked at it with a piecemeal attitude and a pigeon-sized cranium. Yvette Charbeau was new, she had an excuse. Jayne Beauregard was obsessed by major league baseball. The Toronto Blue Jays, more so than the Detroit Tigers. A more formal analysis of the breadth of human resources available at Penmaen Lithography relied pretty much on a questionnaire Thom and Sophie distributed to their employees once a year in the week prior to summer vacation.

The preamble advised: 'The following is a list of questions which may be of assistance in considering the nature of your employment at Penmaen Lithography. The questions are intended to be neither daunting, nor exhaustive. It is not necessary to answer all of the questions, nor is it necessary to limit yourself to these suggested topics, but please do remember that annual employment review is intended to provide an opportunity for you to influence possible wage increases and other changes to the terms and nature of your employment.'

Philippe LeBoubon took exception to the tenor of the document in the summer of 1988 and took upon himself, aided and abetted by the nefarious Miss Lorrie Wright, the responsibility of convening a meeting of Penmaen employees...

('On company time, at company expense,' Thom whined.

'Zut alors, c'est vrai!' Philippe insisted.)

... to correct the perceived bias and misleading wording of the odious management 'interrogation', as Philippe characterized the document.

Two years earlier, in May of 1986, Philippe LeBoubon had started work at Penmaen Lithography.

LeBoubon had applied for the pressman's job once before, a year earlier still, when Young Lucky quit unexpectedly at a tender age to take the Grand Tour. Which was not a half bad idea on young Lucky's part, at the age of twenty-three.

Young Lucky had the money.

Lucky was like that, with money, and the kid had all the time in the world and then some, but Young Lucky quit Penmaen Lithography with the minimum two weeks' notice after five years on the Heidelberg, which caused Thom some considerable difficulties in meeting prior commitments with no time to consider training an apprentice. The pressure of which Thom resented, and coloured Thom's attitude to energetic applicants with inadequate experience.

Philippe LeBoubon was energetic. He arrived at the shop on Main Street one morning in April, 1985, to announce that not only did he live in the village, himself, 'in person', but also that he had decided to accept the pressman's job advertised in the classifieds of the Glendaele *Gazetteer*.

'How much will I be paid?' LeBoubon continued. 'At which hours do I make my commencement?'

'Do you have experience?' Thom inquired, sceptically. 'We're looking for someone with experience.'

Thom had not done well in language studies at school. Not at primary school in the west end of Montreal, not at high school in NDG and not at university in Toronto. Fourteen years of mediocre grades en français wouldn't have garnered Thom much more than a plate of poutine in a brasserie. Thom did, however, recognize the accent.

'En voilà-t-il,' replied Le Boubon.

'On what kind of press?' Thom persisted.

Philippe LeBoubon was born in Burgundy, the youngest in a family of six. Philippe's father was a respected physician in the parish, as were each of his two older brothers. His one sister was a registered nurse. Rumour in the diocese had it there had been a Boubon in attendance at Versailles, at the court of the Sun King, Louis the Fourteenth. Philippe doubted the story but it was undeniable that the Boubons were resident in Burgundy since the time of the Crusades.

Philippe did not feel destined to be a physician. Philippe LeBoubon toyed with a course of industrial design at a polytechnique in Rennes, then abandoned his studies abruptly to wander the oceans of the world by tramp freighter until he met his fiancée in Canada, quite by chance, in Toronto.

'I'm sorry,' Thom continued. 'I must apologize. We're looking for someone with sheet-fed experience, preferably someone with time on a twenty-five inch Heidelberg KORD.'

'Mais non!' LeBoubon insisted. 'Je désire. I want, to see the kind of a press that makes the printed pages!' LeBoubon had experience, apparently, on a flexo press in the wallpaper industry. At MichaelAngelos, in Brampton.

Thom Penmaen did not know much about wallpaper. Other than that the stuff was frequently cited as the root cause of marital discord and that wallpaper was printed on huge multi-colour web presses that were more massive in themselves than the entire building that housed puny little Penmaen Lithography. Web presses of that size were manned by teams of unionized employees who traded shifts. It was clear to Thom that Philippe LeBoubon's experience at MichaelAngelos, while interesting, was in no way applicable to the rigours of a single-colour sheet-fed Heidelberg KORD.

'Mais non!' Philippe was not to be dissuaded. 'You understand nothing of what there is!'

Thom took exception to LeBoubon's odd choice of phrase, but in the end he did relent and allow Philippe a look at the Heidelberg and a short talk with Young Lucky. Thom did not, however, offer LeBoubon an interview.

PHILIPPE LEBOUBON

In retrospect, he probably should have.

Young Lucky was replaced by John Barleycorn, a personable sort of a fellow who lived in the Village, had years of experience running all manner of sheet-fed presses in the City, looked great on paper, talked an even better line and was prepared to take a sizeable cut in pay from his previous employment.

'For the convenience,' so Barleycorn explained.

Thom should have been suspicious.

Prospective employees that seem too good to be true on paper usually are, just that. John Barleycorn never did bother to exert himself much beyond room temperature, and he resigned the very day his one-year drunk-driving licence suspension, which he had not previously thought to mention, expired.

Twelve months after twenty-three-year-old Young Lucky left the Village, Penmaen Lithography still received sporadic postcards. From Vienna, at first. Then Yugoslavia, Istanbul, Beirut, and then finally Israel where Lucky had apparently met a girl of a certain persuasion and taken a job running a Heidelberg on a kibbutz in the Negev.

When John Barleycorn quit, after twelve months to the minute, with a scant five days' notice, Thom was starting to think that he was not so much looking for a closet alcoholic with KORD experience and a spotty driving record as maybe just a warm body.

Local, preferably with some initiative.

In May of 1986, Philippe LeBoubon applied for the pressman's job at Penmaen Lithography a second time.

'I was here a year ago and you didn't make me a courtesy with the interview,' Philippe complained.

'You weren't qualified,' Thom countered. 'You didn't deserve an interview a year ago.'

[69]

'Mon dieu! The guy who qualified didn't do the expectations so good like Napoleon or the guy who qualified wouldn't be in exile on Elba at this very instant!' Philippe replied, mixing his metaphors with a vengeance.

LeBoubon had a point, about Napoleon. Philippe also had initiative, and a lump-sum pension buyout coming his way from MichaelAngelos so he could afford to offer to work the first month at Penmaen for the legal minimum six dollars in lieu of experience provided he was guaranteed two-dollar-an-hour raises at the end of each of the first three months.

Philippe cut himself a deal.

Thom accepted it.

Two years later LeBoubon had talked himself up to thirteen and a quarter an hour. He had forgotten completely the convenience of riding his bicycle to work in Glendaele Village and he took it upon himself to redraft the Penmaen Lithography employment review questionnaire from his own, uniquely bitter, perspective.

The newly varnished document was presented to Sophie, rather than Thom, at break time on the last afternoon before holidays. Sophie smiled and assured LeBoubon that she would review the material with her husband.

'Mais non!' Philippe disagreed. 'That may not be adequate, or acceptable to the employee committee,' Philippe LeBoubon insisted, 'or to myself as lead person.'

'I said,' Sophie repeated herself, 'that I will discuss your thoughts with Thom. I will do what I said I will do, and I will not attempt to do anything more than I said I would do. Thank you. Very much.'

* * *

Two of the Penmaens' largest and most impressive artworks were lithographs hand-tinted by the Ottawa printmaker Jennifer Dickson. 'Hunter's Moon, Bowood' featured a detail of the famous garden in Wiltshire designed by Capability Brown in the eighteenth century. 'Venus of the Parterre d'Eau, Blenheim' depicted a sculpture that was probably commissioned for Blenheim Palace in Oxfordshire, and completed as recently as 1930.

Jennifer Dickson was born at Piet Retief in the Republic of South Africa in 1936. She studied art at Goldsmiths' College in London, England in the early fifties and later apprenticed in Paris at the prestigious graphic workshop Atelier 17 under the direction of the late S.W. Hayter. Dickson's exhibition, 'El suspiro del Moro', was scheduled to open at Wallacks Gallery in Ottawa on Bank Street, Saturday, July 23, close to the mid-point in the Penmaens' two-week summer break.

Thom let himself be persuaded.

'It's going to take for*ever*,' Sophie protested, but Thom was not to be swayed from the northern route to Ottawa – up across Highway 9 an hour to Holland Marsh and then north to Lake Simcoe, partly because there was no particular hurry to arrive at the mouth of the Rideau at any set time, but mostly to avoid the traffic on the 401.

The correct number of lanes to a highway, in Thom's estimation, was two – 'the one that gets ya there, and the other one', as he said in what he thought might pass for a Newfoundland accent, given some confidence by the knowledge that Sophie had never been to Newfoundland. Four-lane highways had been known to give Thom panic attacks. Similarly with forty-foot transport trucks passing at any sort of speed, and portable concrete abutments positioned anywhere within a metre of a hubcap.

'If we go the northern route, we can stop at Sharon Temple,' Thom countered. 'Take our time. Relax. Do the see-sights. We are *supposed* to be on vacation,' Thom added, mimicking his wife in a tone she did not find congenial.

Sophie was not to be mollified. 'Did I *ask* to stop at Sharon Temple?' Sophie asked. 'Do I *know* anything about Sharon Temple? Do I *want* to stop at Sharon Temple? Where is Sharon Temple anyway?'

'North of Newmarket,' Thom replied.

Sharon Temple, as it happened, was closed to the public that very day.

Sophie uncreased the text of LeBoubon's revised employment questionnaire, and started to read aloud in the car. Thom continued the drive north, towards Jackson's Point.

'How can you do that?' asked Thom.

'Do what?'

'Read from a piece of paper in a moving vehicle,' Thom continued. 'Doesn't it bother your inner ear? Or your stomach?'

Sophie shrugged.

The first question had been expanded by LeBoubon and company to ask 'What, in your own words, is your current position? What percentage of your time do you feel you spend at each part? At which part do you feel most adequately trained? And which part the least? On which of your position's responsibilities would a clearer understanding be helpful? How should it be presented?'

A whole lot of verbiage, from Sophie's perspective, scanning just the top of the thing quickly. Much too much ado, about nothing. The other questions continued in a similar vein, often tainted with the underlying implication that management, Thom and Sophie, were remiss, deficient, or incompetent.

'"Two,"' Sophie read aloud. '"Penmaen Lithography does not have a cash incentive for suggestions programme. Do you feel you have made suggestions during the past twelve months which have improved productivity or efficiency and which should be considered in a wage adjustment? Could you put a precise cash value on your suggestions?" — I think I know what LeBoubon is driving at here,' Sophie commented.

'Pray tell,' Thom's knuckles whitened on the steering wheel.

'Philippe was asking to see copies of Whyte-Hooke invoices with Kimwipes billed on them,' Sophie replied.

'LeBoubon thinks that productivity is measured with industrial-strength Kleenex?' Thom was confused.

'I don't know for certain what he thinks he's going to do with the information, but for some reason Philippe was *very* interested in the unit cost of Kimwipes,' warned Sophie. 'The Nubtex cloths, as well.' She continued to read, '"Three. Do you find there are adequate opportunities in your work to use and develop your abilities? Which of your abilities are currently under-utilized and how could they be maximized?"'

'LeBoubon talks a lot about Napoleon,' Thom offered. 'We could maybe take a vote, make him Emperor of Penmaen Lithography. Il Duce.'

'Thom!' Sophie warned. '"Four. Are there aspects of your position for which you will require more experience or training? If there was a training programme available would you be willing to take it? What portion of the costs — in terms of dollars or hours — would you be willing to contribute? Is there any training programme in particular that could benefit you personally and/or the company? Five. Do you feel there are changes that will be required to make your position and the overall company more efficient, productive and enjoyable?"'

'So what now?' Thom demanded. 'LeBoubon wants bigger doughnuts with his expresso?'

'The word is espresso, not expresso,' Sophie corrected her husband. '"Six. Do you feel that your wages are fair compensation for your position in the company? If not, why not? Please compare your position to other similar ones within the

GREAT EXPECTATIONS

company, the village, or the industry. What would you characterize as fair compensation?"'

'Naturally I can't wait to hear what the prick has to say in response to number six,' Thom cursed.

'Why is this such a big problem for you?' Sophie asked. 'I really do not understand why wages have to be such a big problem year after year after year. I thought you told me that Philippe is already making more than any KORD pressman in Wellington County?'

'True story,' Thom confirmed, 'but he's greedy.'

'How do you know that, for sure?' Sophie challenged.

'Because I asked the paper salesman from Whyte-Hooke to check it out,' Thom's voice rose a notch. He tightened his grip on the steering wheel. A roadside billboard advertised 'The Briars, twelve km.'

'Does Philippe know that?' Sophie continued.

'What?'

'That he's the highest-paid KORD operator in Wellington County,' Sophie clarified.

'Damn right!' Thom insisted.

'How so?' Sophie was not convinced.

'Because Philippe bribed the Whyte-Hooke guy to check it out too!' Thom replied. 'Asked Jim Dunne to find out the same thing I asked Dunne to check. Only I didn't pay for the information.'

Sophie was still not convinced.

'We buy $80,000 worth of paper a year from the Whyte-Hooke guy,' Thom explained. 'LeBoubon slipped Dunne twenty bucks. Jim took the twenty bucks and gave Philippe the same information he gave me for free, only LeBoubon didn't get the answer he thought he was going to get. Philippe's always suspicious that we're taking unfair advantage of him, even if we aren't. So naturally I'm suspicious that LeBoubon's taking unfair advantage of us, just because

[74]

he's suspicious. It takes one to know one.'

'So Philippe is already the best-paid KORD pressman in the county, and he knows it, and he bribed Jim Dunne to confirm it. So what's his problem?' It was Sophie's turn to be confused. 'Why don't you just talk to Philippe? Reason with him?'

'Because I don't like the jerk,' Thom replied. 'Read on.'

'"Seven,"' Sophie continued. '"Do you feel that your personal level of productivity is making the company more profitable? How would you measure that level? How much profit do you feel you have personally contributed to Penmaen Lithography in the past twelve months?"'

Thom rolled his eyeballs.

'Keep your eyes on the road,' Sophie chided. 'The straight and the narrow. "Eight. Do you feel that you know enough of the company's short and long range scheduling to understand how your current assignment makes you part of the team? If not, what information do you feel you are lacking and how could it be better presented?"'

'Bigger doughnuts, with expresso coffee,' Thom interjected. 'I'm telling you, this whole employment review thing is winding up to the size of the hole in the middle of Philippe's doughnut. We're talking centimetres. Millimetres.'

'Espresso,' Sophie replied. 'I told you before, the word is espresso. "Nine. Would you be interested to learn other aspects of the business? Which ones? Why? Ten. Are there considerations such as travel, flexible working hours, holiday scheduling, family and personal needs or benefit plans which could be taken into account to enhance your working environment?"'

'Oh, for Christ ...' Thom began his summation.

'So why do we have to put up with this guy?' Sophie continued, crumpling the newly revised employment-review document into a tight little wad not much bigger than a table tennis ball. 'You don't like him. I don't like him. How are we supposed to tolerate someone with a chip on his shoulder the size of a block and tackle? Why don't we just fire him?'

'Wrongful dismissal, for one reason,' Thom suggested, changing his tack just about 180 degrees where Highway 48 turned back south to meet up with Number 7 east to Peterborough. 'Constructive dismissal, for another. LeBoubon's had the thrill of his employee coven, he's gotten his way a little bit. Let's let the four harpies fill out whatever they want on their report cards and see what we get back in August. Little Lorrie Wright, for one, is spineless. I think we can count on that. Push Philippe at this point just when he's got a bucket of steam up to boil and you're looking at a union for sure, maybe even a human rights tribunal!' Thom warned. 'And guess who would be captain of the contract negotiating team, *and* the grievance committee.'

'If you were Arthur Campbellford,' Sophie challenged, 'you'd fire LeBoubon in a minute. Arthur Campbellford would fire him, you know that.'

'Campbellford is a lawyer,' Thom replied, 'that limits significantly the potential for legal expenses in a suit.'

'What is Philippe's problem, exactly? You're the one who's supposed to know how men think,' Sophie challenged.

'I know how men think,' Thom agreed. 'But I'm not convinced that it's just Philippe by himself that we're up against here.'

'?' Sophie asked.

'There's Imogene LeBoubon, masquerading as the long suffering house-frau, and then there's that poisonous little wench Lorrie Wright and I do not, as you have indicated yourself many times, have the faintest idea how women think. And you're forgetting that I was hopeless in French,' Thom replied.

'I'm not forgetting. That's where we met, remember? In

PHILIPPE LEBOUBON

Professor Neuman's tutorial. Neuman asked if anyone had any questions about the first two French lectures of the semester and you put up your hand and admitted you hadn't understood a word of either one. No one in the class could believe you had the nerve to be that honest. Everyone laughed at you.' Sophie's recollection of the incident was not incorrect. 'What's French got to do with it?'

'Philippe LeBoubon is French. And I did *not* understand a word of either lecture. I was telling the truth,' Thom confirmed.

The first night on the road to Ottawa the Penmaens stopped in Peterborough. Thom was disappointed that Sophie steadfastly refused to consider modelling salacious lingerie in a motel room in which the breeze-block walls perspired and the shag carpet had a certain odour to it, though even Thom was forced to agree that the walls were damp and the carpet probably did support a greater range of biodiversity than might normally be expected in Astroturf.

The next morning in the car, en route to lunch in Perth, there was considerable conjugal discussion about the relative merits of doing 'things right' as opposed to doing 'the right thing'. The debate began as a squabble about the alleged depravity of males, and degenerated rapidly into a spitting match about accounting.

To do 'things right', as Thom understood it, was to sort your pocket change into nickels, dimes and quarters, to balance your chequebook, to file the books in your personal library alphabetically by author, things like that, to 'rearrange the deck chairs on the *Titanic*' as a noted accountant once suggested. Desirable pursuits, but not so critical as doing the 'right thing', which often required the conscious and deliberate evasion of pocket change, monthly bank statements and trolleys of unfiled library books, to ensure that, if nothing else, the *Titanic* does not hit the iceberg.

Sophie, for her part, remembered each of the times Thom failed to file Workmen's Compensation reconciliations on time and revisited those shortcomings with astonishing clarity. Thom, on the other hand, had been known to ask Sophie to deliberately delay a VISA payment or maybe a municipal tax bill, often with a view to fluffing up a fiscal year-end or hoodwinking a loans officer.

Sophie had difficulties with the verb 'to hoodwink', and she was incapable of comprehending the effective use of fluff as a negotiating tactic in dealing with chartered banks.

Sophie was born in Germany, in a small village on the Rhine not far from Königswinter. She had a deep-rooted mistrust of officialdom of any kind, a distaste for the completion of official-looking forms and an aversion to unpaid bills in excess of her fear of documentation and mistrust of bureaucracy combined and factored to a power of two.

Annual employment reviews were looming in August, so 'surely', Sophie argued, the thing to do was to do 'things right' and attend first to personal obligations to the employees as human beings.

'Philippe LeBoubon?' Thom asked. 'Surely you're not trying to suggest that trained baboon is human?'

'Thom!'

'OK OK OK, but why don't we just postpone the damn employment reviews until after we know for sure what's happening with Pegaesean?' asked Thom. From his point of view this was a completely reasonable sort of a delay if Pegaesean really *was* contemplating the purchase of Penmaen Lithography at an early date. Maybe September? Possibly October? 'So maybe employment review this summer is inappropriate because how can we ever hope to convince Jayne Beauregard to be happy with an increase of fifty cents an hour if Philippe

LeBoubon figures he's soon to be working for Galen Nicholas Aldebaan and exercising preferential stock options in Pegaesean, Springfield, Confederate Glass and Hessen.' Thom was frustrated. 'Little Lorrie Wright and friends get to meet Big Daddy Warbucks and there he is, right out of the funnies, diamond stickpin stuck in the middle of his silk cravat,' added Thom. 'And if that is to be the new reality, then surely the "right thing" to do at the moment has to be the financial stuff requested by Daddy Warbucks' personal emissary Geoffrey Bowles, no? Maybe postpone the odious personnel reviews?' Thom suggested. 'I'm starting to pull together an organizational flow chart for Penmaen.'

'So?' Sophie grimaced.

'I'm calling it "The Rain in Spain",' Thom replied, grinning in spite of himself.

Sophie was having none of it. No rain, no Spain. Sophie disagreed all the way through Havelock, Madoc and Kaladar, through lunch in Perth and on to Ottawa in the heat of the afternoon. 'It's just not right,' she insisted, 'and anyway, what's the difference?'

'The difference between what and what?' asked Thom.

'Between doing things right and doing the right thing dammit,' Sophie replied. 'Haven't you been paying attention?'

'I'm paying attention, I'm paying attention,' Thom repeated. 'It's the difference between working *in* a business, and *on* a business. That simple.'

'Who told you that?' snapped Sophie.

'Grant Robinson,' Thom replied, in a bit of an elevated tone. Thom knew that Sophie would accept much of what their accountant advised virtually without question.

'So. What did Grant mean when he said that?' Sophie was unsure.

'If you're working *in* the business, you're busy with the

busy-ness of tiresome stuff like Workmen's Compensation reconciliations and you don't give yourself the space to step back and consider the expanse of the water going over Niagara Falls – like how much do we figure Penmaen Lithography is worth if we're going to sell?' Thom replied.

'Does that mean you've decided we're going to sell?' Sophie asked, a little too ingenuously for Thom's mood.

'That is not what I said!' Thom insisted. 'You know damn well that is *not* what I said.'

'What did you say?' Sophie persisted. 'Don't get your knickers twisted. We owe it to Jayne and to Philippe, to Lorrie and to Yvette Charbeau to put their concerns first,' Sophie resumed the refrain. 'Especially now you've gone and raised their expectations by letting them rewrite the questions on the stupid employment review form.'

'Why do we owe it to them?' Thom raised his eyelids.

'Because they're people, dammit, you dolt. Human beings. That's why!' Sophie exclaimed, with an uncharacteristic level of conviction.

'So what about Aldebaan?' Thom countered. 'Maybe he's human too?'

'Not the same thing!'

'Because?' Thom challenged.

'Have you met him? No. Do you know anything about him, really? I mean, personally. No. For all you know for sure, Mr Penmaen,' Sophie added, 'Galen Nicholas Aldebaan is a figment of Geoffrey Bowles's fertile imagination. Maybe, just maybe, my Thom, Galen Nicholas Aldebaan doesn't even exist!' Sophie rested her case.

'Grant Robinson said he met Aldebaan once,' Thom volleyed again.

'Where?' Sophie was suspicious.

'In Bermuda. At the Royal Bermuda Yacht Club,' Thom answered impatiently.

PHILIPPE LEBOUBON

'When did Grant tell you that?' Sophie was still suspicious. 'He didn't. It's in the foreword, page seven. You haven't read the foreword yet?' Thom was starting to suspect that maybe doing the 'right thing' was a thing that males did for some genetic reason and that doing 'things right' was a concept so alien that only a female could begin to understand it. Thom was also starting to suspect that Sophie was the sort of creature who actually enjoyed rearranging living room furniture, and navigated by landmarks rather than the points of the compass.

'Do you even *own* a compass?' Sophie asked in her defence, then answered her own question: 'No. So what do you mean you navigate by direction? Which direction?'

'East,' replied Thom, pointing in the direction of the Rideau Canal.

★ ★ ★

Jennifer Dickson's latest suite of lithographs took as its point of departure the Puerta de la Justicia in the south wall of the 'Qal'a al-Hambra', literally the 'Red Castle', the storied Alhambra palace in Granada, Andalusia, in the south of Spain.

It was not unaccustomed for Dickson to do such a thing, to seek out the sanctuary of an exotic culture and to walk purposefully through an ancient portal intent on the conservation of history and most particularly of sites that include gardens as magnificent as those of the Generalife, the so-called 'Gardens of the Architect' attached to the east wing of the Alhambra palace.

The first image in the suite of Dickson's lithographs highlights a single white keystone, probably alabaster, embossed with the image of a baroque locksmith's key and set directly above the arch of the Puerta de la Justicia. The portal leads to the Plaza de los Aljibes, Sophie and Thom read from the printed tablet that accompanied each lithograph in the exhibition.

The Torre Quebrada is named after the huge crack in its foundation, which may have opened during the earthquake of 1522, and then yawned wider with the explosion of a powder magazine that added to the misery of pestilence and plague in the valley of the river Darro later in the sixteenth century.

The artist illustrates the extent of the chasm with a detail of purple acanthus growing in profusion in the cleft.

The Broken Tower defines the eastern limit of the Alcazaba, a fortress overlooking both the Arab district of Granada and the older gypsy district, Sacromonte, but the plainness of the citadel in no way prepares the visitor for the intricacies of the arabesque motifs and filigreed cartouches of the Alhambra that would inspire the poet Francisco de Icaza.

> Dale limosna, mujer,
> Que no hay en la vida nada
> Como la pena de ser
> Ciego en Granada.

✺

> Give him alms, woman
> For there is nothing in this life so cruel
> As the grief of being
> Blind in Granada.

✺

To the north, we pass the Torre del Homenaje, the Keep, which served as a prison for generations of pirates from the Barbary Coast, for collaborators with the French of various sorts, and for the infamous Juan Alvarez de Mendizábal, an economist and one-time Chancellor of the Exchequer to the court of the Nasrite kings. Also a noted fraud.

Directly to the east, the Machuca Court leads into the Mexuar, the Court of Justice, and from the Mexuar to the Myrtle Court, which features a narrow reflecting pool lined on either side with boxwood clipped to a height of three feet. 'This is a public place, a court of petitions and of audiences, of dispensations and of ambassadors,' Sophie read aloud.

'An auspicious spot to conduct annual employment reviews,' Thom observed wryly, bending to look closely at the image. 'The emissaries of His Eminence M. Philippe le Boubon have arrived, from Burgundy. I have seated them in the Mexuar where they await your kind ministrations.' Thom was thinking out loud.

'What are you giggling about?' Sophie asked. 'You don't normally giggle.'

'I'm not giggling,' Thom replied. 'I don't giggle. I never giggle. I don't even know how to giggle. Can't. Don't have the facial muscles for it. Even if I wanted to, which I don't.' Then Thom added, 'Do you think Philippe LeBoubon has lice?'

'Lice? What *are* you talking about?'

'Nothing. Leave it now,' was what Thom answered, but it wasn't really what he was thinking. Emissaries from Burgundy to the court of the Nasrites in the early fifteenth century would have been obliged to endure the humiliation of a delousing before gaining admission to the grandeur of the Myrtle Court. Thom found the notion amusing. LeBoubon had recently taken to opening the screen in the door to the pressroom whenever either of the adjacent properties had their septic tanks emptied. The stench of the methane quickly permeated the entire shop, particularly the bindery and the office on the ground floor. Thom felt convinced that LeBoubon opened the window deliberately, on such occasions. Sophie was equally convinced LeBoubon was absentminded, rather than malicious. Thom was also suspicious that

LeBoubon deliberately left the water in the pressroom sink running so as to overflow their own septic tank.

Sophie thought Thom was paranoid.

By the mid-fifteenth century the dynasty of the Nasrids in Granada had begun to unravel. Muley Hassan was smitten with the charms of a Christian princess and considered repudiating Queen Ayesha, mother of his heir Boabdil, in favour of the many courtesies of the heathen Zoraya.

Conjugal jealousy and concern for the regal birthright of Boabdil forced Ayesha first to flee the city, which was already consumed with feuds between the family of the Abencerrajes in support of herself, and of her son, and those of the Zegris in support of Zoraya.

Mother and son were not long in returning to Granada where they succeeded in dethroning the adulterer Hassan and his brother with him, but fatally split the loyalties of the kingdom in the victory. Preying on this weakness, the Christian Fernando the Fifth of Aragón managed to detain Boabdil, the Boy King, then bartered the safety of His Regal Person for the favour of military disengagement while the Catholic monarchs annexed ever greater tracts of Moorish Andalusia.

Boabdil had little choice.

The heir to the Nasrite throne turned at the end on his allies, three dozen of whom reputedly died by his hand in the infamous Hall of the Abencerrajes. The treachery greased an erosion of civic morale that manifested itself when Ferdinand and Isabella laid siege to Granada and then entered the city at the Holy Feast of the Birth of the Christ Child virtually unopposed. The Christian conquest of the last Moorish stronghold in Spain was completed mere months before Christopher Columbus set sail for the New World in the spring of 1492.

Boabdil fled to the south, to the Alpujarres mountains

where it is reported that he turned for one last look at the glory of Granada, which had been his to rule. His mother took offence at his weakness and full advantage of the opportunity to publicly vilify her son, accusing him of weeping 'like a woman, for what you could not hold as a man,' Sophie read from the last of the tablets.

The stony outcrop in the foothills of the Alpujarres mountains to the south of Granada faces at a distance both the southern rampart of the Alhambra Palace and the southern exposure of the infamous Hall of the Abencerrajes. It is called, not inappropriately, el Suspiro del Moro, the Moor's Sigh.

* * *

August 1 was a Monday, the midsummer civic holiday. The simmering feud between George Bell and Jimy Williams had finally erupted the previous Tuesday in Minneapolis when Bell failed to hit the cutoff man on a routine Kirby Puckett single into the gap with two on and the Jays leading 3-0. Bell golfed a lazy moonshot over second base on in to the catcher on two bounces, the Twins scored a run on the play and the base runners advanced to second and third on the error. Both runners scored later in the inning and the Twins went on to win the game 6-3.

This sort of incident was not uncommon, for Bell, but this one time Williams seized the opportunity to explain in some explicit detail to his star outfielder just precisely what the manager thought of his fielding, his attitude, his batting average and the smell of his game socks.

George Bell was riding the pine tar the next day when the Jays unexpectedly managed to eke out a win against Frank Viola pitching for the Minnesota Twins. Bell was still on the bench when the Jays travelled to New York for a weekend series with the Yankees. The Toronto sport pages were full of little else the last week of July.

GREAT EXPECTATIONS

PARTY IS FINALLY OVER FOR BELL.
GEORGE'S WAR OF WORDS — BLOW BY BLOW.
BYE BYE BELL! JAYS FANS SAY.
WILLIAMS GETS FANS' BACKING IN DISPUTE.

Monday there was no newspaper.

Tuesday there was no mention of Pegaesean in the *Globe*. Nor Wednesday.

'Nothing?' Sophie asked. 'Again? Are you completely sure? Geoffrey Bowles did say the first week of August, didn't he?' Then she added, 'His name was John Beresford Tipton.'

'Whose name?' Thom wasn't paying attention.

'The millionaire. You asked me the name of the philanthropist on the television show *The Millionaire*, you remember? John Beresford Tipton, that was his name.'

'I'm impressed,' Thom answered. 'I am truly impressed, but what I really wanted to know was the name of the guy who delivered the cheques for Tipton, Michael ... ?'

'Anthony,' Sophie replied.

'Michael Anthony. I think you're absolutely right!' Thom applauded.

'Why don't we offer Jayne a one-dollar-an-hour raise retroactive to August 1 and have done with it?' Sophie added, changing the subject dramatically.

'On the basis of what, precisely?' asked Thom. 'I thought I said fifty cents? I'm sure I said fifty cents.'

'Maybe you said fifty cents, I don't remember. On the basis of nothing more than a feeling, a gut feeling. The same sort of reason I just came up with the name Michael Anthony. Instinct. Last time Jayne got a raise it was a dollar, so maybe a dollar is the right number, or maybe it isn't. Maybe it's just a number that's close enough to get a discussion started,' Sophie answered.

'OK, you've got a discussion started, but why a buck? What

[86]

about a thousand-buck bonus, cash up front, and have done with the thing for a year. No raise, but Jayne gets some money in her pocket and over the course of twelve months we save maybe $800 off what a buck-an-hour raise would cost,' Thom fantasized.

'How many hours does Jayne work in a year?' Sophie asked.

'Are you assuming she'll book off sick most afternoons on Friday and half the Mondays in the morning?' Thom challenged Sophie.

'Thom!' Sophie warned her husband.

'If you give Jayne a buck, you'll have to give LeBoubon a buck and a quarter to be sure.' Thom switched his tack. 'Jayne and Philippe are like brother and sister ... Jayne will be happy with just about anything we offer so long as it's more than Philippe gets, and Philippe will be more than content so long as he can be convinced he's getting a premium on whatever it is that Jayne gets. And then what do you do with that little snit Miss Lorrie Wright?'

'But that's not fair!' insisted Sophie. 'Forget Lorrie Wright, I don't care about Lorrie Wright. Philippe hasn't been with the company as long as Jayne, he doesn't know anything about computers, he *never* helps with the garbage ...'

'... because he considers garbage to be beneath his station,' Thom interrupted. 'He's French, remember, and his family has lived in Burgundy since the time of the Crusades. And he's distantly related to some sort of poisoner who was tight with the court of Louis the Fourteenth. Courtiers, my sweet, do not *do* Glad bags.'

'Practitioner,' Sophie corrected Thom, 'not poisoner. Medical practitioner.'

'At Versailles,' Thom replied, 'there was a difference?'

'What does Burgundy have to do with wage review?' Sophie inquired. 'Or Versailles?'

'We weren't talking about wage review, we were talking about garbage, remember, and don't call it "wage" review either, that's what LeBoubon calls it. Call it "employment" review, please!' Thom insisted.

'And the subtle difference, which at this very moment escapes me, is ... ?' Sophie inquired.

'The difference is,' Thom paused to align his marbles. 'Remember we used to print books for the francophone publisher from North Bay? And I thought M. le directeur-generale was a bit dim because he knew nothing about page imposition, but M. le directeur-generale was equally convinced that I was a nobody because I didn't have a private office, let alone a secretary with an appropriately sized bosom!'

'You,' Sophie advised, icily, 'are in imminent danger of exile to Englehart. I happen to think Jayne Beauregard has a very pleasant figure.'

'You mean Thessalon, don't you? Not Englehart. It's Thessalon that's a hundred miles from the edge of civilization as we know it. And so does Jayne, think she has a nice figure, but M. le directeur-generale wasn't impressed, and Jayne really does not need the support of those lacy double-D bra straps she's ever eager to flaunt,' Thom replied.

'Which you ogle,' Sophie countered.

'The difference,' Thom changed the topic, 'is that wage review happens when LeBoubon holds a cocked pistol to my temple and rags me in some tedious detail about the ruinous cost to his immediate family of the prescription pharmaceuticals essential to curbing his wife's ample appetite.'

Sophie pursed her lips.

'Employment review, on the other hand, happens when I hold a cocked pistol to *his* temple and explain to him in a mannered tone that he can't have a buck-and-a-half increase in wages because he doesn't buy in to the corporate mission statement, he isn't a team player and he apparently suffers from an undiagnosed allergy to polyethylene because he never takes out the garbage,' Thom suggested.

'Polypropylene. You mean polypropylene, don't you? Not polyethylene.'

'Whatever,' Thom snarled.

'So maybe LeBoubon doesn't get a buck and a half, maybe he gets a buck even but we offer some kind of health package?' Sophie replied.

'That includes weight-loss pills? And season tickets to the Blue Jays for Jayne Beauregard to watch George Bell and Jimy Williams squabble? I don't think so, sends all kinds of ambivalent messages to the employees, but even if you *do* decide to offer some kind of benefit package, remember what Grant Robinson said about benefit packages,' Thom cautioned.

Sophie raised an eyebrow.

'Grant said that employees compare their employment situations with other employees by comparing wages, or salaries, but they don't necessarily bother to consider intangibles like benefit packages and whether or not this package or that package includes or does not include weight-control pharmaceuticals or Blue Jays tickets on the first base line. Grant's point was that even if you do decide to add a benefit package you're always better off to share the costs fifty-fifty with the employees.'

'Because that way it costs half as much?' Sophie asked.

'That too,' Thom agreed, 'but that's not what Grant meant. The thing is that if Penmaen Lithography pays 100 per cent of a benefit package, Jayne Beauregard rapidly comes to take the benefit for granted and we lose the advantage of the incentive. You can see it yourself...'

'... but we don't *have* a benefit package,' Sophie interrupted.

'Not really, but sort of ... you serve the employees coffee and doughnuts at breaktime,' Thom replied. 'Real doughnuts.

With big holes. And you pay them an extra week off between Christmas and New Year's.'

'... well, that's hardly anything ...'

'It's hardly anything? Like hell it's hardly anything! Do you really think Henry Ford personally passes out apple-cinnamon muffins at 10:00 a.m. on the line in Oakville?' asked Thom. 'Do you have any idea why the waitresses at Witherspoon's aren't allowed to work more than twenty-five hours a week?'

'Ex*cuse* me. Auto workers at Ford make more than $13 an hour. Even my father made more than $13 an hour at Ford, and that was in the 1960s!' Sophie replied. 'Why are the waitresses at Witherspoon's limited to twenty-five hours a week? Are the waitresses at Witherspoon's not allowed to work more than twenty-five hours a week? I didn't know that. How could I possibly be expected to know that?'

'Philippe makes $13.25,' Thom insisted, '*before* doughnuts.'

'OK OK OK, $13.25. Auto workers at Ford make *way* more than $13.25.' Sophie refused to concede. 'Why are the waitresses at Witherspoon's limited to twenty-five hours a week?'

'Quite so,' Thom agreed, 'and Henry Ford personally rents out the cafeteria concession and claws back fifty cents a cup every time someone wants a coffee. A nickel more if they want cream. Fifty-seven cents if they want white and sweet, sixty-four cents for double double. And the waitresses at Witherspoon's aren't allowed to work more than twenty-five hours a week because if they did, then Ebenezer Witherspoon would have to pay them eight hours for Christmas Day, which he doesn't!'

'So what do you expect me to do?' Sophie asked in exasperation, 'put a tin cup beside the coffee urn? I don't care what the Witherspoons do to their staff, I want to treat our people right.'

'It's a thought,' added Thom, 'about the tin cup. But you can't because it's too late now. My point is that I can't remember the last time Philippe LeBoubon thanked you for his free coffee and doughnut and neither can you, so you've lost the incentive value of the premium.'

'Is there a cafeteria where Grant Robinson works?' Sophie challenged.

'I think so, like a lunchroom, yeah,' Thom replied warily. 'Cafeteria might be too grand a word.'

'Is there a coffee urn in the lunchroom?' Sophie continued to press her advantage.

'I remember a framed reproduction of a Ken Danby watercolour on the wall, of a kid in blue jeans standing beside a wooden horse on an old circus carousel. And there's a plaque that says the painting was commissioned by the City of Guelph to celebrate its 150th anniversary and underneath the plaque there's a coffee urn,' Thom acknowledged. 'And now that you mention it, I distinctly recall seeing a cup, filled with quarters.'

'You're making that up!'

'What?' Thom turned his palms face up.

Thursday morning, there it was. Not in the Business section where Thom had been searching in vain all week, but in the Arts section. A small item buried on page 6 right opposite 'Blondie', 'Mary Worth' and 'Gasoline Alley' – 'PEGAESEAN BUYS RESPECTED LITERARY PUBLISHER'. Thom almost missed it.

'What does it say?' Sophie wanted to know, though she wondered if she did, really.

There were three short columns, each maybe three inches deep, one of which was a file photograph of Nicholas Aldebaan done up in his best Savile Row Sunday go-to–St Paul's Cathedral attire. 'Each of the principals declined to divulge details of the sale,' Thom read aloud, 'but Aldebaan allowed as to how he felt "lucky to strike a deal with the most creative and the best publishing company in Canada." ... That's a bit thick, wouldn't you say?'

For their part, Thom read further, Duckworth & Osborne, Labellarte were convinced that 'The company will maintain its editorial independence and direction. Everything will stay the same, but Pegaesean will give us the financial base to allow us the freedom to do what we love to do even better.'

Aldebaan apparently agreed with the sentiments expressed on behalf of D&OL by Will Duckworth. The article ended with Aldebaan quoted as saying 'I don't think it would be advisable for me, from an investment standpoint, to interfere with what I consider to be a winning formula.'

'There it is,' Thom crowed. 'We're rich!'

Chapter Four
Will Duckworth

William Duckworth, like many of his zealous, but chronically overworked and underpaid colleagues in the Canadian publishing industry, was not an easy person to reach by telephone.

Duckworth's aversion to the use of digital switching equipment was, in part, a stress management technique designed to keep expectant authors, patient suppliers and earnest loans officers all at a respectful distance for however long it might take for the annual infusion of cash from the Canada Council to arrive. In Duckworth's long and colourful career in publishing he had learned, if nothing else, that cheques from the Canada Council do not arrive by telephone.

Very little, in fact, of what might be construed as good news by the Canadian publishing industry arrives by telephone. It cost Thom Penmaen three full days of dogged trial by telephone-answering-device, but Thom finally managed to reach Will Duckworth at the offices of Duckworth & Osborne, Labellarte the following Tuesday, August 9.

'How are you?' Duckworth asked, relieved to be talking to someone who wanted to discuss anything other than schedules of payments for accounts past due. Duckworth fingered the plunger on a mechanical timer on his desk as he cradled the receiver to his ear.

'Still in business,' Thom replied. 'Same business.'

'You're kidding,' Duckworth took up the challenge, leaning back in his armchair. 'That well? You don't say! So how much of my busy day do you intend to waste explaining how perfectly dissatisfied you are, after fifteen years, that you still haven't screwed up and that Penmaen is still in business?'

'An hour?' Thom suggested, tentatively, skirting the playful banter.

'An hour!?' Duckworth protested. 'Sixty minutes? Whatever are we going to find to talk about for sixty minutes? I'm sure you're a fascinating fellow, a prince of an entrepreneur, and possibly even a borderline genius, but you need an entire hour to recite a litany of your many achievements? Could we do the trailer? Rather than the whole CV?'

'OK OK OK, not an hour. How 'bout half an hour? Fifteen minutes if you promise to talk fast. Very fast. I *have* to talk to you. I have questions. My *wife* has questions,' Thom tried to convey something of the immediacy of his plight.

'I hear you. Believe me, I hear you. Tuesday afternoon next week. The 16th, 4:30. Half an hour,' Duckworth suggested. 'I'll talk fast.'

Duckworth's office at D&OL was on the second floor of a partially renovated Victorian townhouse on the north side of Sullivan Street just east of Spadina and a block or two south of the Victory Burlesque.

William Duckworth was a short man with a salt-and-pepper beard and a nervous tic above his left eye.

Duckworth was also inordinately proud, as he rarely failed to mention, that the view to the southeast from his office window ... across a vacant lot, to the right of a large horse chestnut and down the alley between two nineteenth-century row houses ... included a bit — 'just a little bit, but a bit nonetheless' — of the distinctive white retractable roof of the Skydome. Future home of the Toronto Blue Jays' American League franchise.

Duckworth himself was a noted local intellectual, a man whose breadth of vision was reflected in the catholicism inherent in the D&OL publishing programme. Duckworth was also an unlikely but avid baseball fan, who had personally championed the publication of *Bases on Balls*, an exhaustive statistical account of the Jays' 1984 season.

'So what do you think about Jimy Williams benching George Bell in Minneapolis the other week?' Thom Penmaen asked, hoping to break some ice with the notoriously difficult publisher.

Duckworth lifted a bushy eyebrow over the rim of a thick pair of black-framed reading glasses. 'I hadn't realized you were a baseball fan?' he responded, quizzically.

'I'm not,' Thom replied. 'I'm a printer. Don't have much time for spectator sports. And I've never attended a game at the CNE myself, but I do follow the baseball a bit in the *Globe*. Mostly to be able to commiserate with my secretary.'

'She's a baseball fan?' Duckworth asked. 'Your secretary?'

'Oh, Jayne Beauregard usually tries to wheedle the afternoon off for opening day in the spring. Normally I don't think much of the idea. And normally Jayne whines and wheedles until she gets her way. I'm not completely convinced she would be quite so keen if the opening game were played on her own time rather than during working hours, but she's a fan, yeah. Jayne Beauregard can quote you batting averages a lot quicker than she can type you a letter. More accurately too, I'd guess, not that I'd have any way of knowing for sure if her batting averages were spot on. Her spelling could be better. Her diction too,' Thom complained.

'Bell screwed up in Minneapolis,' Duckworth took a swing at the topic. 'Williams was right, Bell should have hit the cut-off man. Close only counts in horseshoes, and Bell wasn't within sixty feet of a play at the plate. Thing is, though, that Bell is hitting .357 with 47 RBIs, .397 with men on base.'

'That's good?' Thom Penmaen did not in fact know a great deal about the game, or the Toronto Blue Jays franchise, though he did pride himself on owning a genuine copyright felt Blue Jays ball cap. Size seven and a quarter. Thom despised the more common, but cheaper, imitations with the adjustable plastic headbands. Thom liked to wear the ball cap for gardening.

'Not as good as last year, but the Jays didn't have anyone hitting any better up to the all-star break. Right at the moment, *no* one in the American League has anyone hitting any better, and Jimy Williams doesn't hit. He's the manager. Managers don't hit .357 and they don't pocket $1.9 million a year. Nobody, not even Pat Gillick, is ever going to sell tickets to anyone on Front Street to watch a manager work a chaw of Red Man Plug in the dugout.' Duckworth paused to savour the righteousness of his analysis.

'So you think Bell is going to get his way?' Thom was relieved that Duckworth was talking. Not that Duckworth was talking about anything Thom wanted to know, particularly, but at least Duckworth was talking.

'Bell stays put, this season. Bell can hit a ball. It's probably not fair to Williams, and Bell really should have hit the cutoff man in Minneapolis, and it's going to cause some bickering in the clubhouse, but Williams is out of there for sure, and sooner too, rather than later. He won't be able to pull the plug quite so quick but if Pat Gillick is smart he'll be looking to unload Bell too, maybe in the spring – maybe trade a Dominican attitude problem for a pair of young arms, that wouldn't be half bad of a deal. Good pitching beats good hitting two times out of three. Give the ball to Dave Stieb, that's all you really need to know.' Duckworth rested his case.

'Is that a fact? About the pitching and the hitting? Two times out of three? Do you wager much on the games?' Thom was surprised. 'I thought Williams took Stieb out early, last week, in New York.'

'I didn't say that I gamble. You said that. I'm just trying to explain to you how the game that Abner Doubleday may or may not have invented works at the major league level. Did you ever play on a sandlot,' Duckworth asked, 'when you were younger? And how did you know that Williams pulled Stieb early in New York? I thought you said you didn't follow baseball much?'

Thom squirmed in his seat. 'I used to be able to throw a ball pretty well, at one time. I spent whole summers when I was seven, maybe eight, throwing pitch and catch to myself against the chimney of my parents' house in Montreal. Drove my mother crazy, so she said. Wound all the kinks out of my shoulder though. But I couldn't run, or hit, for beans. I wasn't very strong, and I don't think my eyes were quick enough. Hand-to-eye co-ordination wasn't great.'

Duckworth laughed. 'So what happened to your beautiful throwing arm in the end?'

'I ripped the rotator cuff throwing a stick for a Border collie. The ligaments healed, more or less. It took a long time, and the arm was never the same after that,' Penmaen explained.

'It happens,' Duckworth agreed, then changed his tone. 'Apart from the burning question of which team has a prayer of catching the Tigers at the top of the AL East, which is presumably not the reason you called this meeting, what else would you like to know?'

'I feel a bit like a mouse, looking up at the working underside of an elephant's hoof.' Thom prided himself on his unique ability to tell the truth, most of the time, in almost any situation — though he rarely had much to lose, in any given situation, much of the time. Thom plunged onward. 'How much can you tell me about Galen Nicholas Aldebaan? The man, the deal, the tenor of the negotiations ... I dunno, could we go somewhere on Spadina? Could I buy you a drink?' Thom offered, awkwardly.

'I am a member of Alcoholics Anonymous,' Duckworth replied.

Thom cringed.

'I've been on the wagon seven years, so, no, thank you, not a drink. I don't think that would be helpful. But if you feel like a mouse, then D&OL is probably not much bigger than a mole. I spoke to Rebeca this afternoon before you arrived. We spent, between us, maybe $20,000 for a mergers and acquisitions guy to piece together a management contract...'

'Twenty thousand dollars!?' Thom interrupted. 'You spent $20,000? Before you even had a deal signed with Aldebaan?' Thom wished, in retrospect, that he had not suggested the drink on Spadina.

'I know. Twenty thousand, that's the number. Big number.' Duckworth did not mince words. 'And what the thing says, basically, stripped of the participles, the legalese and the subordinate clauses, is that Rebeca and I each get a salary of $75,000 a year, effective starting day one. Which wouldn't impress Dave Stieb, or Ernie Whitt.'

'That's a hell of a lot more than you've been making up to now, surely?' Thom speculated that Sophie might be encouraged to hear such a number.

'It is,' Duckworth continued drily, 'more than we've been accustomed to bleeding the company in the past, but now we no longer own the company. Aldebaan owns it. The contract also says that it's D&OL that has to pony up the $150,000 in management salary — and that's Duckworth & Osborne, Labellarte, mind. Us. Rebeca and I. Not Pegaesean, corporately, and certainly not Aldebaan personally. Basically what the agreement means at the end of the day is that Rebeca and I have just bloated our overhead well beyond any distant possibility of profitability....'

'Surely Aldebaan is aware of that?' Thom queried.

'I don't know,' Duckworth was surprisingly reflective. 'You

would think someone with a background in Canadian publishing would know that, but I couldn't really say for sure. Pegaesean made a lot of money with Aldebaan's own history of the prime ministers, and Bowles keeps harping on about cost controls to the point I sometimes think.... No, never mind what I think, that would be nothing more than conjecture on my part and I don't honestly know.' Duckworth retreated from any further analysis.

'Geoffrey Bowles isn't one of those clowns who thinks the only thing wrong with Canadian publishing is that he, personally, isn't involved?' asked Thom. 'I hope?'

'We hope not. Rebeca hopes not. Let's all hope not,' Duckworth agreed, 'but in the meantime you better have a look at this management contract thing. Rebeca says she's OK sharing it, she likes you. We'll white out the specifics, of course, but at least you'll get a look at the range of issues that come into play. A bunt up the third base line is quite different from a single through the gap into right, though the result may well be identical, but all of this is premature until you get your own best shot past Geoffrey Bowles. Have you done the lunch thing with Geoffrey yet?'

'Just the once. Bowles phoned, and then subsequently he came up to Glendaele Village. We did grilled cheese on white, Heinz on the side, but I wasn't left with much of an impression. Who is he? What's he like? And where in God's name does he come from? Sophie talks intuitively about Bowles like he fell off some adjacent planet,' Thom told Duckworth, 'which may well be true for all I know, but the thing I would like to know is – which planet?'

'Take a careful look at your inventory,' Duckworth advised. 'Sharpen your pencils. Bowles has this thing about dead spruce on the balance sheet, otherwise he's not that meddlesome. Geoffrey used to work for Stephen Roman at Denison Mines. And his wife, Stephanie, is an utter knockout, did I mention that earlier? Geoffrey himself doesn't seem to know a great deal about the publishing business. Like, for example, I'm trying to get him to understand the concept of an author's advance on royalties,' Duckworth sighed, 'with not much luck so far.'

'An author's advance, that's not so complicated, what's to understand?' Thom was confused.

'That it's an investment in talent, and in future growth. That an advance is an investment, an asset, and not an expense. Name-brand authors command big advances. Publishers don't set the agenda any more. They did, at one time, when the Ryerson Press was the only show in town. It's different now. You've got to spend money to make money,' Duckworth continued. 'An author's advance is an investment in human resources. And that's another thing,' Duckworth added. 'Get the dead spruce out of your inventory, and then bring your personnel review files up to date.'

Thom groaned. 'And Bowles doesn't understand that, about the author advances?'

'Geoffrey is pretty cautious on the financial side. And he's adamant that an author advance is an expense, not an asset, but I guess Denison Mines probably does sport a healthier cashflow than D&OL. Maybe Bowles is just conservative by custom and not by choice. We're into it now. We'll see how it plays out.' Duckworth dropped the subject.

'Geoffrey Bowles wears cleverly tailored suits, I did notice that much,' Thom agreed. 'What was the name of the actor who played John Steed in *The Avengers*?'

'The what?'

'*The Avengers*. British television, maybe 1960, 1962? It was Macnee, wasn't it, something like that? Patrick, maybe. Patrick Macnee?' Thom speculated.

'So?' Duckworth was not following Thom's thread.

'The thing that I don't understand, and my wife Sophie

understands even less,' Thom changed the topic, 'is why me? How in the hell does a merchant banker the size of a Galen Nicholas Aldebaan even know that I exist? Penmaen Lithography? In Glendaele Village? I think I'm improbable.'

'I told him,' Duckworth answered, matter-of-factly.

'*You* told him?' Penmaen was thunderstruck. The Canadian publishing industry was small, Thom was aware of that. Incestuously small, perhaps, at times. But William Duckworth was an individual Thom knew only by reputation.

'I told him, so what? I told him. Rebeca and I were in Bermuda, at Aldebaan's place – on his ticket too I might add and Aldebaan asked if we knew any printers. Nicholas also asked if we knew anyone in radio, or in television, and in magazines. Aldebaan asked a lot of questions. I think he and Bowles are looking to buy Wigwam Canadiana too.'

'From Elsbeth and Sue Cobblestone?'

Duckworth nodded. 'Amongst other things. And I think they're looking at *Sunday Evening* magazine.'

'But D&OL deals with all kinds of printers ten times bigger than Penmaen, whatever possessed you to think of me?' Thom asked. 'Of us? Of Sophie and me?'

'You weren't the only one,' Duckworth admitted, 'don't flatter yourself. But at the time we *were* in Bermuda.'

'You were in Bermuda?' Thom repeated. 'So?'

'You remember the UNIX seminar you attended at the Golden Dog Press?' Duckworth asked. 'Years ago. And do you have any recollection that Rebeca Labellarte was in the same class?'

'At the Golden Dog? ... I do, you know, now that you mention it. I wouldn't have, before you mentioned it, but I remember. I remember Ms Labellarte was wearing a leather miniskirt that was *extremely* short,' Thom admitted, bashfully, 'even by the standards of the day. Of all the many things I've forgotten from that whirlwind of a computing seminar, the length of Rebeca Labellarte's leather miniskirt is probably the one single least forgettable.'

'Rebeca has a way of doing that,' Duckworth half apologized, 'to men. It's genetic. Something to do with her Latin heritage. I would even venture that she does it consciously, and deliberately, at least half of the time.'

Thom was confused.

'You remember the anecdote you told the class at the Golden Dog about the Bermuda Triangle?' Duckworth asked, and leaned forward.

'As it applies to the design of books?' Thom replied. 'Yeah, I remember the story. I don't remember telling it at the Golden Dog and I certainly do not remember seeing the famous editor Rebeca Labellarte sitting in the audience.'

'You told the story. And Rebeca was there. And Rebeca told Aldebaan about it mostly just because we happened to be in Bermuda at the time and the venue seemed appropriate,' Duckworth explained.

'Galen Nicholas Aldebaan wants to buy puny little Penmaen Lithography because of a second-hand version of a fable that was three-quarters horse manure when I invented it four years ago?' Thom asked. 'That's ridiculous. Here all along I'd been thinking this deal must have something to do with the location of Geoffrey Bowles's hobby farm outside of Glendaele Village!'

'That too,' Duckworth agreed. 'It does. And the MGB. You're a clever fellow and you're absolutely right about that last bit. Location, location and location. All equally important when buying or selling real estate. And don't underestimate the tax implications of Bowles's MGB, but apart from Bowles, Aldebaan himself was amused by what Rebeca could remember of your Bermuda Triangle story.'

'I'm a little small-town printer,' Thom protested, 'from Glendaele Village.'

'You're not, you know,' Duckworth corrected Thom. 'You're not a printer so much as a philosopher who just happens to know how to operate a printing press, lucky for you. Employment in philosophy is currently not as plentiful as it once was in Athens or Rhodes. Gutenberg was a printer too, but I don't think Johannes would be happy managing a Kwik-Kopy franchise and neither would you,' Duckworth warmed to his topic. 'Aldebaan wants to change the way literature is published in this country, and he wants to change it quite dramatically. He needs you, in a funny kind of a way, and your little shop just happens to be located within a kilometre of the most likely spot in southwestern Ontario for Geoffrey Bowles to be able to claim a legitimate tax deduction on the personal use of his MGB. Congratulations! Do you have any idea what it costs Bowles to buy genuine British auto parts for that clunker?' Duckworth asked.

'Congratulations?' Thom asked. 'Congratulations for what? What's that supposed to mean? What about you guys? Why did Aldebaan pick on Duckworth & Osborne, Labellarte? What have you done to warrant the attention of Geoffrey Bowles and the very famous Galen Nicholas Aldebaan?' Thom was intrigued more by Aldebaan's motives than with Bowles's MGB.

'Nothing. We didn't. Aldebaan had some cash. We needed some equity capital. D&OL has one of the most prestigious literary lists in the country, you know that, and Aldebaan is a man in a hurry. He didn't want to wait fifteen years to build a list from scratch to rival what D&OL already has in place, so we swapped him. A bit of his money, up front, in exchange for the cachet Rebeca and I have built with fifteen years of bloody hard work.'

'Not to mention the Canada Council grants?' Thom chided. 'That simple? Tat for tit?'

'Not really, there was some other stuff. Like I think maybe

Aldebaan is enamoured of Rebeca,' Duckworth added.

'You're kidding. You have got to be kidding.' Thom shook his head in amazement. 'Aldebaan is smitten with Rebeca's suede miniskirt too?'

'No, no, no,' Duckworth smiled. 'Not that I know of anyway, but Rebeca is....'

'Oh yeah,' Thom remembered, 'the niece....'

'No, no, not the niece. Rebeca is a cousin once removed of the Colombian novelist Gabriel García Márquez. *One Hundred Years of Solitude*. Aldebaan mentioned the book when we were at his place in Hamilton. I personally think Aldebaan was enchanted with Rebeca's wit, her brains, and especially with her literary lineage.'

'And not her cleavage?' Thom was joking. It was not a particularly successful joke.

'Cleavage is not Rebeca's strong suit.' Duckworth frowned. 'Are you familiar with the expression *gros jos*?'

'I don't think so,' replied Thom.

'I thought you grew up in Montreal?' Duckworth asked.

'I grew up in the extreme west end of Montreal in a minuscule Catholic English-speaking enclave in the middle of a very much larger English-speaking Protestant ghetto. Maybe I didn't grow up in Montreal so much as I grew up in a suburb of Montreal. How did you know that I grew up in Montreal?' Thom asked.

'Don't remember. Maybe you told me? Someone must have told me. Anyway there's this marketing anecdote about an American food packing company that sold a line of kidney beans they called "Big John" beans in Vermont. So when they had the label redone for a test market north into Quebec they had "Big John" translated as "Gros Jos".' Duckworth snickered.

'I don't get it,' Thom admitted. 'I wasn't much better at French than I was at baseball.'

'"Gros jos" means big tits. How many cans of beans labelled "Big Tits" do you suppose an American packer from Vermont would likely sell to your average Quebec housewife? Your average *Catholic* Quebec housewife,' Duckworth added. 'Big tits on porcelain. "Ici, mon cheri, les gros jos." How do you think that would go down in a kitchen at Lac Saint Jean on a Saturday night?'

'You're making that up,' Thom admonished Duckworth.

'I am not making that up, why would I make that up?' Duckworth insisted.

'What about your employees?' Thom attempted to lure Duckworth back to the business at hand. Thom remembered that Duckworth had triggered a timer on his desk twenty minutes earlier. 'How many people do you have working here at D&OL? Aside from Rebeca and yourself?'

'Eight, full time, and a couple of freelancers,' Duckworth answered. 'In the summer we take on a few extra interns for cheap, gearing up for the fall season.'

'Eight,' Thom repeated. 'OK. And you're not concerned that any one of the eight isn't about to up and decide that he or she deserves a substantially bigger slice of Aldebaan's pocketbook and tilts your pay scale all out of whack?' The expectations of Thom's employees, both real and presumed, were never far from Thom's mind.

'We treat our people well,' Duckworth resisted the suggestion.

'Yah, yah, I believe you,' Thom shrugged. 'I try to treat my people well too. I make maybe four dollars an hour myself, and there is not one of my employees who earns less than double that, and some a lot more but I'm convinced that if we sell Penmaen to Aldebaan there's going to be at least two, maybe three, of our senior people looking for very substantial raises in the near future. Sophie, for one, is going to be fascinated to learn that Rebeca Labellarte now makes $75,000 a year!'

'That may be a problem in your shop, and it will be if you haven't been paying market value in the past, but I don't anticipate any problems of that nature at D&OL,' Duckworth responded drily. 'What goes around, comes around.'

Idiot, Thom thought to himself. 'What about your independence? What about your editorial integrity? What about the authors on your list? What do you anticipate your authors are going to want in terms of advances for next season?' Penmaen pushed his theory. '... now that they figure you've been handed the combination to Aldebaan's safety deposit box.'

'We just don't see any reason for concern.' Duckworth took off his glasses and placed them, deliberately, on his desk. He appeared to be losing patience, rapidly.

Thom changed his tack. 'Have you seen a copy of Pegaesean's latest annual report?' Thom asked. 'The one with the naked aboriginal on the cover?'

'Panning for gold in a mountain stream. Singularly inappropriate, I thought,' Duckworth admitted. 'Politically incorrect. Poor taste, too. Sends out all kinds of confusing signals to the stakeholders, but yes, Bowles gave me a copy. Almost apologetically, I thought, as I took it from him. I don't think Bowles himself had much to do with the cover design,' Duckworth speculated.

'From what I read in there, it looks like your perennial cashflow problems just vaporized!' Penmaen exclaimed, 'and Bowles used to be in gold mining, didn't he?'

'You know, Thom,' Duckworth pushed back, away from his desk, 'after we signed the papers and did the press conference thing in the bar on the roof of the Park Plaza I took Aldebaan, that same afternoon, to introduce him to our loans officer at the bank. D&OL had a $200,000 revolving credit line in place, financing sales of $1.3 million. Aldebaan himself, on the other hand, personally, had $40 million in short-term GICs in the same damn bank the day we went calling. That's the kitty for Geoffrey Bowles to acquire this "horizontally integrated communications company" you've heard so much about.'

'It's not going to cost Aldebaan anywhere *near* that much to buy Penmaen Lithography!' Thom interjected.

'I wouldn't doubt it,' Duckworth continued, resolutely. 'So I introduced Aldebaan to this myopic dimwit at the bank and explained we'd be retiring our operating line within the week and replacing it with a cash advance from Pegaesean and you know what dumbkopf's response was?'

'Heart palpitations?' Thom offered. 'Pol Brut Roger on ice? Jubilation?'

'You might have thought. *I* might have thought the twit would be pretty quick to ingratiate himself with Aldebaan. Offer some services, a beer after work, a shoeshine, a hot stock tip, something like that but no, what dumbo said was ... you're not going to *believe* this ... what he said was: "I'll need a cashier's cheque." Can you compre*hend* this donkey? Aldebaan's got $40 million dollars in cash in the vault but the junior clerical staff don't trust him to kite paper for $200,000! How many times does $200,000 divide into $40 million?' Duckworth pursued his point.

'I'm not accustomed to working with numbers much over ten thousand myself,' Thom had to admit. 'How many zeros are there in a million?'

'Banking at one time was an honourable profession,' said Duckworth. 'Account managers used to be right up there with house league hockey referees and volunteer fire chiefs. Veritable pillars of the community. Now they're nothing more than numerically challenged bookkeepers with a fancy for polyester.'

'There's a portrait of Aldebaan in a suit printed as a duotone on page 2 of the Pegaesean annual report,' Thom advised. 'The fabric doesn't look like polyester to me.'

'I don't think the bespoke tailors on Savile Row have ever

even *heard* of the stuff,' Duckworth offered. 'Maybe in Hong Kong? Maybe not even in Hong Kong, maybe in Kowloon?'

'Kowloon?' Thom asked.

'Kowloon.' Duckworth reached for his desk timer. 'Dead spruce, and personnel reviews,' he concluded. 'Remember.'

★ ★ ★

'So what do you think Philip LeBoubon will want?' Sophie asked Thom.

'At his employment review?' Thom turned to face his wife. It wasn't that Thom couldn't hear, but even Thom was aware that he could hear more clearly if he could simultaneously watch the vowels forming on a person's lips. 'The moon, the stars, both of the inner planets and whatever it is that we may eventually discover on Jayne Beauregard's wish list, factored up to a power of two, maybe three. Maybe a few fringe benefits on the side. Ketchup for his poutine.' Thom made no attempt to disguise his personal distaste for the subject, and its object. 'Do you know the prick tried to underbid me on the chamber of commerce brochure?'

'I thought you told me you don't enjoy printing brochures for the chamber of commerce?' Sophie reminded Thom.

'I don't, the ingrates. But I don't like getting my price undercut by my pressman who's got a little Multi 1250 hidden in his basement. On which he doesn't,' Thom added dramatically, 'trouble himself to pay business taxes, or sales taxes, or holiday pay for that matter, or workmen's compensation.'

'LeBoubon is not stupid,' Sophie noted. 'Wasn't that the first press you learned to print on? A Multi 1250? Maybe he's just trying to follow your example.'

'Stupid? OK. I agree, he's not stupid. Maybe I'll put that down on the personnel assessment we're apparently supposed to prepare for Bowles – LeBoubon, Philippe: Pressman. Cheat, thief, and moonlighter. Stupid, not,' Thom sneered, 'and it wasn't a Multi 1250, it was an AB Dick. The Multi 1250 came later.'

'Leave it now!' Sophie felt blood rushing to her cheeks. 'If you're not prepared to be reasonable we're not going to talk about it. We're just trying to come to some agreement between ourselves about what to expect at his employment review. That's all!' But Sophie continued, in spite of herself, 'and we could do without your snide little marginalia if you don't mind, please and thank you very much!'

'What's to expect? I told you what's to expect. The moon, the stars, Mars and Venus. Mercury too if LeBoubon gets it into his pea brain to get piggy. You heard that the catalogue he printed for Wastrel Editions is chalked all to hell? And you know why? Because M. Philippe LeBoubon himself personally didn't choose to work half a bloody hour overtime to get the fourth run down in the same shift. Half a bloody hour! So now the first three colours have dried hard as the Sahara desert and the magenta won't stick to them. So now we have to buy more stock and reprint the damn thing from scratch. And I am PISSED off!' Thom insisted.

'You're quite sure you're not just PISSED drunk pure and simple?' taunted Sophie.

'!?!'

'So maybe you scheduled too much for one shift?' Sophie challenged. 'So maybe it's not Philippe's fault. Maybe it's your fault. Maybe you asked too much. That would hardly be unlike you, to ask too much from your employees. You can't expect normal human beings to work like you work. No one works like you work. You ask too much of me, for Christ's sake. And you ask too much of yourself too, dammit!' Sophie was on a roll, the words tripped off her tongue like lead from a Gatling gun.

'We discussed the press schedule for that particular week on the Monday, in the morning as you will recall,' Thom

GREAT EXPECTATIONS

insisted through clenched teeth. 'Philippe LeBoubon discussed it, and you discussed it and I discussed it, and I do not recall hearing dissenting voices at the meeting,' Thom paused, took wind and readied himself for the next salvo. 'And it is NOT my damn fault that the magenta won't stick if the cyan, yellow, and black are already too dry. This is chemistry we're talking about. Pigment and vehicle. I am NOT a damn chemist. I don't pretend to be a chemist. I don't manufacture ink and I don't sell bloody ink and I don't know piss all about ink other than that I have to get the four damn colours down in one shift on a single-colour press, or the fourth chalks. Always. Always did. Always will. It's like Creation. Creation wasn't my damn fault either, because I wasn't there!' Thom snarled.

'Philippe LeBoubon shows up on time for work,' Sophie reminded her husband, gently. 'That's more than we can say for some of our employees.'

'You're thinking of Jayne Beauregard?'

Sophie nodded.

'Jayne is a problem,' Thom agreed. 'And Philippe LeBoubon does show up on time, that's also true. So do I. Thom Penmaen himself personally shows up on time, or a bit before time, and I leave a bit after time, and I work on for a couple of hours after supper at night, every night, and I show up on Saturday and I work on Sunday! I do most of my best work on Sunday, come to think of it, when there are no goddamn employees in the shop to distract me with their petty little personal problems,' Thom's voice was rising to meet the colour in Sophie's cheeks. 'And I work most bloody holidays, too!'

'I know you do. And I've told you before I wish you wouldn't.' Sophie flung her two cents back into Thom's face.

'Even Christmas!' Thom continued the rant. 'I work ... what? Eh? What did you say?' Thom stopped up short. 'For

God's sake, Sophie, I thought we were talking about Philippe LeBoubon.'

'*I* was talking about Philippe LeBoubon, his employment here and his impending employment review. You, on the other hand, were indulging yourself in a tirade about absolutely nothing that has anything remotely to do with anything whatsoever!'

'He shows up on time.' Thom ignored the insult. 'So what?' Thom was pushed, and pushing, and veering rapidly out of control. 'You think he deserves a medal? The *Légion d'honneur?* For what? Philippe LeBoubon shows up on his ten-speed from home after a two-minute cycle. Downhill, I might add, on time on a regular basis and you think this is an achievement equivalent to delivering a camel train to an oasis in Algeria?'

'Algeria? What the hell do you think this has got to do with the French Foreign Legion? Stop it, Thom. Just stop it,' Sophie was nearing the end of her humour.

'Stop what? LeBoubon is a punctual but arrogant and aggressive megalomaniac suffering from delusions of grandeur. Do you remember de Gaulle, Charles de Gaulle, shouting from the parapet in Montreal "Vive le Quebec libre"? Do you know what Lester Pearson thought about that?' The pitch of Thom's voice continued to rise through another octave.

'Not much?' Sophie ventured a guess.

'Not much. That's right, not much,' Thom agreed. 'Very clever. Not much,' Thom continued, muttering to himself.

'Philippe came to me privately the other day and asked if we would consider a forty-hour, four-day week for the Heidelberg?' Sophie reported. 'He said he wants to enrol in a course in financial planning that starts in the fall. He needs to have his Fridays off.'

'*His* Fridays? He came to you? That's news,' Thom

admitted. 'Why didn't the creep come to me?'

'Because he can't, you jerk,' Sophie replied. 'You never listen to him.'

'What do you mean "you jerk"? What do you mean "You never listen to him"? Since when do *you* listen to him? Since when are you so sweet all of a sudden on that pompous twit? Is that what you're trying to tell me? If that's what you're trying to tell me why don't you come right out and say it. Say it. Come on, say it.' Thom's blood pressure registered a lifetime high.

'You are *so* considerate of your employees' many personal needs and suggestions,' Sophie sneered. 'You stupid jerk!'

'Stupid?' Thom repeated.

'Stupid, you are stupid. I said "stupid", that's the word I used. You're smart, but you're stupid, simultaneously, at the same time.' Sophie would not, or could not, let it go.

'Jerk?' inquired Thom.

'That too, you stupid jerk. Can't you see that I love you for Christ's sake?' Sophie pleaded. 'Go ahead. Stay up half the night if that's what you want to do. Work on your stupid deal with the fabulously wealthy Galen Nicholas Aldebaan if that's what you think is important in your life. I am going to bed.'

'?!'

★ ★ ★

Thom Penmaen's first late-night attempt to inventory capital equipment on behalf of Geoffrey Bowles was ambushed by a nagging suspicion that neither Jayne Beauregard nor Philippe LeBoubon actually deserved anywhere near the buck-an-hour increase in wages Sophie had proposed, though Thom could not quite finger any one, single, defensible reason for his dissenting opinion.

Working through a preliminary draft of Penmaen's financial statements for the fiscal year ended 31 May, it occurred to

Thom that there were any number of line items over which he felt he had little, or no, control — depreciation, for one. Bank charges, for another. The thought also occurred that the sorts of expenses Thom considered 'overhead' were by no means confined to the so-called 'Administrative' part of his Earnings Statement.

Thom's first, unschooled, attempt to quantify overhead added the sum of rent, utilities, machine and property maintenance, depreciation, travel, advertising, auto, bank charges and interest, insurance, interest on the long-term debt, bad debts, professional fees, office and general and business taxes ... and divided the total by the total number of hours worked in the shop in the previous twelve months. The figure Thom wrenched from the calculation was $6.26, which looked, at first glance, like a perfectly useless number, because it didn't factor in the cost of paid holidays, or vacations, or even the many hours LeBoubon wasted resewing dampener sleeves that wouldn't need such frequent replacement if more attention had been paid to their daily, routine, maintenance.

The lack of tap water.

And elbow grease.

Thom realized, however, that a more useful assessment of overhead was going to have to wait until he finished at least some kind of a rough inventory of capital equipment for Bowles.

Thom's initial attempt to commit inventory to paper produced a list in which 'YEAR' was the date of acquisition, 'COST' was the purchase price inclusive of taxes and installation, and 'DESCRIPTION' included serial numbers of the equipment where available. Thom thought the last bit was a nice touch ... including the serial numbers where he knew them. Real numbers. Verifiable numbers. The numbers lent an air of credibility to the table, from Thom's uniquely biased point of view, even if they wouldn't particularly mean

GREAT EXPECTATIONS

anything to Geoffrey Bowles. Let alone Nicholas Aldebaan. The thought had not yet occurred to Thom that virtually all of his prized equipment was too small to print the volume of product Geoffrey Bowles wanted printed, and hence would be worthless to Pegaesean.

Capital Equipment

YEAR	COST	DESCRIPTION (incl serial numbers)
1975	$2328	Baumfolder 4332 (25x38) #16472 with feeder
1975	702	Smyth National Book Sewing Machine #324
1976	1145	Multi 1250 (10x13) #973591
1976	4080	Sulby AutoMinabinda #A8339
1978	24000	Heidelberg KORD 64 (18x25) #339329
1980	3300	Masseeley Model 33 (12"x6") Foilstamper
1980	2280	Southwind Film Dryer (23") #FD-E80-292
1981	3030	NuArc Platemaker FT26V2UP #223L80-22
1982	18887	Polar Model 72CE Guillotine #5151792 (28")
1983	1500	Beehive ATL-0100 Terminal #L310378
1983	1500	Beehive ATL-0100 Terminal #L310375
1985	3503	GE LinePrinter Model 3S6302AGH4145B1
1986	6500	Apple LaserWriter #A511019M0156
1987	18795	CTS120 mini computer #225284-1MT
1987	1000	Beehive ATL-0100 Terminal #C500273
1987	2370	Cosar Pressmate PIAC3-638372 Densitometer
1987	1300	Hunkeler MBP90 #4315-3 Bundling Press
1987	2100	Air Conditioner
1988	20233	Klimsch SuperVertical camera #215 628
1988	3500	Sola Constant Voltage transformer 63-23-250-8
$122,053		Total

[114]

The table was a beginning, but it clearly wouldn't suffice as a tactic designed to impress Geoffrey Bowles. In the first place because the list included only major pieces of capital equipment, the obvious ones, and didn't take into account the smaller bits of bric-à-brac Penmaen Lithography used on a daily basis.

Like the ink scale and the packing gauge, Thom thought as he worried over the list. The air compressor and any of the software running on the UNIX-box. The database software, for example, that persuaded Thom to deduct undocketable hours from total employee hours before calculating real overhead, then to add back average employee wage expense per hour and undocketable management/employee wage expense per hour to overhead to re-calculate a realistic cost of employment.

The second figure seemed to be $29.18 an hour, as opposed to $6.26.

Though Thom was unsure about the $29.18.

The thought occurred to Thom that if, in fact, Sophie and he were poised to sell the business, they would get the opportunity to sell Penmaen Lithography no more than once, and that once sold, the business would likely stay sold for a very long time. And maybe that wouldn't be such a bad thing, given that Penmaen probably couldn't afford employees that cost $29.18 an hour anyway.

Thom was painfully aware that he was not adept at human resource issues. Some issues more 'less adept' than others, but in general Thom was not good with people, and the incessant bickering in the shop was straining Sophie, his relationship with Sophie, and even his relationship with Kit Carson who assumed ever more defensive attitudes towards her mistress as Thom and Sophie bickered about the bickering.

Perhaps Thom should seize the opportunity — sell, and be done with the likes of Philippe LeBoubon, Jayne Beauregard,

GREAT EXPECTATIONS

Little Lorrie Wright, Yvette Charbeau and the $29.18 an hour it cost to employ each of them. The idea had its appeal, but maybe Thom had best make sure he included *all* of the assets in the list of capital equipment, and maybe he had best get it right the first time, before Bowles started to pick it over and winnow it down.

Some of the stuff was junk. Thom knew that, though he suspected that Bowles would be hard pressed to explain the difference between a densitometer and a press packing gauge. The long list looked more promising to Thom than the short list, though he could see there were problems with the valuations as he plodded through a blizzard of cancelled payables.

Geoffrey Bowles had expressed reservations with Duckworth's allocation of unearned author advances. Thom correctly suspected Bowles would have no trouble discovering that $110,000 of the $150,000 Thom was prepared to call capital equipment had already been depreciated on the balance sheet to rust, so maybe the capital equipment was worth no more than $40,000? Thom thought not.

'No bloody way,' Thom cursed to himself.

The machines also carried a hypothetical value that Penmaen Lithography recorded on its financial statements as a net book value, but that was primarily for tax purposes and had little to do with Thom's understanding of reality. Thom made a list of notations as he opened the twist cap of yet another bottle of Sleeman's Pale Ale and considered the issues.

On the one hand, 1975 dollars and 1988 dollars weren't the same dollars. A used 25-inch Baumfolder could be bought in 1975 for $2,000 and change. Such a machine could not be had in 1988 for less than twice the amount. Not even the same machine, albeit thirteen years later. Maybe the Baumfolder was worth $4,000?

Some of the equipment was good stuff. Penmaen had been offered $48,000 for the Heidelberg KORD, and turned it down, so maybe the KORD was also worth double its purchase price instead of its fully depreciated net book value. The KORD was already eight years old when they bought it in 1978, but the press had been restored to mint condition, with genuine German marks that cost more, if anything, than genuine British pounds sterling.

The computer software, on the other hand, the database manager and the typesetting package, was licensed to the Convergent Technologies machine on which it ran. If the CT-box were to die the licences were toast and Penmaen did not possess the source-code, the expertise, or the copyright to consider porting them to another machine.

The age of the machines appeared to be an issue. The Polar cutter, and the Klimsch camera, had been purchased new — state-of-the-art technology, but at premium prices, so their resale value could naturally be expected to plummet in the first twelve months. The National Book Sewing machine, on the other hand, was built in 1905. There was no modern equivalent of such a machine, so its value was more akin to that of a painstakingly restored Ford Model T than to the rusted-out shell of a Chevy Corvair.

Thom came to recognize that a more useful inventory of capital equipment would have to include the date of manufacture as well as the date of purchase; the acquisition cost, certainly, but also the accumulated depreciation and a realistic approximation of the potential resale value.

Old wine is worth more than old cheddar, but old cheddar is worth more than stale beer.

The potential resale value might even prove to be the most useful number of the lot, Thom reasoned, except that it was also the most subjective. The asset cost, on the other hand,

GREAT EXPECTATIONS

was certainly the most objective of the several sets of numbers, but also the most clearly uninteresting because it didn't reflect Thom's pride in his company, his machines or his maintenance programme.

Will Duckworth and Rebeca Labellarte didn't have machines to sell, Thom reasoned, just a lot of dead spruce cluttering up warehouse space, maybe some premium goodwill and one stellar genealogy. But Duckworth and Labellarte each get $75,000 a year, so I'm damned if we're selling the Heidelberg for honey-coated beer nuts.

Chapter Five
Jayne Beauregard & Co.

'What do you think you're doing?' Sophie asked Thom, who was squatting on his haunches facing the millpond and the sun in the west in the late afternoon.
'Watching Alvin,' replied Thom.
'Alvin?' Sophie inquired. 'Alvin was a chipmunk, no? He made a recording? A hit vinyl forty-five?'
'Alvin the sunfish.' Thom pointed to a spot maybe three or four feet from the edge of the pond. There, sure enough, was a fish. Not a very large fish in Sophie's estimation, perhaps eight inches long, swimming in the sunlight in half a foot of water.
'Alvin?' Sophie peered over Thom's shoulder into the water that wasn't much deeper than a puddle. 'So how do you know Alvin is Alvin? How do you know Alvin is even a sunfish? Maybe Alvin is a perch?'
Thom frowned. 'Alvin is not a perch. Sunfish have iridescent discs on either side of their gills. Perch have vertical stripes down the length of their body. And their bodies are longer, the perch. Not so round. Alvin is a sunfish.' Thom was certain.
'So maybe the fish is a sunfish.' Sophie looked again. The fish in question was still in the same spot, treading water, as it were. 'But how do you know for certain it's the *same* sunfish?' Sophie asked. 'Maybe Alvin is the unwitting victim of multiple personality disorder? Maybe Alvin has a twin? Maybe more than one twin? How can you be so cocksure that Alvin doesn't have more than one twin, Thom? Maybe Alvin is a

composite figment of your astonishing imagination? How do you know, for sure, that Alvin is any more, or less, real than Aldebaan? Or Geoffrey Bowles, for that matter?'

'Habit,' Thom replied, 'and habitat. You can see for yourself that Alvin has excavated a nest for himself?'

Sophie leaned over Thom's shoulder and squinted through the sunlight reflecting off the surface of the millpond. There was, it was true, a small circular area on the bottom of the pond the fish had apparently dug a few centimetres deeper than the surrounding muck by swishing at organic debris with its fins. The 'nest', if that was the correct term for the habitation of a sunfish, and Sophie was not at all certain on that point, was clearly visible because the pebbles on the bottom beneath the muck had been swept clean with dorsal fins. To Sophie's eye the improbable construction looked not unlike a suburban sunken living room, with a faux-marble floor. Sophie decided to keep that observation to herself.

'You see how Alvin keeps turning?' Thom continued. 'Every ten or fifteen seconds Alvin turns himself ninety degrees to the right, always treading water to hold his position in the middle of the cavity. I think he's guarding something, and I think the depth of the nest helps to make him less conspicuous to oncoming fish, or turtles, I don't really know what species of creatures Alvin considers his natural enemies.'

'So how do you know Alvin is a boy?' Sophie interjected. 'Maybe Alvin is actually Agnes?'

'Not possible. I've seen Agnes too, but only the once,' Thom insisted. 'They were screwing.'

'Oh, come on,' Sophie scoffed. 'Give us a break. Really.'

'No breaks,' Thom insisted. 'Gospel truth. Agnes breached almost ninety degrees onto her side and Alvin rubbed his stomach against hers, and they both seemed to be making a good job of it because the thing that they were doing went on for fifteen minutes or more.'

'Even,' Sophie paused. 'Let's just pretend for a moment that I believe you — that you actually spent fifteen minutes of your life watching two sunfish fornicating in a millpond — how did you know which one was Alvin and which one was Agnes?' Sophie paused again, pleased with the underlying perception inherent in her question.

'Because Alvin was on top....'

'Oh, PISS off...' Sophie started to reply.

'I'm kidding, I'm kidding, OK? A joke. Very funny. Ha-ha, a joke. The thing is the male sunfish has a flashy disc thing on its gills. The female doesn't,' Thom replied. 'It's pretty obvious.'

'So have you seen any little sunfish yet?' challenged Sophie.

'No little sunfish yet. And I haven't seen Agnes recently either, but I'm concerned about Alvin,' Thom added, pointing to the crown of a dense clump of cedars overhanging the far bank. 'There's a pair of kingfishers that strafe the millpond every afternoon as soon as the sun comes around far enough for the birds to see clear to the bottom. I don't think the kingfishers would venture to this bank, close to the noise of the compressors at Witherspoon's, and Alvin may not realize how fortunate he is that he's got a few thick limbs of black willow above him, but I really don't think Alvin's little trench is much of a defence against a kingfisher,' explained Thom.

'You're worried about that little fish?' Sophie realized suddenly, pointing into the millpond.

'My fish,' Thom corrected Sophie. 'I'm worried about Alvin.'

'Do you feed it?' asked Sophie.

'Him, not it. I've tried goldfish flakes,' Thom admitted. 'Alvin doesn't seem interested.'

GREAT EXPECTATIONS

Sophie exhaled slowly. 'Dinner,' she told him, 'will be served in fifteen minutes. Be there. Remember you've got Yvette Charbeau coming back at seven tonight for her employment review, and then Jayne Beauregard at 7:30. Busy evening.' Sophie moved off through the garden. 'You're weird, Thom,' she added over her shoulder, then stopped and nearly tripped over a starling on the lawn that scrabbled under the protective leaves of a mature hosta.

'Weird?' Thom turned and addressed the fish. 'Do you think I'm weird, Alvin?'

* * *

Yvette Charbeau was Thom's most recent hire. She had been employed by Penmaen Lithography not even six months, but Yvette was already beginning to suspect that Lorrie Wright, Jayne Beauregard and Philippe LeBoubon were each more than a little cracked. Yvette was tempted to tell Thom what little she understood of LeBoubon's plot to have all the employees ask for the same thing at their reviews, but then she decided against it. Getting herself involved with management was not Yvette's style. No good would come of it.

Yvette grew up in Kirkland Lake. Her father had been a miner. Yvette got herself knocked up accidentally more or less on purpose before she completed secondary school and moved south to Oshawa to give birth to the boy she named Henri, because her father had been an admirer of the great Henri Richard, the Pocket Rocket. Yvette did not know a great deal about hockey. She did know that Henri Richard was not as talented a hockey player as his brother, Maurice, so he had to try harder. Yvette's father had told her that.

Yvette's Henri was likely going to have to try harder also.

Yvette got herself a job in auto parts making distributor caps on an assembly line, and eventually a husband willing to assume responsibility for a second-hand son, but shortly thereafter the auto plant relocated to the maquiladora district of Chihuahua state and Yvette turned to sewing Boy Scout ties for piecework. At a nickel apiece, Yvette was expected to sew 120 ties an hour to reach minimum wage. Two ties a minute, one every thirty seconds. Two in thirty seconds if she stopped for a minute to think about something. From Yvette's viewpoint, Philippe LeBoubon was a little full of himself, with his big ideas about employee power and wringing concessions out of management — full of himself the same way Yvette herself felt stuffed the morning after Thanksgiving turkey, and Little Lorrie Wright was an undernourished poisonous little snit, but Yvette was new to Penmaen so she tried to keep her mouth shut as much as possible.

'You bought a new plant for the shop washroom.' Yvette smiled nervously. She was uncertain of what to expect. Of what she was supposed to say, or not to say. 'The one hanging from the ceiling above the palm tree.'

'The "palm" tree is actually a dracaena, and quite probably an elderly specimen,' Thom elaborated, 'that once belonged to David Cronenberg's wife.'

Yvette was not familiar with the films of David Cronenberg.

'Don't get Thom started on his plants, Yvette,' Sophie cautioned. 'You'll regret it.'

'Why? What kind of plant is it?' Yvette asked innocently, pleased with herself that Thom and Sophie were talking about plants rather than anything to do with her work. Yvette was a bit concerned that maybe her sewing of the book signatures wasn't quite up to production speed.

'A philodendron. A "heart-leaved" philodendron to be specific,' Thom answered. 'First introduced to England from the West Indies on behalf of the Royal Botanical Society by a certain Captain Bligh of the Royal Navy.'

'You see, Yvette?' Sophie interjected. 'You've started it.'

'Lieutenant William Bligh, master of His Majesty's Ship *Bounty*, and lately of Cornwall,' Thom continued, confidently.

'I saw the movie,' Yvette said, 'with Anthony Hopkins as the Captain.'

'The recent version,' Thom agreed. 'Who played the role of Fletcher Christian?'

'Fletcher Christian. I'd forgotten his name. He was the leader of the mutineers, wasn't he?' asked Yvette.

'He was,' Thom answered.

'And did he ever hang, in the end? For the mutiny I mean?' Yvette continued. 'I couldn't tell from the way the movie ended.'

'Dunno. Don't think anyone does, for sure,' Thom replied. 'Who played the role of Fletcher Christian opposite Anthony Hopkins' Bligh?'

'Mel Gibson,' answered Sophie.

'So how come you put the new plant in the washroom above the palm tree?' asked Yvette.

'Dracaena,' Thom insisted.

'So how come you put the new plant in the washroom above the dracaena?' Yvette rephrased the question.

'Because I want William Bligh watching out for Fletcher Christian.' Thom grinned in spite of himself. 'Particularly when Christian has his pants wrapped around his ankles.'

'Thom!' warned Sophie.

'A joke, OK?' Thom apologized.

'You think Philippe LeBoubon is Fletcher Christian, don't you?' – the thought occurred to Yvette.

'Not really. You don't think William Bligh is a philodrendron, do you?' Thom countered.

'Can I ask you a question about the plants?' Yvette struggled to follow the conversation. Much of the time she did not understand Thom Penmaen, or what he said.

'I thought that is what we were talking about. Philodendrons,' Thom professed ignorance.

'You weren't, Thom,' Sophie chided. 'Yvette was talking about plants, and you were talking about Philippe LeBoubon.'

'What was the question you wanted to ask me about plants?' Thom asked Yvette.

'You've got lots of plants in the shop washroom.'

'True thing. Mostly sick, at one time, or ailing, or refugees from the compost heap. I don't do thoroughbreds, only refugees,' Thom insisted.

'But the plants all look great,' said Yvette. 'The philodendron, and the dracaena.'

'The plants all look green, maybe, I'm not so sure about great, but if that last comment was intended as a compliment I'll take it for that and I'll thank you very much.' Thom said that part sincerely. The shop washroom was a space that did not interest Sophie, so it was the one space that Thom could decorate pretty much as he saw fit, and he pretty much always saw it as a greenhouse.

The washroom did not have a lot of windows, but the few that it did have faced south and west, and the building was shielded from the north and the east. The washroom had a conveniently low ceiling, and cheap vinyl flooring that was easy to clean.

'I don't understand,' Yvette continued, 'why the plants in my apartment always die, and the plants in the shop washroom don't. Die, I mean.'

'Probably because you water too much,' Thom speculated. 'I met a plantsman once who advised that if you're not an expert, the correct amount to water houseplants is about half what you'd be inclined to water without thinking about it.'

'But how do you know?' Yvette asked. 'Like, you've got that one little tree on the shelf by the window....'

'The hibiscus?' Thom asked.

'The hibiscus, maybe, probably ... you drown the thing virtually every morning and I know that for sure because I see the water on the floor but I don't understand why it doesn't rot? And then there's the jade on the shelf just beside it and its leaves are so fat and glossy they look like ripe avocados but I swear that you've never watered that plant once in the six months that I've been here!'

'You're observant,' Thom replied. 'I like that.'

'So how do you know when to water the jade?' Yvette prodded.

'I don't. I read the newspaper,' Thom explained.

'The *Glendaele Gazetteer*?'

'I'm not sure I'd consider the *Glendaele Gazetteer* to be a newspaper,' Thom replied. 'I read the *Globe and Mail* myself.'

'That's where it says when to water the jade plant? You're shitting me,' Yvette guessed.

'Not so. The jade is a semi-succulent. It grows in the desert. So how could I possibly be expected to know how often it rains in the desert unless I read the weather in the *Globe*. Every time it rains in Tucson, Arizona, I water the jade, lightly,' Thom replied, not completely dishonestly.

'Tucson, Arizona?'

'It's where the Kansas City Royals hold spring training camp,' Thom explained.

Yvette Charbeau knew nothing about baseball.

'You could try misting,' Thom suggested. 'Clean out an empty Windex bottle, and every time you think your plants need watering just mist the leaves.'

'Jayne Beauregard smokes in the shop washroom.' Yvette changed the subject.

'That's it? That's all you want to tell us,' Sophie asked, 'about your employment here?'

'I like my job. I'm happy that you pay by the hour and not

JAYNE BEAUREGARD & CO.

piecework. I like doing different things on different days. I dunno, I've only been here six months.' Yvette squirmed.

'I don't think Jayne Beauregard smokes in the shop washroom, Yvette,' Thom disagreed, gently, 'because so far as I know, Jayne doesn't smoke. At all. Period. Not in the shop washroom. Not anywhere.'

'Jayne Beauregard smokes in the shop washroom,' Yvette answered. 'That's really all I have to say.'

★ ★ ★

Jayne Beauregard started work at Penmaen Lithography in August of 1982.

Thom advertised for a Baumfolder operator because Sophie had decided that Thom needed 'one less machine to worry about himself', and thought the Baumfolder might be it. Sophie was trying to be helpful. Thom, for his part, was not so convinced that he could teach just anyone to operate the Baumfolder, partly because the machine was built in the 1930s and partly because it was known to be cantankerous as well as aged and complex. That was the rationale. Thom was also not convinced that he really *wanted* to give up running the Baumfolder himself because he feared losing the opportunity to check each press sheet while loading them onto the folder and he was sceptical of the advisability of putting a trainee in a position to ruin hitherto saleable presswork by folding the sheets crooked, or creased, or inside out with the pages within the signature out of order.

Running the Baumfolder was at best a thankless task.

If the operator were skilled enough to cajole the machine into folding all the sheets square, with no creases, no blanks, no jams and no waste, then the work of the day was deemed to be acceptable. No better than acceptable, just acceptable. Perfection, in fact, was a minimum requirement for that particular machine, but perfection on a forty-year-old used folder that had likely been previously abused for at least three decades in any number of high-volume trade binderies, and subsequently discarded for scrap, *and* that required the manual adjustment of three dozen interdependent pressure settings to put three folds at two right angles, a perforation and a score in each press sheet was not exactly easy.

Thom could make the job *look* easy.

But the job was not easy.

Sophie knew very little about Baumfolders, but she assumed that if anyone could teach the complexities of a folding machine to an appropriate apprentice, it was Thom. But Jayne Beauregard knew nothing more about opposing locknuts than Sophie did.

'JB', as she fancied herself, was, on the other hand, in possession of a resumé that included a degree in English literature from Victoria College at the University of Toronto and some considerable secretarial experience at Pennywhite Cards in Mississauga. Jayne was not, apparently, very content at Pennywhite because she characterized her boss as a drunk who insisted she cover his butt as well as her own and passed judgement as well as looks whenever Jayne failed to manage both his job, and hers, to his immediate superior's elastic standard.

Office equipment at Penmaen Lithography in the summer of 1982 was limited to an aged Underwood upright typewriter and the original teller's desk from the post office in neighbouring Hawthorne Village complete with wrought iron grating and a little horizontal slot at waist height through which postage was exchanged in return for handwritten correspondence.

Faced with the unique opportunity of Jayne's stellar resumé, Thom and Sophie decided against offering much in the way of wages, because they correctly figured Jayne would save a thousand dollars a year at least losing the commute to Pennywhite Cards, and also because the Penmaens were reasonably certain that there were not many employers in Glendaele even remotely interested in Jayne's degree in English literature, but they did decide to upgrade the Underwood to a used, plum-coloured IBM Selectric and also decided to let Jayne hold court at the heirloom-quality post office desk behind the teller's grate.

The employee search for a suitable Baumfolder operator was suspended. Much to Thom's relief.

Jayne Beauregard did not, however, consider herself to be a secretary.

She could read, and write, at a post-secondary level.

Jayne could answer the phone, take messages and type. She wasn't much help with the more physical jobs around the shop. She wore an elastic tensor bandage around her right wrist just about every other day – 'wrecked the wrist curling', so she claimed. She watched the Briar on television in the spring, religiously. She wasn't much help carrying boxes or unloading trucks. Sometimes the bindery people, and especially Lorrie Wright, complained that Jayne Beauregard was lazy.

Which was probably not true.

Eccentric, though, she maybe was.

Jayne insisted on having her hair cut once a week, every week, Thursdays, in a barbershop. No highfalutin hairdressing salons for this gal. Cut and paste. A little dab'll do yuh. No perms. No curls. It might have had something to do with Jayne's childhood in Sarnia. Petrochemical-induced brain damage, perhaps. Or wind-borne pollution from Detroit. Her parents were from Sarnia too.

It might even have been genetic.

Jayne also had a thing about trucks, particularly big trucks and most particularly big tank trucks. She could watch, utterly fascinated, for twenty minutes at a stretch while the big Sunoco eighteen-wheeler delivered gasoline to Featherstone's garage directly across Main Street from Jayne's throne behind the teller's cage.

'Lookit the size of that ... sucker.' Jayne talked to herself frequently. Often about tank trucks.

'Betcha you could see a quarter mile of blacktop from the cab of that ... sucker.'

'Dunno how he gets that ... sucker *in* there ...'

... though every week on a Tuesday just about five minutes past three in the afternoon the Sunoco tank truck driver executed pretty much the same three-point pirouette to fuel Featherstone's pumps that he had executed the week before, and the pirouette was remarkably similar to the one he had turned the week before that.

Jayne, for some unknown reason, never lost interest, and never missed an opportunity to watch.

She liked to watch.

It must have been something like vicarious sex, for her, or a strange kind of pharmaceutical dependency. Jayne had one older brother who had suffered through illness for long stretches as a child. JB loved him dearly. She spoke of Jonathan often though he lived in the West and Jayne saw him rarely and didn't approve of his taste in lady friends. She also maybe resented the attention her parents had lavished on Jonathan's childhood illness, and grew up befuddled, somehow, as if the only way she could hope to warrant similar attention for herself was to pretend to be male, and sickly, or both.

JB was ill disposed, frequently. Particularly on Monday mornings, and then sometimes Friday afternoons as well. It wasn't a problem that was noticeable at first, just an annoyance, something Thom tolerated just as he tolerated Jayne's annual contention that opening day of the Blue Jays baseball season was a statutory employee holiday.

JAYNE BEAUREGARD & CO.

* * *

Jayne Beauregard arrived a couple of minutes late for her employment review. She was wearing the brightest, gaudiest, glossiest, most in-your-face shade of red lipstick Thom had ever encountered.

Uh-oh, thought Sophie, assessing Jayne's aggressive choice of make-up, here comes an attitude looking for a problem.

'We've had a complaint.' Thom started the conversation tentatively. Jayne appeared surprised to hear of any such complaint, but didn't trouble herself to rise to the bait. 'Yvette Charbeau mentioned that she thinks you are smoking cigarettes in the shop washroom,' Thom continued.

Sophie watched Jayne's eyes, which did widen, perceptibly.

'What, the hell, does snitty Yvette Charbeau's obnoxious tongue have to do with *my* employment review?' Jayne demanded, right off the bat.

'Easy, please. For Christ's sake don't get your nose out of joint,' Thom backpedalled. 'We've had a complaint. So far as I know you don't even *smoke* for God's sake, so I thought we could get this one little confusion out of the way. Dismiss it straight off?'

'I thought this was *supposed* to be *my* employment review,' Jayne started up, ignoring Thom's attempt at conciliation. 'And if that is in fact the case, and if you are in fact *trying* to make this process more employ*ee* friendly …'.

'Now hold on a minute,' Sophie interrupted Jayne. 'We are trying to make this process more fair, not necessarily employ-*ee* friendly. "Fair" means fair to Yvette and Lorrie, fair to Philippe LeBoubon, fair to Thom and fair to me. Thom and I feel we went out of our way to give you guys the opportunity to revise the parameters of the employment review questionnaire to your liking, so, now, here's your chance. Let's hear what you've got to say.'

'I think it was petty of your husband to prevent me from

buying a new letter-opener,' Jayne snipped.

'Oh for Christ's … ,' Thom interjected.

'Thom,' Sophie warned, 'button it.' Sophie turned to face Jayne, offering her the benefit of body language and rapt attention. 'Why did you feel you needed a new letter-opener?'

'To open letters,' Jayne snipped again.

'Clearly,' Sophie replied, unimpressed.

'I did not authorize,' Thom began with a heavy sigh, 'the proposed purchase of a new letter opener because, as I explained to Ms Beauregard in some detail at the time, Penmaen Lithography is not excessively profitable. A letter can readily be opened with a knife or a ruler, either of which instruments we already have in abundance. A letter opener is not on my wish list for capital expenditures, and I considered the proposal frivolous.'

'It was not frivolous,' Jayne countered, 'it was *my* idea, and we are talking about the princely sum of $4.98!'

'Five bucks?' Sophie asked incredulously. 'Five bucks for a letter opener seems like a lot of money to me. Why can't you use a ruler, or a knife, as Thom suggests?'

'I have,' Jayne sniffed, 'my own personal sense of style. And I really do not see that F-I-V-E whole dollars is such an outlandish request for a simple thing that would make me happy. You people,' Jayne concluded, 'don't have a *clue* how to manage human resources. Just wait until Penmaen is bought out from under you by Pegaesean and we get some *real* management in here. You just wait!'

'If five bucks will make you happy, here's five bucks,' offered Thom, who stood up, pulled his wallet out of his jeans and peeled off a portrait of Wilfrid Laurier. The bill landed on the table in front of Jayne, kingfisher side up – just like her, Thom thought, all beak and a beady little eye. 'But I really don't see that you're any happier now than you were five minutes ago.'

'Stop it,' Sophie insisted. 'Stop it, the both of you.'

Thom glared.

'Surely,' Sophie continued, 'Jayne. You went through the whole exercise of evaluating the terms of your employment here, surely you have something more substantial to suggest than a designated letter opener?'

'I don't like the hours,' Jayne replied, 'and the lock on the shop washroom is broken.'

'What did you say?' Thom reversed the order of Jayne's priorities. 'Why the hell would you wait for annual employment review to tell us the lock on the shop washroom is broken?'

'Possibly because you and your company between you cannot afford the expenditure of $4.98 for a letter-opener. I just naturally assumed the contract services of a locksmith would be well beyond your financial grasp. Particularly as your employees,' Jayne continued, 'have jointly reached the decision that we want flexi-hour employment.'

'Flexi-hour employment?' Thom considered the concept, very briefly. Flexi-hour employment. That would be something akin to 'sanitary landfill' or perhaps even 'synthetic natural gas'. Thom could not make much sense of the proposal.

'The freedom to come and go as I please,' Jayne explained. 'Think of it as a lifestyle thing. Getting my priorities in order. And you, Mr Penmaen, as you probably recognize, are not one of my life's priorities.'

'I don't think your proposal is appropriate to an industrial environment,' Thom tried to retain a measure of civility. 'We can't have one employee waiting for another to arrive in the morning before running a job on the Sulby binder.' Thom smiled. Thom did not smile frequently.

'I don't run the Sulby binder,' Jayne stated. 'Never have, never will.'

'I know that, Jayne,' Sophie interrupted. 'The Sulby

binder was an example, a figure of speech that Thom was using to indicate that two people....'

'Don't bother making excuses for your husband,' Jayne warned Sophie. 'I do not appreciate being compared, even favourably, with the sort of trailer-park trash you've got working in the bindery, and I do not intend to start work at eight o'clock any longer. It's simply not fair to treat me the same way you treat Yvette Charbeau, who didn't even graduate from high school for Christ's sake. You people are going to start treating me with the respect that my education deserves, and you are going to make it plain to Yvette and to Lorrie and to Philippe that I am getting the respect I deserve. I've decided I'll be at my desk at nine, most days, nine-thirty some days if I'm tired, maybe not until one if I think you've not got anything for me to do that morning of interest. I do like to be challenged by my job.'

'You are,' Thom started his reply in a low timbre and built quickly to a crescendo, 'such a goddamn princess.'

'Don't,' Jayne spat back, 'you *ever* say that word to me again, you petty little spiteful man. You don't know how to treat people properly, you don't *care* about the people you work with and I hate you.'

Thom had apparently hit a nerve, face on, which surprised him considerably, because he didn't normally consider himself to be such an astute judge of character.

'Don't! you ever say that word to me again....' Jayne was crying now. Big round teardrops welled up under her eyelids then her mascara gave way under the flow and purple stains streaked the ruby red of her lips.

Crocodile tears, Thom thought, but managed to keep the more acidic of his thoughts to himself.

'We are just trying,' Sophie began again, 'to be fair to everyone...'.

'He called me a princess,' Jayne sobbed, jabbing a finger

repeatedly into Thom's face. 'He called me a goddamn princess.'

'Christ!' Thom announced suddenly to no one in particular after Jayne had left in disarray. 'I've had it with this crap.'
 'So?' Sophie challenged her husband. 'You're the boss, the big cheese. The Gorgonzola. You're even the smell. If you don't like the agenda, change it for Christ's sake, but stop bitching, just *do* something. Make a decision. Either way, I don't care.'
 'You know what?' Thom was sufficiently agitated by Jayne Beauregard's lip that one impulsive decision seemed, all at once, easy enough to get done. 'You know what I'm going to do? I do not want to talk to Lorrie Wright tomorrow night, and I definitely do not want to hear whatever it might be that LeBoubon's got to say so I'm going to give each employee a $500 bonus effective immediately, and then I'm going to postpone the rest of the bloody employee reviews until after the meeting with Bowles.' Thom's voice trailed off.
 'You're going to give Jayne Beauregard a $500 cash bonus tomorrow?' Sophie was incredulous. 'After what you just got finished saying to the woman tonight? That's ridiculous! I don't believe that you are human. Do you bleed, Thom, when you are cut?'
 'Give me a break will you, Sophie, please? Cut me some slack?' Thom replied, slowly. 'Will you not just please give me a break?'

* * *

'I meant to tell you, then I forgot ... I was in at Witherspoon's the other day, getting an ice cream, and I overheard a juicy bit of gossip about your sweetie,' Sophie teased Thom. Sophie was eager to find a topic, any topic, to distract Thom from his extended rant on the subject of employees in general and Jayne Beauregard in particular.

'Who's my sweetie?' inquired Thom. 'Jayne Beauregard?'

'No, no. Your sweetie. Gayle Wicket. I thought you told me she took off her top for you?'

'Gayle Wicket did that, take off her top, and that is not a particularly amusing story,' Thom replied stiffly. 'She flashed me, dammit. She harassed me, sexually.'

'Oh, lighten up, Thom. I thought you liked women with big breasts. You certainly seem to enjoy peering down the front of Jayne's sweaters.' Sophie would not let it go. 'Or you did, until recently.'

'Jayne Beauregard does not have big tits,' insisted Thom, remembering the spectre of Gayle Wicket's boobs drooping over the rail of her second-storey balcony, and her bikini top dropping like a banana peel when she flung it theatrically into the breeze. 'Wu-hoo,' indeed. Boobs wasn't quite large enough a word to adequately describe the pendulous shapelessness of Wicket's chest. Thom found himself at an unaccustomed loss for words.

'Apparently she doesn't allow the employees in her gift shop to talk,' Sophie continued. 'That's what they were saying in at Witherspoon's.'

'What?' Thom asked. 'There's no talking allowed in Wicketware?'

'I know. Apparently there are cracks in the floorboards in her flat above the shop and Wicket lies on the floor and listens for the sound of her employees talking. Then she sails downstairs and chews them out, even when they whisper.'

'What does Wicket think her staff might be whispering about?' Thom asked.

'Who knows?' Sophie answered. 'Her money? Her figure? Who knows? What do you think Jayne Beauregard's problem really is?'

'I don't think Jayne was talking about letter-openers, if that's what you mean.' Thom replied.

JAYNE BEAUREGARD & CO.

The troubles with Jayne Beauregard had started four years earlier when Penmaen Lithography first entered the brave new digital world in the spring of 1984. The trouble began innocently enough. Jayne, Thom and Sophie all enrolled in the same introductory course in BASIC at Glendaele Valley Secondary in a night programme. Sophie wasn't all that interested in computers, but Jayne was adamant that she knew as much, or more, about BASIC than Thom. Jayne was probably correct in that assessment, at the time, but the issue was one of self-esteem more than digital expertise. And of getting rid of Penmaen Lithography's one and only IBM Selectric typewriter. Jayne Beauregard did not like to think of herself as a typist.

Thom had learned to print at the Golden Dog Press in the City in the summer of 1969, when he completed a three-hour introductory course on an AB Dick duplicator. David Golden, top dog at the Golden Dog, lectured about ink and water, off and on, and alluded to a few subtleties of paper-handling that had to do with the niceties of coaxing a sheet of paper, and only one sheet of paper, to pass through the press in a vaguely predictable location on each revolution. This was the summer of Woodstock. Of Jimi Hendrix and Janis Joplin. Big Brother and the Holding Company. Golden Dog books were printed on ph neutral stock by self-acknowledged mindless acid freaks.

Fifteen years later, Thom furthered his computer studies in much the same way – he enrolled in an introductory course at the Golden Dog on a Saturday when Jayne Beauregard was preoccupied with the Yankees in the City for a double-header against the Blue Jays.

Technology had become increasingly complex in the intervening decade, so whereas three hours were considered ample for an introduction to offset book printing in 1969, by 1984 the introductory UNIX course had bloated to a full five hours.

Thom was puzzled.

'Mail' was mail, that part was OK. 'Date' was date, 'who' was them and the difference between 'look' and 'see' was not as subtle as Thom might have thought. 'Ed' was edit, 'grep' was more challenging and 'awk' was an undocumented nightmare, but Thom was encouraged enough to agree to rent a dummy DEC VT 100 terminal that was to be installed in Glendaele and connected via Gandalf modem to the microcomputer at the Golden Dog tucked in an alley off Chippewa Street behind the thirteen-storey den of iniquity called Everdale College.

The terminal arrived at Penmaen Lithography one Sunday in the late fall of 1984. Top dog David Golden delivered it himself in his Jaguar – and right there Thom could begin to see the advantages of this new technology, because David was surely the *only* literary book printer in the country at the time to drive a Jaguar, even second-hand.

David Golden uncrated the terminal and the modem, cabled them together, filed the instruction books away for possible future reference and pecked out –

linefeed, RETURN,
linefeed, RETURN.
DIAL WHAT NUMBER?
1-416-858-1786
DIALLING...
1 4 1 6 8 5 8 1 7 8 6
dialling done, waiting for answer tone.
modem answer tone received,
data mode.

JAYNE BEAUREGARD & CO.

Thom Penmaen had every reason to believe, at this juncture, that Penmaen Lithography had left the carbon-based world of printing ink and entered the bold new silicon age. Thom's suspicion was confirmed when the CPU at GDP flashed a login prompt across the screen of his DEC VT100 terminal in Glendaele Village. Slowly, of course. Maybe the login prompt didn't flash so much as it crept, a single letter at a time. This was 1200 baud, this was 1984. Douglas Engelbart had yet to invent the mouse.

David's brow knotted, however, and his smile creased to a frown as he and Thom watched an uninterruptable stream of curly braces race each other to fill the screen with gobbledegook. Curly braces can be symptomatic of a type of telephone noise encountered when a specific pair of copper wires happen to be located in close proximity to a high volume data-line in the Brampton switching office. But the subject of runaway curly braces was not addressed in any of the available documentation, and in fact they would take months if not years of badgering Bell Telephone to identify, so David Golden and Thom hung up and tried a second time.

The second try worked, so they indulged in a beer to celebrate and then dinner and then a few more Sleeman Pale Ales and then they tried the data link a third time. David left for the City about eleven and Thom hacked on till past midnight, then opened the manual to review the preferred sequence of disengagement – 'Control D results in login: red DATA button up, TR, MR and HS lights switch to TR and MC' – and went upstairs to bed. If for no other reason than because Glendaele is a long-distance call from Toronto, Sophie drowsily asked Thom if he was completely sure he'd hung up the phone –

... red DATA button up, TR MR and HS lights switch to TR and MC, SD and RD are out – Thom got out of bed and went back downstairs to the shop for yet another status check of the TR MR SD RD HS and MC lights. Then Thom retraced his steps

[139]

and suffered the first of a hundred anxious nights racked with dreams about large telephone bills and runaway curly braces. The first large telephone bill arrived thirty days later — $400, of which $350 was spent calling 416-858-1786.

★ ★ ★

Thom Penmaen's first stand-alone computer was delivered to Glendaele Village the following spring. The 'Pixel' was physically bulky, expensive, and already by 1985 supported half a dozen linked workstations. It was also, as was not immediately apparent on delivery, rather less than robust in its internal architecture.

Thom's degree was in English literature, not electrical engineering, and he was rather more familiar with the novels of Mordecai Richler than the pattern a sine wave draws on an oscilloscope, but even the English major was not unaware of the potential for power contortions in the local feed from the Glendaele Public Utilities Commission.

Particularly from the Glendaele PUC.

In 1978 Penmaen Lithography had replaced a twenty-four-inch ATF 'Chief' with a twenty-five-inch Heidelberg KORD 64. Both presses required a nominal industrial-strength 220 volt three-phase service, but the Chief was a clunker of an American-built machine. Suspect, in its design and tooling, and capable of close register only in the most clement of conditions but tolerant of Tombstone-quality frontier electric power. The Heidelberg, on the other hand, was German. Manufactured on the banks of the River Neckar and dramatically less tolerant of voltage fluctuation to the point of bursting into flame on the first night of installation.

A nominal 220 volts plus or minus 10 per cent was measured at 250 volts and rising the morning after the fire in the Heidelberg. The Glendaele PUC were quick to acknowledge that they wanted no truck with unhappy clientele and advised little Penmaen Lithography that Thom could shut up, relocate the business, or abandon the offensive service in favour of whatever alternative power supply seemed most appropriate. Windmills, perhaps. His choice.

The hydroelectric potential of the West Credit River did not appear to offer a viable alternative at the time, so the compromise between the scorched Heidelberg and the intransigence of the Glendaele PUC was the first of what would eventually grow to be an extended family of constant-voltage transformers installed at Penmaen Lithography.

Mindful, therefore, of the noxious odour of burning Heidelbergs, Thom Penmaen cautioned his hardware supplier in 1985 of suspect power and was advised to install power filters, isolated ground and yet another SOLA constant voltage transformer. Penmaen Lithography complied, notwithstanding the worrisome reluctance of the local electrician who was intimately conversant with augers, heat cables, farm equipment of all sorts, water pumps and the like, but not so tight with isolated grounds.

Thom had been advised, however, to check for orange plugs, and the plugs, as installed, were in fact orange. Obviously. Even to an English major, who might well be pressed to distinguish burnt sienna from over-ripe mango.

Seven months later the embryonic CPU cannibalized sizeable chunks of its own operating system.

Hitherto unheard-of files with cryptic names like adb.881, ccom20.81, libPW.a and libsocket.a were reported as missing each morning after the overnight backup to magnetic tape. The last one, 'libsocket.a', bothered Thom somewhat more than the others because it sounded as if it might have something to do with wrenches, and wrenches, in Thom's estimation, could often be critical.

The diagnosis was uncertain.

It was clear, however, that the Pixel had developed an acute case of gastric indigestion that led rapidly to internal hemorrhaging and thence to an untimely death exacerbated by business pressures attendant on the simultaneous production of the two volumes of a set of philosophical ruminations entitled *Ibo*, which had been in production for several years at this juncture, but had reached a critical stage when the author, a Czech journalist of some repute, had unexpectedly been diagnosed with a terminal illness. Wastrel Editions, the publisher of the collection, as well as the journalist's widow-in-waiting, were united in their fervent desire to see the book in print before the author went to meet his maker. There was an added concern, from Thom's point of view, that if Penmaen failed in its efforts to thwart death in this matter, interest in the publication of *Ibo* might well be expected to wane after the journalist's demise and the chances of Thom collecting his receivable might wane with it.

Thom contacted the service department of the hardware supplier on a Thursday afternoon and was promised that their 'Senior Man' would return the call when he got back from the Coast late Friday.

Monday, Thom phoned again and discovered that the service manager he had spoken with on Thursday was no longer 'in the employ of the firm', and that the Senior Man, whose name was Yakushin, Alexei Yakushin, had in fact returned from Vancouver 'as predicted' late Friday but was out on call and would be in touch Tuesday.

Tuesday, Jayne Beauregard mentioned in passing to Thom that Philippe LeBoubon was anxious about the status of his electronic timesheet entries with payday fast approaching.

LeBoubon wanted it made clear to management that he had recently accelerated his mortgage payments to a weekly basis in a concerted effort to accumulate wealth and maximize his RRSP contribution and he was not prepared to suffer any delay in payment of wages due. LeBoubon was also not inclined to discuss his concerns with Thom or Sophie personally, partially because he didn't want to hear any excuses about alleged computer problems, but also because he preferred to relay his thoughts through Jayne Beauregard, whom he considered to be 'middle management'.

None of the above was welcome news for Thom, though he did appreciate the happenstance that he had not been called upon to critique LeBoubon's latest tirade personally.

Wednesday, Thom phoned the service department of the hardware supplier once more to discover that their Senior Man had been dispatched unexpectedly back to the Coast, 'on business', but that their Junior Man was at the very moment thinking about looking up the telephone number for Penmaen Lithography. The Junior Man did express some trepidation at the prospect of travel beyond the City limits at Steeles Avenue, but Thom was able to persuade the fellow that Glendaele Village was nowhere near as far as Seattle and that assurance apparently mollified the Junior Man sufficiently that he would at least contemplate the trek to Wellington County.

Thursday, the Junior Man arrived in Glendaele Village.

Thom was in the basement on the Baumfolder at the time, but he rushed upstairs on hearing the news, searched expectantly around the office area and couldn't find the lad.

At first Thom thought perhaps the Junior Man had returned to his car for wrenches, or possibly manuals, maybe even an oscilloscope, then he noticed Jayne Beauregard shaking her head and pointing with a crooked finger up, over the top of the customer service counter, and then down. Thom followed with his eyes the motion of Jayne's finger, up, over the top of the customer service counter, and then down and that's where Thom found him. The Junior Man. Who might have been five feet tall but probably wasn't.

The Junior Man's name was Obi. Thom was quite certain of that because he had him repeat it twice and then finally asked Obi to write out his name on a piece of paper because Thom couldn't follow his strange sing song of an accent and also because Thom had not been expecting a diminutive palindrome for *Ibo*.

'But you can call me Ben, Mr Penmaen,' Obi smiled.

'Ben?' repeated Thom.

'People call me Ben,' explained Obi.

Thom helped Obi/Ben up to the failing Pixel with the aid of a small stepladder.

Ben pulled some printed circuit boards, set a rubber eraser to work on the contacts, overwrote the directory /lib from the installation tape and by four o'clock Penmaen Lithography was running payroll.

At four-fifteen, Obi left for Steeles Avenue and the comfort of civilization as he remembered it.

At four-thirty, the Pixel crashed.

That was Thursday. Jayne reminded Thom that she was incapable of typing a letter without the full service of 'her' computer. Which was true. Jayne had finally succeeded in having the antiquated IBM Selectric escorted to the village landfill.

Saturday Obi returned with a refurbished, factory-warrantied 40-megabyte disk drive. It took some time, in 1985, to rebuild a 40-megabyte system from scratch – isolating bad blocks, partitioning the drive into appropriately sized filesystems and bootstrapping the basic files required to begin loading the operating system.

Thom managed to bribe Obi to stay on past five o'clock, with pizza and beer, but by nine o'clock an unexpected late November snowfall had begun in earnest and Obi, wild-eyed at the prospect of driving in crystallized rain without the benefit of streetlamps, reminded Thom repeatedly that he was at least an hour north of civilization as he remembered it. 'Even if it wasn't snowing!'

Obi was clearly beside himself.

'Resident alien,' Thom thought as he continued to watch a scroll of incomprehensible file names being appended to the refurbished Winchester drive.

At ten o'clock the process came to an abrupt and disconcerting halt with an error message – NO SPACE ON /DEV/DOC – which was, as it turned out, the wrong spot to be loading root in the first place, and hence completely predictable that root would not fit into the partition.

'It's apparently quite obvious,' Thom explained to Sophie, who by ten o'clock on any given Saturday night would normally be in the process of reviewing the contents of her lingerie drawer. 'That root won't fit on /dev/doc.'

'/dev/doc?' Sophie was unsure.

'I know. I started to wonder about Obi/Ben when he ordered pineapple for his pizza.' Thom attempted to sympathize with Sophie's apparent confusion. 'I think he's from an alien star system.' Thom attempted a joke. 'Maybe Hawaii?'

The lingerie was not having the accustomed effect. 'Star system?' Sophie was less than convinced.

At eleven, his marriage the subject of an impending review with possible negative implications, Thom cleared the hard drive of the previous two hours' worth of tape, and started anew. By 3:00 a.m. Thom had finally succeeded in loading all of root and the user directories and tried to run an internal file system integrity check called fsck – just for a lark really, but also to assure himself once and for all, before he himself crashed for the night, that Penmaen Lithography was back in the payroll business.

Fsck attempted to disembowel part of root.

On Monday, Thom asked Jayne Beauregard to put in a call to Obi/Ben.

'Could you write down for me,' Jayne asked Thom, 'a list of all the computer things you learned this weekend? I wouldn't want to fall behind.'

Thom looked at Jayne as if she had recently taken leave of Venus.

The problem was eventually traced to a wonky Winchester controller board that might or might not have been winged by a faulty Tycor power filter.

Not that there was much to be said about the relative karma of Tycor power filters.

'A happy light is a happy light. And a happy light that glows in the dark is about as content as happy lights get to be, in the absence of persuasive evidence to the contrary,' advised the Senior Man, whose name was Yakushin, and he traced the ground fault with the aid of a schematic he drew with coloured pencils.

Chapter Six

The Horseshoe Inn

The first meeting between Aldebaan's emissary Geoffrey Bowles and Thom and Sophie Penmaen together was scheduled for the first available Thursday after Labour Day — dinner for four at the Horseshoe Inn in Cataract, a sleepy hamlet a few kilometres east of Glendaele. On the road to nowhere, in point of fact, though at one time Cataract had been a busy railway junction where the Credit Valley main line north from the City to Cheltenham, Inglewood and Orangeville met the spur line west to Glendaele, Hawthorne, Fergus and Elora.

There was a waterfall in the hamlet, a cascade of nearly twenty metres that had powered a succession of hydraulic mills from as early as 1820 to as recently as 1947, when the remnants of the Caledon Electric Company were dynamited and Cataract Lake was flushed down the valley through Brimstone, Glen Williams and Huttonville and on out into Lake Ontario at Port Credit.

There had been a hand-cranked turntable for steam locomotives in the earlier years, and two hotels, of which the Horseshoe Inn was the older and smaller. The grander, three-storey 'Junction House' had been built by Frank McAlister in 1886 but fell on hard times when Peel County voted in favour of prohibition shortly after the turn of the century and was razed to the ground with the approval of the populace in 1908.

The station at Cataract Junction was closed in 1932 in the midst of the Great Depression.

Passenger service to the City was discontinued in 1970.

The Penmaens arrived early, as was their custom.

'Your tie is crooked,' Sophie advised Thom.

'Never mind about the tie, OK? Please. Let's just never mind about the tie right at the moment, Mrs Penmaen. It's hot, and I am *trying* to be cool,' Thom replied.

'Are you nervous? Thom?'

'Nervous? What's to be nervous? Me? Why would I be nervous?' asked Thom. 'What's to be nervous about?'

'Well, are we going to sell, or not going to sell?' inquired Sophie. 'The business. You know, the business?'

Thom made a pretence of considering Sophie's question, then offered: 'To sell or to sell, not. That is the question.'

'Don't be a dolt.'

'I'm not being a dolt!' Thom protested. 'I thought we'd already agreed we could be equally happy either way? Sell the business, or don't sell the business. So if we're already agreed that we don't care if we do sell the business or don't sell the business, then the busy-ness of selling the business doesn't matter much this way or that, in the first place; and in the second place we're here tonight to listen to an offer and hopefully sting Bowles with a significant portion of the bill for a very elegant dinner. An *initial* offer for God's sake, and we're not even talking to the Main Man, just his hired popgun. So what's to be nervous?'

'Then why are you so crabby?' Sophie snapped.

'I am not crabby. Just leave my tie alone. Please,' Thom pleaded.

'Don't let Mr Bowles pay for the dinner. I wouldn't want Bowles to think we're beholden,' Sophie continued.

'Beholden?' asked Thom. 'Beholden for what? You don't think Aldebaan gave Bowles an expense account?'

'Whatever. Maybe yes, maybe no. I don't want to be beholden.' Sophie was not to be dissuaded. 'And don't you dare take more than two glasses of wine with dinner.'

THE HORSESHOE INN

Thom did not reply.
'And no Pernod with your coffee, either.'

The Penmaens shifted warily in the drive under the shade of an elderly sugar maple, looking, at first absentmindedly then more closely, at a sizeable limestone cistern.

> F & S M^cALISTER
> 1891

'What was it?' Sophie asked, pointing. 'For horses?'
'No. Don't you remember?' Thom replied. 'For trout. It was used for trout.'
'Trout? How am I supposed to remember trout? What trout? I remember a book called *Trout Fishing in America*.'
'Richard Brautigan. Great book, but it has nothing to do with the cistern. There was a photograph in a history we printed called *The McAlisters of Credit Valley*, or something like that. I don't quite remember the title,' admitted Thom.
'It had a green cover?' asked Sophie.
'Pale green, that's the one. Washed-out schoolbook lime green, the colour of a condensed lime rickey. Looked like hell, actually, now that I think of it.' Thom mused.
'Lime rickey?' asked Sophie.
'You didn't drink lime rickey in the sixties?' Thom was surprised. 'Better than cherry Coke, and not as sweet. The tart aftertaste was unusual, refreshing. The cover of the McAlister history was hideous, really, but the book did include a couple of curious photographs and one of the photographs in particular was a photograph of this cistern thing. I remember a caption about the stone pond that had something to do with keeping trout from the Credit River fresh before the cook pan-fried the fish for dinner.'

'When was this we're talking about?' asked Sophie.

'Eighteen ninety-one, I guess,' Thom answered, pointing at the inscription.

'Smartass!' replied Sophie.

'I can read, that's true, but I seem to recall there was something else remarkable about the inscription, other than the date. "F" is Frank, I'm pretty sure – I remember Frank had a British-colonial-sized handlebar moustache – and "S" was Sharon, or Stephanie or Samantha, I can't quite remember, but I *do* remember it was considered unusual at the time for the wife's name to be carved into the stone.'

'Typical,' Sophie sniffed. 'But her name can't have been Stephanie, because that's Mr Bowles's wife's name.'

'How is it that you happen to know the name of Geoffrey Bowles's wife?' Thom inquired. 'I don't remember telling you.'

'When Bowles phoned to confirm the dinner. I asked him what his wife was going to wear. He mentioned her name.'

'What is it his wife is going to wear?' asked Thom.

'Mr Bowles said he didn't know,' Sophie answered. 'Oh, damn!'

'What,' asked Thom, impatiently. 'What now?'

'I forgot my glasses in the car.'

'Are you sure you need them?' Thom whined. 'Really?'

'I need them, believe me, or you'll be reciting the menu to me three times over. And I don't want to traipse back to the parking lot in my heels....'

'OK, OK, OK,' Thom answered. 'You need your glasses, I'll go get your glasses for you.'

* * *

Geoffrey Bowles and his wife Stephanie walked up the drive from the lot behind the Horseshoe Inn and set the conversation immediately back to where it had been not five minutes earlier.

'What is this thing?' asked Bowles, pointing at the cistern.

'Careful,' Sophie cautioned. 'Thom knows more about the history of Cataract Junction than you likely want to hear.' Sophie cast a lowering glance in the direction of her husband, hoping to convince Thom to refrain from a rambling dissertation on the economics of nineteenth-century railways while they all stood awkwardly in the setting sun.

'I'm not so sure about that, Sophie,' Stephanie smiled. 'Knowing Geoffrey, he probably wants to hear every single detail. All that Thom can remember, and then some. We could be here for some time. Perhaps we should fetch a glass of wine before we let the men get started in on it?'

Stephanie Bowles was a stunning woman. Tallish, with the longest, thickest, most raven-black hair. Sophie Penmaen thought she recognized Stephanie from somewhere, but couldn't quite place the face.

Thom took one surreptitious glance at the height of Mrs Bowles's spike heels and the cut of her leather jeans and thought immediately of the British actress Diana Rigg playing the role of Emma Peel in *The Avengers*. The episode in the Hellfire Club, in particular. Will Duckworth had not exaggerated in the least. The storied Mrs Bowles was a looker.

'So,' Stephanie continued, after the couples were seated and Geoffrey Bowles had ordered a bottle of surprisingly expensive Australian chardonnay. 'How is it that you came to know so much about the history of Cataract Junction, Thom?'

'I don't, really. Know much, Mrs Bowles. Sophie and I printed a history for a family called the McAlisters a while back, and before that we printed a *History of the Credit Valley Railway* for another local author.'

'And you are blessed with a photographic memory?' Stephanie prodded.

'Photographic? In a way I suppose I am,' Thom answered, 'but not in the way you're thinking, and I wouldn't agree that I am blessed. This was ten years ago. I ran the printing press myself, then. History books, particularly family history books, tend to include lots of photographs, so the pressman has to pay close attention to the printed sheets watching for hickeys.'

'Hickeys? I thought hickeys were a skin condition that afflicts adolescent girls on Saturday nights?' Stephanie teased.

Thom decided Mrs Stephanie Bowles was something of a flirt, which was not entirely welcome news because Thom often felt awkward in the company of strangers, particularly female strangers, and most particularly attractive female strangers who knew how to flirt to effect, and did so.

Thom shifted in his seat.

'Don't look now,' Thom announced to no one in particular, primarily to divert attention from his discomfort, 'but who is that man sitting at the far end of the dining room?'

'Which one?' Stephanie asked, looking directly at Thom.

'The guy facing south,' Thom nodded in the appropriate direction. 'At the table by the window. This is a Trivial Pursuit question.'

'Trivial Pursuit?' Geoffrey Bowles interrupted. 'You mean he's Roy Orbison, or Phil Everly? Someone like that?'

'Not quite.' Thom frowned. 'But you're getting warmer. Who was the shortstop for the Detroit Tigers in 1954?'

'This gentleman by the south window was the shortstop for the Detroit Tigers baseball team in 1954?' Geoffrey Bowles whispered.

'Nope. Wrong. But the stranger by the south window at one time knew who did play shortstop for the Detroit Tigers in 1954, and it got him a job, once, working for Conrad Black,' Thom replied.

'Working where, for Conrad Black?' Geoffrey Bowles inquired. 'Doing what?'

'Come on, come on! If I tell you *where*, or what, you'll know who it is for sure,' exclaimed Thom. 'No fair.'

'Where?' Stephanie asked. 'We don't have a clue. We three.'

'Sherbrooke, Quebec.' Thom relented.

'Sherbrooke, Quebec,' Geoffrey Bowles repeated. 'Didn't Conrad Black once own the newspaper in Sherbrooke, Quebec? Maybe even his first newspaper?'

'Yup, and the name of the sports editor for the Sherbrooke *Record* in 1971 was ... ?' Thom continued.

'That's the sports editor of the Sherbrooke *Record* from fifteen years ago sitting across the room?' Sophie asked. 'So what? Who cares?'

'He's famous,' Thom replied.

There was a pause at the table. Sophie, Stephanie and Geoffrey Bowles each looked at Thom expectantly. Thom leaned forward. 'Scott Abbot. You've heard of Horn, Abbot? The publishers of a board game called Trivial Pursuit? He's Abbot,' Thom pronounced confidently, pointing discreetly across the room.

'What's he doing here in Cataract?' asked Geoffrey Bowles.

'I think Abbot owns a piece of a golf course on the escarpment,' Thom speculated. 'The Devil's Pulpit.'

'You're kidding.'

'What are hickeys?' Stephanie Bowles leaned towards Thom and touched his leg a few inches above the knee.

'In offset printing,' Thom replied stiffly, 'hard bits of ink or paper sometimes get stuck on either the plate cylinder or the blanket cylinder. The image stops printing in that specific area and then the pressman is left with a black dot in the middle of a white halo – a doughnut, I call it, but I'm not certain that's as appropriate a term as "hickey".'

'I'm having a problem following the connection between "hickeys" and the history of Cataract Junction.' Geoffrey Bowles admitted. 'Though I must admit that I am likely more interested in the latter than the former.'

'Oh, God, don't let Geoffrey start in on railways or we'll be here past midnight. As if it wasn't enough that he's built a hundred yards of track in the back pasture, now he's threatening to add a spur line into the solarium!' Stephanie Bowles reached out to touch her husband's arm, affectionately.

'Crystal Palace,' Bowles intoned. 'Next station stop.'

'You're building a railway on your hundred acres? Outside Glendaele?' Sophie was incredulous. 'Surely not?'

'Railway may be too grand a term for a handcar, one semaphore and a hundred yards of track,' Bowles apologized. 'Pegaesean, for example, is fast on its way to becoming a sizeable enterprise, but it isn't yet close to anything I would call an empire. I'm reading a biography, at the moment, on the life of William Van Horne....'

'Oh, God,' interrupted Stephanie. 'William Van Horne, the empire builder. Now we're in for it! Duck.'

'The Credit Valley Line was sold to the CPR,' Thom lectured. 'In 1883. Was Van Horne still working for the railway in 1883?'

'Not two of you, surely!' Stephanie exclaimed in mock horror. 'You were telling us, Thom, about hickeys.'

'Hickeys show up on the press most frequently in photographs, not so often with simple text,' Thom replied. 'That's why I remember most of the photographs I printed when I was running the Heidelberg myself, ...'

Sophie pulled a face. 'Thom may be back running the Heidelberg himself again soon if we don't settle a wage dispute with the pressman. We're due for annual employment review soon. Philippe LeBoubon is not exactly happy.'

'Perhaps Mr LeBoubon would feel more comfortable in the workplace if he knew something about the future of Penmaen Lithography?' Geoffrey suggested. 'Perhaps this time next year Mr Boubon will be shift foreman at the new plant?'

'Maybe. Maybe not.' Sophie answered. 'The employees are aware of your proposal. We're not trying to be secretive. Their reaction so far is mixed. Decidedly mixed.'

'More likely Philippe will want twice as much money to work for you as he's earning now, working for Penmaen, which is already twice as much as I'm currently making with him working for me,' Thom protested.

'Thom,' Sophie cut in, 'you're exaggerating.'

'LeBoubon doesn't take home twice what I make in a year, that's true,' Thom corrected himself, 'but Philippe sure as hell pockets a lot more than I do. For less hours, no risk, and piss-all investment.'

'Entrepreneurs often earn less than their senior employees,' Bowles agreed. 'Look around this dining room for example. I'd lay odds the maître d' has a part ownership. You can tell. Just watch. He knows most of his clientele by name, and he's trying hard to please. I'll also bet that he doesn't file a T-4 anywhere near as hefty as any of the senior waiters, and that's acknowledging that the waiters are unlikely to be reporting quite 100 per cent of their cash tips to Revenue Canada.'

GREAT EXPECTATIONS

Geoffrey Bowles's spot analysis of the various compensation packages available in the dining room at the Horseshoe Inn was interrupted by the arrival at table of one of the aforementioned presumed tax frauds with a lengthy list of the specials of the day.

The appetizer was a choice between a 'Local Produced Chèvrai' with fresh herbs, cracked black pepper, arugula and smoked pepper vinaigrette, and the 'Horseshoe Caesar' with crisp romaine, smoked bacon, padano walnut croutons and creamed garlic dressing.

The main course was a choice between the 'HoneyComb Balsamic Glazed Capon', the 'CharGrilled Atlantic Salmon' with Niçoise vegetables, air-dried tomato tapenade and grilled lemon, and the 'Grilled Alberta Beef Tenderloin' with essence of roasted garlic and grilled red onion rings served over buttermilk-whipped Yukons.

'It's pretty clear,' Thom continued, after the waiter had finished the recitation, 'that we've already made a great deal more progress on this purchase agreement than meets the eye.'

'How so?' Sophie hoped against faint hope that Thom was not about to launch into one of his more tangential diatribes. Sophie opened her glasses case.

'The first time Geoffrey and I met for lunch in Glendaele the choice of entrées was a toss up between the burger and fries, with or without the gravy, and grilled cheese with fries. But the potatoes weren't from the Yukon and I don't remember the ground beef being imported from Alberta either,' Thom jested.

'Thom, you twit,' Sophie interrupted. 'These are my sunglasses, not my reading glasses!'·

Geoffrey Bowles thought Thom's analysis of the deal as it stood amusing enough to provide an opening to the topic at hand. 'So did the two of you find time to discuss my proposal while you were on vacation?' he asked.

'We talked about it.' Sophie understated the truth of the matter.

'... and I bought the *Globe and Mail* every morning the first week of August just as you suggested,' Thom added.

'*Pegaesean Buys Shares of D&OL*, I know,' Bowles acknowledged. 'I read it too. But did you notice the *Globe* piece ran directly opposite the funnies? Pegaesean got as much space for the Duckworth deal as Blondie and Mary Worth together, and if it hadn't been for the piece above us about Lauren Bacall singing at Leonard Bernstein's birthday party, we might have had as much space as Blondie, Mary Worth, Gasoline Alley and Rex Morgan too!' Bowles thought this happenstance amusing.

Thom pulled the clipping out of his jacket pocket and read aloud: 'The Pegaesean Corporation today announced the acquisition of the publishing firm Duckworth & Osborne, Labellarte, buying 100% of the shares outstanding but leaving William Duckworth and Rebeca Labellarte in place as managers of the Toronto-based company.

'"Both Rebeca Labellarte and I are pleased with this unique opportunity," Duckworth, president of Duckworth & Osborne, Labellarte, said yesterday. "The company will maintain its editorial independence and direction. Everything will stay the same...",

'Everything will stay the same?' Thom repeated, sceptically.

'Why not?' Bowles challenged. 'If all the stakeholders go into the deal with their eyes open? We're talking about clever people here, honourable people.'

Thom continued to read from the clipping: '"I feel fortunate to be able to strike a deal with the most creative and the best publishing company in Canada," Nicholas Aldebaan, president of the $600-million Pegaesean Corporation, said yesterday. "For the first decade, much of our cash flow was built on publishing and for this reason it feels perfectly natural to want to return to our roots."

'Neither Aldebaan nor Duckworth would discuss terms of the acquisition. "It will ultimately involve quite a bit of financing, but they (William Duckworth and Rebeca Labellarte) will be totally involved in running the whole show," Aldebaan confirmed.

'And precisely just how much of this piece are we expected to swallow whole?' Thom asked. '"... *everything will stay the same"?* If Aldebaan wanted to buy a bankrupt publishing company, why didn't he simply step back and let Duckworth and Labellarte fall on the sword? Everything is *not* going to stay the same, surely.'

'Will Duckworth could stand some help with the numbers, you're right about that part,' Bowles allowed. 'Duckworth is not a numbers man. I'm working with him. I'm trying, for example, at the moment, to convince Will that an advance against royalties is an expense, and not an asset.'

'How so?' Thom asked, feigning ignorance.

'An advance is not quite the same sort of a thing as a pre-paid expense,' Bowles replied. 'It's not like an insurance policy that you could arbitrarily choose to cancel in mid-term and reasonably expect to collect at least a partial refund. Author advances aren't like that. The money goes out. It never comes back. An unearned advance is an expense.'

'Are you winning?' asked Thom.

'Winning?' Bowles did not understand the verb in the context Thom used it.

'Winning your point. Does Duckworth get it?'

'Oh, quite so, I'm winning, sure I'm winning. Will Duckworth's OK, other than he does prattle on about baseball. The Blue Jay Birds, apparently, are winning too, at the moment.

THE HORSESHOE INN

I'm not saying anything against Duckworth. We get on fine. He just doesn't have a great deal of business experience outside the circumspect confines of the publishing world, which doesn't, to be truthful, look much like any other kind of business I've ever known,' Bowles answered.

'Geoffrey used to work for Stephen Roman,' Stephanie explained. 'Denison Mines. We lived in Perth, in Australia, and Geoffrey travelled all over the Outback laying stake for Denison. Ellendale, Glenroy, Noonkanbah ... places like that.'

'Which was a fair bit easier than buying publishing companies for Aldebaan, I must say,' Bowles added.

'Bullion sounds more lucrative than fiction,' Thom broke in. 'Why didn't you stay in Perth? Take up twelve-metre yachting. Isn't yachting what they do, in Perth?'

'Thom!' Sophie was not pleased with the drift of the conversation.

'Yachting is what they do, in Perth,' Stephanie Bowles smiled fetchingly. 'Tell me, Thom. Are you familiar with Boyle's law?'

Thom looked to Sophie for support. Sophie shrugged.

'No,' he answered.

'This is precisely the sort of anecdote that is considered amusing, in Australia,' Geoffrey Bowles advised. 'Tell me. Would you consider Hell to be exothermic or endothermic?'

'This was a question, apparently, on a chemistry examination at the University of Brisbane,' explained Stephanie Bowles. 'Most of the candidates answered it in terms of Boyle's law.'

Thom's face registered a blank.

'Gas cools when it expands, and heats when it contracts,' Geoffrey Bowles extrapolated.

'So to address the question of Hell,' Stephanie continued, 'first we might want to consider the mass of the place, ...'

'... and in particular the growth or depletion of the mass as it ebbs and flows over time,' her husband completed her theorem.

It was clear, to Sophie at least, that the Bowleses had played at this particular charade many times in the past, and equally clear that they each enjoyed the playful cut and thrust of the repartee.

'Boyle's law explains that the temperature and pressure in Hell will remain constant only so long as the volume of Hell expands in direct proportion to the mass of each new soul added.' Stephanie smiled seductively.

'Which,' Geoffrey Bowles continued, 'given the statistical improbability of stasis in the known universe...'

'... is not bloody likely,' Thom concluded.

Sophie winced.

'Presume, therefore, that Hell is expanding at a slower pace than the rate at which souls are condemned to eternal grief,' Stephanie Bowles resumed the thesis.

'Then the temperature and pressure in Hell would increase until all Hell breaks loose!' Geoffrey Bowles exclaimed.

'Which hasn't happened yet,' Stephanie countered.

'But it could,' Thom suggested. 'At some point in the future.'

'If, on the other hand...' Stephanie made a casual show of admiring her manicure.

'Hell is expanding at a rate faster than the increase in souls sentenced to damnation...' Geoffrey Bowles continued.

'Then the temperature and pressure will drop precipitously until Hell freezes solid,' Stephanie concluded.

'If we accept the postulate given to one candidate by the object of his affection during his freshman year at the University of Brisbane...' Bowles continued.

'That it will be a frosty night in Hell before the beloved would consider reciprocity,' Stephanie smiled. 'And given some personal acquaintance with the predatory nature of the typical Australian male ...'

'Then by virtue of the presumed truth of the candidate's reluctant admission of failure in his pursuit of Miss Manners ...'

'We conclude that Hell cannot possibly be endothermic,' Stephanie reasoned.

'Hence, it must be exothermic!' Geoffrey Bowles exclaimed.

'Australia is a fascinating place,' the pitch of Stephanie Bowles's voice dropped an octave. 'Ayr's Rock. Alice Springs. Magical places, all of them, but we were in the Antipodes five years. We wanted to come home.'

'Stephen Roman may have been a curmudgeon,' Geoffrey added, 'and he was probably a couple of other things not as flattering, but he was a clever curmudgeon. Even when Stephen passed away last spring, he arranged to have himself buried in the robes of the Order of St Gregory the Great.'

'Which is?' Thom asked, screwing up his eyebrows.

'I'm surprised that you would ask. I thought I remembered correctly that you attended a Jesuit secondary school?' Bowles asked. 'In Montreal?'

'I did, unhappily so, and I'm more than just a *little* bit surprised that you would know about that ...' Thom replied.

'I made some enquiries.' Bowles dismissed Thom's concern with a wave of his hand.

'Just like Pierre Trudeau and René Lévesque, true enough, and the Order of St Gregory is ... ?' Thom prompted.

'The highest Order the Vatican can bestow on a lay person. Stephen Roman had friends in *very* high places.' Bowles smiled. 'He had enemies too. Did you ever read about the time he called Lester Pearson a sonofabitch to his face?'

'Ah, no?'

'That may have been a bit before your time, Thom,' Bowles

replied. 'In any case, there we were in Perth, a long way from head office in Toronto, and we'd been in Australia five years and Stephanie was tired of having her buttocks groped in the queues at the supermarket....'

'Geoffrey!'

'We received word that Roman wasn't well. He wasn't that old, just barely into his sixties, but he'd been in and out of intensive care with heart problems, and we weren't at all clear on what was going to happen at Denison Mines if, or when, his daughter took control, so we decided, for the one reason or the other, that what we really wanted was to be back in Canada,' Bowles explained.

'Geoffrey, that is simply, unequivocally, not true,' Stephanie insisted. 'Helen Roman-Barber was perfectly capable of taking control of Denison Mines and you know that. Helen's business expertise had nothing to do with our decision to return from Australia and she's been with Denison since 1976, for God's sake, man, get your story straight.'

'That's true, quite true, since 1976, but Helen's first job with Denison Mines was executive assistant to the chairman of the board,' Geoffrey countered. 'Which is not quite the same as learning a mine from the pit.'

'So? Helen was Stephen's daughter, his eldest child. Maybe Stephen Roman wanted her to have a job? Maybe he wanted to give Helen an opportunity that he never enjoyed himself when he was younger. Is this so difficult to understand?' Stephanie challenged.

'What about Stephen Junior? He had a degree of sorts in geology from Laurentian, and he actually worked in a hard-rock mine for a while, at Elliott Lake,' Bowles replied.

'Stephen was a dear boy who enjoyed flying his father's Cessna Piper Apache,' Stephanie turned to Sophie. 'He was a party animal, not a CEO, and I think his father was sufficiently astute to accept that, much as it may have disappointed him.'

'Elliott Lake?' Thom interrupted. 'I didn't realize Elliott Lake was a Denison mine. I was in Elliott Lake once.'

'I've never been there myself,' Geoffrey Bowles answered, 'but from what I've been told you can't have been on your way to anyplace else in the world because Elliott Lake is sixty miles north of the Trans-Canada highway and that's it. The end of the road. Then there's the bush.'

'It was a long time ago,' Thom explained. 'I was a poet. I think I must have been the *most* junior member of the League of Canadian Poets at the time. I was on tour. It was winter, February. I did a reading one morning at the high school in Elliott Lake, then I remember I had to drive back south to the Trans-Canada Highway, then west to Thessalon and north again to Chapleau. I was scheduled to meet up with another poet who was flying a Twin Otter into Chapleau. Five miles north out of Thessalon there's a sign that says…'

Thom held out his hands for effect.

> CAUTION: NO CIVILIZATION
> NEXT 120 MILES

'… that's pretty sobering,' Thom continued. 'In the late afternoon. In February. In an aging Volkswagen Bug. With a cloud bank closing in from the northwest.'

'But you're still with us,' Stephanie Bowles observed. 'Stephen Roman, on the other hand, is not.'

★ ★ ★

Sophie asked Geoffrey Bowles what he expected to discover in each of the various communications companies Galen Nicholas Aldebaan apparently wanted to purchase.

'The usual,' Bowles replied. 'The sort of thing Stephen Roman wanted when I worked for Denison Mines. The same sort of thing that Jake Wellcock is looking for at Hessen Atlantic.'

'Which is?' Sophie persisted.

'Mining, broadcasting, printing ... the principles are all the same. Pegaesean is an investment company. We're looking for three to five years of steady profitability. Some sort of a track record in other words, something we can measure.'

'And?' Sophie prodded. 'Surely your criteria are more elaborate than your railway?'

'Not that much more elaborate: a decent balance sheet, for a start. We do not wish to make a deal with some yahoo who spends the stuff faster than he earns it, no matter how fast he earns it. Great management. Growth. And vision,' Bowles answered, ticking off his wish list on the fingers of one hand.

'And yet you seem to think for some incomprehensible reason that Penmaen Lithography has ever enjoyed even *one* year of decent earnings?' Sophie was suspicious.

'Sophie!' Thom interrupted. 'Whose side is it that you are supposed to be on?'

'That's just the point, my Thom,' Sophie replied. 'I really do not know whose side it is that I am supposed to be on. I don't know that I want to work for the fabulously successful Galen Nicholas Aldebaan, or not, and I don't even know whether I prefer working for the fabulously unsuccessful Penmaen Lithography, or not. And I *really* do not understand why Aldebaan wants you, or us, to work for Pegaesean. Why would he? What've we got that's so special? What's in it for Aldebaan?'

Geoffrey Bowles and his wife shared a knowing glance at the interchange. 'The courage that comes with your convictions?' Stephanie speculated. 'Heart?'

'Do you each have a will?' Bowles asked.

'A will?' Thom asked. 'You think someone at this table is about to become deceased?'

'Not at all. But we were talking about Stephen Roman earlier,' Bowles persisted. 'And he's deceased. Recently.'

'If I die, she gets it. If she dies, I get it. It's a pretty simple will,' said Thom. 'Sophie came into a modest inheritance from a refugee couple who lived at one time in the cottage across from Dominion Lumber. They were from Latvia, originally. She was a lawyer, in Riga, and he was a chemist at the university. They got caught in Germany during the 1940s and then ended up as domestics in Canada after the war. I inherited some books, and a brass sundial. Oh yeah, and a few charcoal nudes he had sketched of her when she was younger.'

'Thom!' warned Sophie.

'What?' Thom continued. 'Sophie inherited what the two of them liked to call "the price of a plane ticket home". One condition they wrote into their will was that their executor formalize our wills before Sophie got her money, or I got my sundial. This is turning into a complicated story,' Thom apologized. 'They were strange people. They planted a lot of daffodils, when they were older. Acres of the bulbs.'

'The printing of family histories is not *quite* as lucrative as mining gold.' Geoffrey Bowles switched tracks. 'We recognize that. Naturally we're going to want to look closely at the financial side, do the due diligence and poke at the skeletons in the closet, but from the little we already know, Penmaen Lithography has been supporting the two of you quite adequately since 1974 – that's fifteen years, in a business that has an average profit margin so close to zero we can't measure the difference.'

'You're thin, Sophie,' Stephanie added. 'Actually you're more than thin, girl, you've got a waist to die for. But you're not anorexic. Do you pump iron?'

Sophie was embarrassed by the question, horrified even, by the idea. 'Iron? Ah, no, I don't pump, anything. But I do carry a lot of paper, up and down stairs, in boxes, and I help unload trucks. The mill delivers paper in 120-pound cartons, which we carry by hand, so I guess I can bench-press sixty pounds, that's true.' Sophie was uncomfortable talking about her figure, which was svelte rather than buxom.

'That's the thing, exactly.' Geoffrey Bowles warmed to his thesis. 'We're looking for people, entrepreneurs, who are managing, by themselves, just fine. We want to invest in people who don't need us, at the moment, but people who are capable of stepping outside their immediate challenges to understand that a little intervention from Pegaesean could make their lives *quite* a bit different.'

'I can think of a few things in my life that could stand improvement, that's true.' Sophie brightened at the prospect.

'Such as?' Bowles prompted.

'Such as it would be pleasant if Thom could manage to quit work at five o'clock and walk Kit Carson with me, and it would be nice if he could take Sundays off instead of doing earnings statements, and I can think of a few clients who could pay their bills a little more promptly,' Sophie speculated, thinking of Wastrel Editions, and Beaver Books.

'Those are all localized, short-term goals. What about the big picture?' Geoffrey Bowles spread his arms in an expansive gesture.

'The big picture?' Sophie was surprised that Geoffrey Bowles would ask such a question. 'Thom and I operate a little printing company in a little village and print mostly little poetry books for little poetry-book publishers who don't have any money. The Big Picture is nothing more than a walk on a Sunday in the woods in the provincial park across from the Cataract. There's a brick chimney in the forest, a ways downstream from the falls and up a bit onto the escarpment, just off what is known as the "Dominion Trail". Sometimes we sit there, in the forest. I wonder if maybe that's all that's left of the original McAlister cabin,' Sophie answered.

'Sophie found a pair of cedar waxwings in the forest a few weeks ago,' Thom explained. 'Actually Sophie didn't, Kit Carson found the birds first underneath a tree.'

'It looked as though they'd just fallen out of the nest,' Sophie added, 'but then it appeared that they were Siamese. The two little birds seemed to have only three legs between them.'

'What did you do?' asked Stephanie.

'There's a woman in Primrose who takes in birds,' Sophie elaborated. 'Not professionally, though she sometimes asks for donations to pay for the feed. She was able to determine that the birds actually weren't deformed but two of their legs had become intertwined with a bit of fishing line in the nest. She cut them apart with tweezers.'

'And did the birds survive?' Stephanie Bowles had never heard of such a thing before.

'The one was probably going to lose a leg,' Thom answered, 'from gangrene. But the bird lady said that's not a terminal problem for a songbird. They can survive easily enough on one leg. You're wrong though, Sophie' – Thom turned to his wife – 'about the McAlister cabin. The age of the ruin is about right, but as I remember it the McAlister homestead was on the other side of the river, just about directly across the stream from where the ruin of the chimney is now.'

'You're sure?' Sophie asked.

'Positive. Because the Credit Valley main line to Toronto ran directly through the McAlister property. And the tracks are on the west side of the river.'

Sophie allowed herself to be persuaded. Thom generally knew more about geography, and maps, than she did.

'How do you remember this stuff?' asked Stephanie Bowles.

'I don't,' Thom answered, 'remember *all* the stuff. Just the interesting bits. I remember the McAlister farm in particular because there was a spring on it that was considered significant enough to warrant a mention on a very early map of the township. Someone hit on the idea of bottling the water and it sold quite well. And then subsequently the spring, and the McAlister farm with it, were both bought up by Canada Dry.'

'Canada Dry?' Geoffrey Bowles found the story unlikely.

* * *

'What was the thing?' Stephanie Bowles turned towards Thom, then leaned forward conspiratorially. '... about the Bermuda Triangle story?'

'It's a bit of a chicken-and-egg kind of a question,' Thom admitted, 'because I can't actually remember how much of it is history, and how much was fictionalized for the benefit of Phil Marchand when he wrote a piece on book technology for the *Toronto Star* years later.'

'Phil Marchand?' asked Stephanie Bowles.

'Philip Marchand. Book columnist for the *Toronto Star*. But the Bermuda Triangle story goes back years before that,' Thom explained. 'My younger brother was studying mathematics at the University of Guelph in the early 1970s. Sophie and I were just getting started in the book printing business and I was looking for some magic numbers we could use to determine the most aesthetically pleasing sorts of trim sizes.'

'Magic numbers?' asked Stephanie. 'In book binding?'

Thom continued, 'Not so magic perhaps. The maximum sheet size of a Heidelberg KORD is eighteen by twenty-five inches. Fold the eighteen inches in half and you're left with nine. A minimal eighth-of-an-inch trim off the head and tail of a nine-inch sheet leaves you with eight and three-quarter inches, that's the height. But the optimum width of the finished book is not so readily apparent,' Thom explained. 'Twenty-five inches divided by four less an eighth-of-an-inch trim would leave you with a book that's six and an eighth inches wide, which would be an efficient use of the mill-size sheet, but my hand is small and at the time I still smoked a pipe so I preferred a book narrow enough to hold in one hand while I smoked my meerschaum with the other.'

'You *used* to smoke a pipe?' Geoffrey Bowles interrupted.

'I wish I still did, if I could, but twenty years of Erinmore Flake pipe tobacco has left me with a distinct breathing disability,' Thom admitted.

'So you quit?' Bowles asked.

Thom nodded.

'What does this have to do with the Bermuda Triangle story?' Stephanie interjected.

'Nothing, maybe,' her husband answered. 'You were telling us about the diminutive size of your right hand and its relationship to literature, Thom.'

'Actually it was my left hand. I held the pipe in my right hand, and books in my left. The thing was, that I was looking for some sort of elegant pseudo-mathematical justification for a standard trim size narrower than six and an eighth. My brother hit on the idea of drawing a theoretical diagonal across the face of a book trimmed to eight and three-quarters high, by five and nine-sixteenths.'

'So?' Stephanie Bowles was not following the logic.

'I can't remember the precise numbers,' Thom continued, 'but the two angles defined on either side of the diagonal, permuted and combined into each of all possible variations of longitude and latitude, just so happen to describe the precise geographic location of the Bermuda Triangle.' Thom allowed himself the unaccustomed frivolity of a shy grin.

'That's bullshit, right?' Stephanie Bowles smiled back seductively. 'You're pulling my leg?'

'You know, the truth of the matter is, I don't remember,' Thom continued. 'My brother invented the idea in the first place, and I embellished it into a little story that I included in a catalogue for an exhibition of small press books mounted at the Fisher Library at the University of Toronto. Marchand reviewed the exhibition and wrote a piece about book technology that was published in the *Toronto Star*. Some professor at George Brown College wrote in to the *Star* taking Marchand to task for believing my story, so then the little fiction started to take on a credibility all its own.'

'You're clever, aren't you?' Stephanie asked.

Thom shrugged.

'Bull. You're smart, and you know it,' Mrs Bowles pronounced judgement confidently. 'You've got brains.'

'I was asked to try the admission test for membership in MENSA – this was years ago, when I was in school. I took the test, I passed, I was offered membership and I was flattered to be offered membership but in the end I declined. I wouldn't have felt comfortable in MENSA. I'm smart, maybe, but only borderline smart, not seriously smart. I don't play chess at all well and I still don't *really* understand why Rebeca Labellarte would have told the Bermuda Triangle story to Nicholas Aldebaan.' Thom looked inquiringly at Geoffrey Bowles.

'Explain to me,' Sophie turned to Geoffrey Bowles as well. Sophie found any consideration of Thom's intelligence or lack of it embarrassing, unseemly, and too personal by half for public consumption. 'Explain to me what happens to the buildings we own on the Main Street in Glendaele Village if, for example, we decide to accept Aldebaan's offer. Presumably the space won't be near big enough to house the size of printing plant you envision?'

'The space will not, no,' confirmed Geoffrey Bowles.

'So Thom and I live above the printing shop at the moment, which is OK so far as it goes, up until now, but if Pegaesean doesn't want the space then presumably, what? We rent it out to someone else?' Sophie continued. 'But what if we can't rent the space? Or what if the only viable commercial tenant we attract is a billiards parlour that decides to apply for a liquor licence? Do I really want to sleep directly above a legalized speakeasy?'

'You live in a flat above the shop in the one building?' Geoffrey Bowles asked Sophie. 'Let me just try to get your present situation clear in my own mind.'

'We live in a flat above the shop in the one building,' Sophie confirmed. 'The light machinery, the bindery, and the darkroom are on the ground floor. The heavy machinery, the press, the folder and the guillotine are in the basement. You took the tour. You've already seen all there is to see.'

'The guillotine?' asked Stephanie.

'For cutting paper, and trimming the edges off bound books,' Sophie explained. 'The last stage in the production process. The other basement, across the alley, we use as a warehouse. The ground floor above it is rented out to a music store, and there's a single-bedroom rental apartment upstairs.'

'How are you doing, Sophie? In the rental business, I mean,' Bowles inquired.

'Covering the mortgage, the principal and the interest, but not the operating expenses yet,' Thom replied for his wife. 'We don't have a great deal of choice. We can't run our own business effectively without the warehouse space in the basement next door, in the short term, and in the long term the rental building is our pension plan.'

'How old are you, Thom?' asked Bowles.

'Thirty-nine, pushing forty, but what does that have to do with the rental building?' Thom was confused.

'Not a thing. It's just that I doubt there are many thirty-nine-year-old entrepreneurs in Glendaele Village who have given much thought to the notion of a pension plan,' Geoffrey Bowles was impressed. 'Of any sort.'

'Pension plan is really too grand a notion for what happened,' Thom confessed. 'Sophie came into a little money, we mentioned that, earlier. Penmaen was renting the basement across the alley for warehouse space. The building came up for sale and the thought occurred that we could easily lose the use of the space depending on who might buy the building, and for what purpose, so we decided to put the inheritance into a down payment. The pension plan idea was just a story I dreamt up after the fact to help convince the bank that we knew what we were doing, when actually we didn't have a clue. The pension plan story has about as much to do with reality as the Bermuda Triangle story.'

'But once the mortgage is retired, you'll have a steady income stream, more or less indexed to inflation, in perpetuity,' Bowles observed.

'It's a commercial mortgage, so we couldn't stretch it past a fifteen-year term. The mortgage is scheduled to disappear when I turn fifty,' Thom acknowledged. 'Which would be bloody wonderful, if it turns out that way.'

'So you've obviously given some thought to your future,' Bowles insisted.

'A little,' Sophie interjected. 'Thom and I have talked about it a little, Mr Bowles, but what are we going to do with the investment properties if we sign on with Pegaesean? Part of the reason we do as well as we do with the rentals is that we're there in person, right across the alley, all the time, so we can keep an eye on the comings and goings. If Thom is going to be working night and day at your new plant in the industrial park, we won't be able to pay such close attention.'

'What are the buildings worth, Sophie?' asked Bowles.

'I can tell you what we paid for each of them,' Thom answered. 'Probably 10 per cent too much in either case, but what they're worth is a philosophical question that depends on what you might be willing to pay to take them off our hands!'

'What about the assessed value, for municipal tax purposes?' Bowles asked.

'That'll tell you what an assessor thought they were worth in 1965,' Thom responded, 'but that is not useful information. We know, for example, that the rental building sold as recently as 1971 for as little as $18,000 but property values in the village soared right after because we bought our first building three years later for $39,900 and then ten years later still we bought the rental property for $154,000, so go figure – from $18,000 in 1971 to $154,000 just about fifteen years later. What's it worth?'

'Sounds to me like you would have been well advised to have bought your rental property in 1971, for $18,000,' Stephanie laughed.

'Should have, and probably could have, because the down payment at the time was only a thousand bucks, but didn't,' Sophie shrugged, 'because we were both just barely finished university. We were accustomed to renting flats. A hundred and twenty dollars a month, as I recall, was our limit. The most we felt we could afford to pay for rent. What does a flat in the City near the university cost now?'

'Don't know,' Bowles replied, 'and I'm not sure how we're going to go about putting a reasonable sort of a value on your buildings.'

'This might be an OK time to think about selling,' Sophie offered, 'from our point of view.'

'How so?' asked Stephanie.

'We're having trouble with a neighbour on the one side,' Sophie explained. 'First she wanted a parking spot, for free, and then she built an eight-foot-high privacy fence on the lot line when we wouldn't give her one. A parking space, I mean. The fence blocks some sunlight but it doesn't bother us a great deal and the properties are zoned commercial so eight-foot fences are legal, but now she's threatening to close the right of way in the alley and recently she's taken to flashing Thom from her balcony.'

'Flashing Thom?' Stephanie Bowles was incredulous. 'The woman sounds like a regular Wicked Witch of the East.'

'Wasn't the Witch of the East the one who died in the tornado?' Sophie queried. 'Maybe this lady is the Wicked Witch of the West?'

'She died too, in the end,' Stephanie offered by way of sympathy.

'We can only hope,' Sophie agreed. 'Unfortunately, Gayle Wicket seems to be wealthy for some unknown reason. Independently so. For the present she doesn't appear to have anything better to do with her time. And she is Evil.'

Sophie's rant was interrupted by the arrival at table of the waiter with a recitation of the temptations of the day: chocolate mousse with armagnac, ginger cranberry sherbet, orange and port sabayon, or Caledon apple tart. The Penmaens, and the Bowleses, agreed to pass. Coffee. Four coffees. Thom remembered, much to Sophie's relief, to forgo his usual Pernod – 'straight up, in a brandy snifter' as was his custom.

'Apart from the buildings, how are we going to put a reasonable sort of a value on Penmaen Lithography?' Thom asked, in as casual a voice as he could manage under the constraints of the circumstances.

'What were your assets on the balance sheet at year end?' Bowles replied. 'Pass the cream, will you?'

'Current assets? or total assets?'

'Thanks. No, no, not current assets. Total assets,' Bowles specified.

'Total assets.' Thom paused to think for a second. 'This is a number I should be able to remember because we just finished up the year end with our accountant not even a month ago. $176,000, something like that.'

'One hundred and seventy-six thousand, OK. And how much are you showing in your depreciation account?' asked Bowles.

'Eighty-one thousand, and it increases a thousand dollars a month which I think is much too high considering that most of the equipment was bought reconditioned and if anything has appreciated rather than depreciated in value. Grant Robinson doesn't see it that way. We have this disagreement every year about the same time,' Thom replied. 'Grant's concern is tax liability. My concern is to show as little profit as possible, but enough to keep the bank off my case.'

'Eighty-one thousand, OK. So maybe Penmaen Lithography is worth the difference between total assets and accumulated depreciation – maybe $95,000,' offered Bowles, 'just off the top of my head and without the use of a calculator.'

'Oh, no, it isn't,' Thom replied confidently.

'I beg your pardon?'

Sophie cringed.

'It ain't. Because I'm not going to sell Penmaen to you for $95,000. That simple. Open and shut. No deal.' Thom took hold of the courage of his conviction.

Bowles smiled. 'Take away Bell Telephone, Northern Telecom and the chartered banks, and every other business in the country is a family business, and every family business in the country is one day going to be sold, internally or externally, voluntarily or involuntarily. Think of the Molsons, the Bronfmans, the Eatons. Think of Denison Mines. Total assets less accumulated depreciation is a formula we use in mergers and acquisitions to get close to the "book" value of a company. It's a number, and it's a useful number, but there are others – we could look at asset value, market value, the value of Penmaen Lithography as a going concern, normalized earnings before tax, EBITDA... we could even look at "liquidation" value but I don't expect that would be appropriate in this case.'

'Damn right it wouldn't!' Thom agreed. 'We may be small but at least we're not in hock up to the eyeballs like Duckworth! We're also not getting closer to figuring out what Penmaen Lithography might be worth, or Sophie's real estate for that matter. And what the hell is EBITDA?'

'Earnings before interest, taxes, depreciation and amortization, but we are, actually, closer than you might think, though you could start to pull together some numbers for me,' Bowles went on. 'I'd like to see your earnings statements and balance sheets for each of the last five years, and you might want to annotate the balance sheets. If there's an abundance of surplus IBM Selectric typewriters in your inventory we'd rather know about the fluff sooner rather than later.'

'No typewriters, no problem,' Thom agreed. 'Jayne Beauregard already saw to it that we got rid of all the typewriters. Jayne Beauregard has a thing about typewriters. And there's no dead spruce, either, on the balance sheet. Duckworth warned me. I'm working on the inventory, but I'm not so comfortable with EBITDA. Penmaen Lithography is worth the exact number of zeros on the cheque Aldebaan signs, to the last decimal point,' Thom suggested.

'In a way that's true, and there's no denying it, but what we're trying to do here is to remove the financing aspect of Penmaen Lithography from your operating results,' explained Bowles. 'If you owned a highly leveraged business with a lot of debt in it, you could be showing pretty dismal earnings and still have a business that is actually performing quite smartly. On the other hand you might own a young business. The banks might not like it, but the business might be viable and Pegaesean might like it a lot better than the banks. Or you could have a business, typically an older business, that runs itself entirely on equity and could look, on paper, like it's very valuable and it probably would be, because an investor like Aldebaan could buy it and leverage the equity into something quite a bit more expansive than was there before.'

'Penmaen Lithography is a young business,' Thom admitted.

'That's hardly a surprise,' Bowles agreed.

'So, let's cut to the chase ... what do you want to know?' asked Thom.

'Take your net income after taxes,' Bowles explained, 'add back anything you paid out in income taxes, interest, depreciation or amortization then adjust the number to restate the management salary to fair market value and Pegaesean will pay between four and six times the normalized EBITDA. Less the outstanding debt that we'll doubtless be asked to assume.'

'You're not expecting Thom to come up with those numbers out of his head, I hope,' Sophie was concerned that Thom was likely not prepared for the complexity of this exercise.

'What do you mean by interest?' Thom asked. 'You mean interest on the operating line or interest on the long-term debt, or both? And who gets to decide whether it's *four* times or *six* times the number?'

'I do,' said Bowles. 'I decide. I review the quality of the underlying asset backing and I make my recommendation to Nicholas, then he flips the shilling. Do you do cash flow projections?'

'If you are going to be reviewing the quality of the assets, do you mind if I ask if you know the difference between a Heidelberg and an AB Dick?' asked Thom. 'But not really, no, we don't do cash flow projections that would resemble anything you would recognize as such. When we've got money, we spend it, and when we don't have money, we don't.'

'So there's no point in trying to do income or cash flow projections at this point because they'd be fictitious, is that what you're suggesting?' Bowles prodded.

'Totally fictitious,' Thom agreed. 'No point whatsoever.'

'But you could put something on paper about your personnel – how long they've been with you, what kind of remuneration they expect, what they're contributing to Penmaen at the moment, what you think they might be capable of doing for Pegaesean in the future. You mentioned that Philippe LeBoubon is unhappy, what could we do to change that around?'

'Simple. Pay him more money,' Sophie interrupted.

'It may not be quite that simple, Sophie,' Bowles disagreed. 'You can increase an employee's wages – that will normally pacify them for a month or two, but if you increase an employee's wages above the employee's ability to generate a return on their labour, then at some point you are going to have to decrease their wages back to reality and most employees do not take kindly to the rigour of the exercise and some might even try to make a case for constructive dismissal. Increasing an employee's wages can, sometimes, lead to more trouble than you might anticipate.'

'Will Duckworth mentioned that he and Rebeca each just got quite a hike at D&OL,' Thom offered.

Bowles ignored the comment, pointedly. 'You could also tell us something about your clientele, who you are printing for now ... Pegaesean may want to retain some of that volume if the margins are there, and you should also have a careful look at your capital equipment. You mentioned that you don't agree with your accountant's method of depreciating the printing presses.'

'I don't,' Thom agreed. 'I'm on the case. Give me a week or two longer. I'll send you some stuff. To the office on Scollard Street? Or to the farm?'

Chapter Seven

Dominion Lumber

'"Morning at La Residencia",' Sophie read aloud, then paused to wait for Thom's full attention. '"You awaken to the whisper of birdsong and a sigh of mountain air reaching under the wooden slats of drawn shutters. You stretch and yawn in a mahogany four-poster bed larger than your imagination. Slowly, your eyes open. Eventually, and at a pace that can be set only by yourself, you wend your way down the cobbled staircase to an upholstered wicker armchair on the terrace where the most elegant of wait staff offer the local oranges freshly squeezed into a glass."' Sophie stopped reading.

Thom waited expectantly. 'Oranges? Seville oranges? What kind of oranges? I don't like oranges.'

'You don't agree the idea of Majorca sounds anything other than utterly romantic? In October, maybe, or more probably November when it will be out of season. Majorca will undoubtedly be cheaper in the fall,' Sophie speculated.

'Majorca?' asked Thom. 'Where in the hell is Majorca? I mean, OK, OK, I know it's in the Mediterranean somewhere off the coast of Spain, but whatever gave you the utterly bizarre idea that you want to visit Majorca? Whatever gave you the idea that I want to visit Majorca? Did I say I wanted a vacation? I don't remember saying I wanted a vacation. I thought I heard you telling Stephanie Bowles just the other week that your idea of paradise is a walk on a Sunday afternoon at Cataract? On the Dominion Trail. Majorca is an island, for Christ's sake. An island not that much bigger than Bermuda, and you remember what Grant Robinson had to say about Bermuda?'

[179]

'That's just my point,' Sophie continued, equally self-assured. 'I've never been there, to Bermuda, and if I did – go – there wouldn't be convicts, and the convicts wouldn't be executed. No helicopters,' Sophie insisted. 'Why do you always insist on painting a black cloud above each and every silver lining? Listen to this: "The eagles soar on thermal updrafts a thousand feet above the lozenge-shaped swimming pool."'

'Eagles?' Thom cut Sophie's reverie short. 'Eagles are a northern species. I highly doubt there would be eagles on an island in the Mediterranean off the coast of Spain. And I very much doubt that thermal updrafts are caused by lozenge-shaped swimming pools! What kind of pap are you reading anyway? That doesn't sound like *National Geographic*.'

'So how do you know for sure that eagles are a northern species?' Sophie asked impatiently. 'And now that I think of it, why do you always have to be so damn cocksure of yourself anyway? Sometimes I think the appendage between your legs interferes with your limited ability to reason.'

'Not me,' Thom protested his innocence. 'Grant Robinson told me.'

'What?' Sophie demanded. 'About lozenge-shaped swimming pools, or Grant Robinson told you there are no eagles on Majorca?'

'Nope. Of course not. Grant Robinson told me he saw eagles one time when he was fishing for salmon on a converted minesweeper anchored off the Queen Charlotte Islands.'

Sophie raised a pencilled eyebrow. 'So?'

'The Queen Charlottes. Just south of Alaska. Like, north, you know?' Thom explained to Sophie. 'Like, in the parlance of the local folk: way the hell and gone far north.'

'So?' Sophie feigned puzzlement.

'So if eagles are native to the Queen Charlottes, and it must be so because Grant Robinson said that it's so, then I have difficulty with the idea that eagles could also be comfortable on

Majorca, in the teeth of a breeze scratched off the Algerian desert!' Thom rested his deposition.

'I'm telling you, Thom Penmaen,' Sophie continued, 'what is printed in this magazine, no less, no more,' Sophie paused to catch her breath. 'Have you ever been to Majorca? No. Are you some sort of expert ornithologist with a minor in rapacious predators? No. And there's a photograph. Look at the photograph will you? What bird other than an eagle could possibly have a wingspan that wide?' Sophie challenged, pointing to the magazine.

'A turkey vulture?' Thom ventured.

'Turkey vulture?' Sophie could not believe her ears. 'It says in this magazine that there are eagles over the swimming pool at La Residencia and yet you insist on calling the eagles vultures. Turkey vultures. What is it with you? Why do you insist on taking such a blackened view of any and every innocuous occasion?'

'Because my genes don't adjust quickly to disappointment?' Thom suggested. 'Something to do with my Jesuit education? Or, alternatively, because I prefer the Cajun cuisine?'

'"... eucalyptus, jade, geraniums. Hedgerows of high, thick rosemary".' Sophie pointedly ignored Thom's feeble attempt at humour. '"Cypress, bougainvillea, carob, lilacs, figs, mock orange, hydrangea, hibiscus, iris, cornflowers ..." Which part do you figure, from your uniquely blackened point of view, will be the most injurious to your tortured Catholic sensibilities?' asked Sophie.

'Let me see the picture of the gardens.' Thom reached for the magazine, and continued, 'It says here that this Residencia place is owned by Richard Branson and his ex-wife. Richard Branson and his *ex*-wife.' Thom emphasized the prefix.

'So, OK, so who is Richard Branson?' asked Sophie, who did not recognize the name.

'Branson is OK ... Virgin Air, Virgin Rail, Virgin Records ... the guy started in 1969, with a single mail-order phonograph outlet, and now he's already got a piece of a hundred different companies in entertainment, travel and publishing. Branson is a regular Oliver Blakeley, and reported to be a balloon pilot too, but it says in this article that La Residencia is a joint venture between Branson and his *ex*-wife, so how can that possibly be romantic? Particularly seeing as to how Branson's ex-wife is German!' Thom concluded his argument.

'Thom Penmaen, you do have a knack for twisting virtually any opportunity to expose the utterly unexpected but inevitable hairline crack in the Rosenthal,' Sophie accused.

'Not me,' Thom protested. 'I never. It says in this article that the author, George Sand, took Frédéric Chopin to Majorca in the winter of 1838, "for a restorative cure" in a monastery overlooking Valldemossa.'

'And what's wrong with that, pray tell,' asked Sophie. 'A restorative cure might be just the tonic that I need.'

'It was an OK idea, maybe, but a bad move nonetheless,' Thom replied. 'It rained, so it says in this article, for three months solid in the winter of 1838, and washed out the only road down from the monastery. At a thousand feet above the beach, it was cold, in February. The monastery was not heated. By the time George Sand got poor old Chopin out of their love nest in the spring, the composer was close to death.'

'You do have a unique talent,' Sophie said, grimacing, 'for annoying me.'

'So just what the bejesus do you think we'd do with our time, then, in a place like Majorca?' asked Thom. 'On an island, for a week. We'd be bored to tears.'

'Keep reading,' replied Sophie.

'Reading about what?' Thom asked, scanning the magazine article quickly to the end.

'About Robert Graves,' continued Sophie.

DOMINION LUMBER

'Robert Graves, author of *The White Goddess?* British poet,' Thom confirmed, 'but I thought he was dead?'

'He's dead, OK? Graves is dead, you're right about that. You are often right. Not as often as you think, though. You don't know everything about everything. Like, for example, that Graves's son Tomás still prints poetry books at the Seizin Press in Deyá. That's what you could do, with your abundance of leisure time after we emigrate. You could work with Robert Graves's son making beautiful books of poems at the Seizin Press, and I could watch the eagles soaring above La Residencia,' Sophie waxed uncharacteristically poetic.

'But the Seizin Press is a letterpress shop.' Thom was still reading the article. 'Wait a minute, what did you say? Emigrate? Did you just say emigrate? I don't know anything about letterpress, and they print on an Albion, for God's sake! That's archaic. Just because I'm pushing forty doesn't necessarily mean I'm archaic! I know offset. I know Heidelbergs.'

'Forty isn't old,' Sophie demurred, 'if you're a tree. Not old at all if you're an oak. I'm thinking about our future, man. I'm thinking about what happens to us after you sell your stake in Penmaen Lithography to Aldebaan and get yourself unceremoniously dismissed by Geoffrey Bowles because you can't cope with Jayne Beauregard and her drinking problem or Philippe LeBoubon and his wife's many expectations.'

'Thank you ever so much for that timely bit of advice,' sniffed Thom. 'LeBoubon has rescheduled, again. I'll keep your helpful hints in mind.'

'Thom Penmaen, you are impossible. You are male. You are almost forty and you may very well be prematurely archaic, but I, right now, have endured more than I care to suffer of your personality disorders for one evening,' Sophie concluded her analysis of good and of evil.

Of Majorca and Glendaele.

Of freedom, and of poverty.

Of the Old World, and the new.
Of heaven, and of hell.

* * *

'You guys want the usual?' the waitress asked, as Thom and Geoffrey Bowles settled into their accustomed table by the south window at the Holmewood.

'The one clear advantage of a small town,' explained Thom. 'Order a grilled cheese from Sally Ann more than twice and you're already marked for life.'

'Do you have any specials on today?' Bowles asked the waitress.

'Just the usual specials, honey,' Sally Ann replied, and offered what she considered a passable imitation of a Bunny dip.

'Which is?' Geoffrey Bowles was not paying close attention to the gratuitous display of cleavage.

'Grilled cheese. You boys'll be wanting your Kraft slices grilled on brown or white, with or without the Holmefries?'

'White with fries for me,' Thom specified. 'Hold the gravy.'

'What momentous event occasioned the crêpe paper and the balloons on the ceiling?' Bowles frowned. 'Is the Holmewood booked for some sort of extravaganza tonight?'

'Looks like maybe we're already past late for the party,' Thom pointed to the litter of burst balloons on the floor.

'You're too late,' Sally Ann confirmed. 'Dirk McTavish hosted a stag for his cousin Sterling here at the Wood last night. Young Sterling is set to be married later this very afternoon.'

'Balloons?' Geoffrey Bowles persisted.

'Part of the theme, like, you know?' Sally Ann screwed her mascara into a question mark. 'Young Dirk McTavish let it all hang out. Even rented a striptease artist lady from Bramalea who let the boys prick at her rubbers one at a time until she was standing there buck naked in front of Sterling except for the one big red balloon tied between her legs and Sterling got to pop that one himself, like, personally, you know, and out plops a maraschino cherry that bounced once on the table and ended up in Sterling's soup. Beef barley.'

'Indeed?' Geoffrey Bowles was genuinely horrified at the thought. 'You don't say. The balloon dance is some sort of local tradition?' Bowles directed his question at Thom.

'Oh, no, honey,' Sally Ann interrupted, pleased that Bowles was appreciative of something that she had to offer. 'Not traditional at all in these parts. Most stags here just rent a movie. Very rare for the local bucks from Glendaele to be able to afford a real, live doe of any sort, never mind a professional lady all the way from Bramalea!'

'White with fries for me,' Thom repeated. 'The grilled cheese, I mean. And a small Coke,' he added, hoping maybe Sally Ann would clue in to the idea that Geoffrey Bowles had already heard more about the McTavish stag than Thom thought appropriate to the occasion.

'What's this I'm reading in the *Globe*,' Thom turned his attention to Geoffrey Bowles and his back to Sally Ann, 'about Oliver Blakeley and a dogfight with Hessen Atlantic over Springfield? I thought you told me Springfield was a subsidiary of Pegaesean, and I also thought that Oliver Blakeley was your operations guy. That's what you said, right? About Blakeley? I remember that correctly? Sounds to me like maybe you've got trouble stewing in corporate paradise.'

'"Dogfight" may not be the most appropriate word to describe what's taking place at the moment,' said Bowles. 'In fact the whole idea of the alleged "dogfight" may well have more to do with the *Globe* romanticizing Blakeley's military background than it does with the business relationship between Pegaesean and Springfield, or between Springfield and Hessen Atlantic. Or even the personal relationship between Oliver Blakeley and Jake Wellcock. And I wouldn't be too confident in the accuracy of that article anyway,' Bowles smiled, knowingly, as if to invite Thom to pursue the topic.

'How so?' Thom took up the invitation, relieved to be rid of Sally Ann.

'Any number of reasons, but the one that comes to mind is the part in which Galen Nicholas Aldebaan supposedly reacted in a hostile manner when asked about his relationship with Oliver Blakeley,' replied Bowles.

'?' Thom rose to the bait.

'I very much doubt a journalist from the *Globe and Mail* would have access to Aldebaan's private telephone number in Bermuda,' Bowles answered. 'And I'm not totally certain that Aldebaan is in Bermuda, at the moment, but even if he is I still doubt that Aldebaan would react in a hostile manner to a story such as that because I don't think Nicholas would react at all, in any manner. A terse "No comment" would be more likely, given what I know of the man.'

'But there must be something going on,' Thom persisted. 'Or coming down. What about Wellcock? How does he fit in? The dogfight piece was three times the length of the coverage you got when Pegaesean swallowed Duckworth and Labellarte. Maybe bigger. The *Globe* thinks it's got a story. A better story than Blondie and Dagwood.'

'That's what the *Globe* thinks. Maybe so. You, on the other hand, think of it as a family thing,' Bowles insisted. 'Four years ago Springfield was conceived as a $400,000 joint venture between two entrepreneurial individuals, Nicholas Aldebaan and Oliver Blakeley. Four years later, here we are. Springfield is worth $900 million and it employs six thousand people working at thirty-six plants spread all over southern Ontario. You don't get here, from there, without quite a bit of creative financing. So maybe the workout boys at Hessen Atlantic are not so happy with the numbers Blakeley reported at the end of June, so what? So maybe Blakeley and Springfield weighted the statements a bit to the side of future growth and that cut into the dividend stream the boys at Hessen were projecting. So maybe the boys in the red suspenders were greedy, or maybe Hessen Atlantic got itself stretched a bit in bauxite in Brazil? Caught in a peso squeeze? Who knows? Who cares? Hessen Atlantic is not an Evil Empire, just a dozen shrewd investors who eke out what they consider to be a superior lifestyle from merchant banking,' Bowles finished up as Sally Ann arrived with the grilled cheese, freshly sliced dill pickles on the side. 'Think of Hessen Atlantic as a family thing, and stay away from it. Don't let it bother you. Just don't think about it.'

'I'm having a bit of trouble,' Thom felt queasy with Bowles's cavalier dismissal of the problems at Springfield, 'with the concept of EBIDTA. Ebitda, is that how you pronounce it? that you outlined at the Horseshoe Inn.'

Bowles nodded affirmatively.

'So let's take Penmaen's fiscal year ended just this past May.' Thom swallowed, with difficulty. 'We may as well talk about reality rather than fantasy, no? Net earnings were $143.30.'

'That's low,' Bowles noted. 'The boys at Hessen would not be impressed.'

'I'll bet. It's low,' Thom agreed, embarrassed and eager to both acknowledge and to rationalize the low number, 'because our accountant has Sophie and me sucking as much money as possible out of Penmaen in management salary in order to maximize our personal RRSP contributions.'

'It's an investment strategy,' Bowles agreed, 'that probably makes sense for Sophie and for yourself. I wouldn't know for sure, but I'd imagine your accountant knows what he's doing, though I doubt your banker is content with corporate earnings of a hundred bucks.'

'The bank does not appear to position our personal financial future at the top of its corporate agenda, that's true,' Thom acknowledged. 'We've been warned, more than twice.'

'And if you're pulling cash to maximize RRSP contributions then you're probably understating Penmaen's real corporate earning potential, so we may decide to adjust management salary before settling on a realistic estimate of EBITDA,' suggested Bowles.

'Even so,' Thom continued to read from his notes. Whenever Thom felt challenged by a social situation, he preferred to read from notes. 'One hundred and forty-three thirty, plus $3,079.91 in bank charges most of which was interest, $1,855.45 in long-term interest and $9,368.36 in depreciation, less $2,230.25 in income taxes recoverable ... the number you're looking for is $12,216.77 ... times four is $48,864, times six is $73,296, but there's no damn way I'd consider selling Penmaen Lithography to Nicholas Aldebaan for $73,000. That would be idiotic,' Thom insisted. 'I get up in the morning and I walk down half a flight of stairs and I'm on the job. I don't punch a clock. I report to no one other than Sophie, and I don't really even need a car, so surely you can understand that I'd be crazy to give up the kind of independence I already enjoy for the favour of a one-time $73,000 payday, half of which I'd lose in capital gains tax anyway!'

'Maybe we'll have to consider a new vehicle as a signing bonus,' Bowles agreed, 'but you'll be well advised to steer clear of MGBs or the mechanics' charges will deplete your windfall faster than you can bank it. Did you check the numbers for the previous year end, to determine if 1988 was an anomaly?'

'I looked, believe me. I checked,' Thom looked down at his notes. 'Last year was a little better. One thousand eight hundred and seven dollars and fifty-three cents in earnings, plus $1,605.19 in bank charges, most of which was interest, $1,938.21 in long-term interest and $12,356 in depreciation, less $2,451.25 in income taxes recoverable ... so now we've got $15,255.68. Times four is $61,020, times six is $91,530, but I also know that I've got $150,000 worth of capital equipment and only $17,000 in long-term debt outstanding, so I'm damned if I'm going to sell Aldebaan $133,000 worth of printing machines for $91,000! That simple!'

'Only $17,000 in long-term debt,' Bowles chortled. 'That's a rather different kind of a situation from the one we were facing at D&OL. And I'm starting to think that maybe in your case we'd best look a bit harder at the underlying asset value of Penmaen Lithography, which was also *not* the case at D&OL!'

'Dead spruce?' Thom brightened.

'In their case, yes. Will Duckworth's revenue stream was higher than yours of course. There was some cash flow there, I don't deny that, but his payroll was significantly higher than yours too. Will and Rebeca didn't own capital equipment, and their debt was a hell of a lot higher than $17,000. What about accumulated depreciation? Do you know what your printing machines are worth on the books?' asked Bowles.

'I looked at that number too,' Thom acknowledged. 'I've looked at lots of numbers. This number, and that number. So many numbers my brain aches and I'm not at all convinced that I'm any further ahead. We were showing $81,000-plus in accumulated depreciation at year end, but that doesn't take into account certain specific local realities. Like, for example, the Heidelberg I bought in 1978 for $24,000 is worth easily twice that on a resale. Maybe $50,000 if the press is sold in Sao Paulo in Canadian dollars. I understand accumulated depreciation is a number accountants need for income tax purposes, but I don't think it will be much help if you're trying to get me to part with my Heidelberg. What is Aldebaan going to make of this sort of evaluation? And when do we get to meet the great man himself?' Thom changed the subject. 'Sophie was asking about that. You do understand that if Sophie is not happy, there's no deal?'

'I'm sure she was,' Bowles sympathized, 'asking. And I'm sorry to say I can't help you much on that score. Aldebaan is a bit of a chameleon. He will see you when he wants you to see him, and not before. I don't think Nicholas enjoyed the publicity around the Duckworth deal much, and he left the country shortly thereafter. By boat, so far as I know. Aldebaan is fiercely protective of his privacy. He's probably somewhere in the Gulf Stream as we speak, sailing to Bermuda.'

'You've been to Aldebaan's place in Bermuda, right? With Duckworth and Rebeca Labellarte?'

'Just the once,' Bowles admitted.

'And?'

'And?' Bowles repeated the question.

'So what's it like, Aldebaan's place in Bermuda?' Thom persisted.

'In a word, ostentatious,' Bowles confirmed. 'Grecian columns and ginkgo trees, and filigreed gold mosaics. A veritable monument to the magnificence of his business acumen.'

Thom was unsure how he was expected to interpret Bowles's hyperbole. Or the allusion.

'Sophie has decided she wants a holiday.' Thom said apologetically to Bowles. 'In Spain.'

'So? What's the problem?' asked Bowles. 'Don't dither. Go to Spain.'

'But what about Aldebaan?' Thom equivocated. 'I don't think I'd want to be caught out of the country, unavailable, if there's any possibility of a deal about to be going down!'

'I remember a demonstration Stephen Roman staged at Denison when he was trying to teach his daughter Helen the rudiments of management. Stephen always did have a game plan, and he was a decent communicator. This one afternoon Roman arranged a pile of fist-sized rocks on the boardroom table and I guess the managers in the room thought the quiz was going to address the quality of ore samples,' Bowles paused.

Thom listened.

'Then Stephen produced a one-gallon mason jar with a wide throat from under the table and very carefully placed the rocks one at a time into the jar, and he must have practised the stunt the night before because by the time he reached the rim there weren't any rocks left on the table. Then Stephen asked his senior people — Helen was in the room too — if the mason jar was full.' Bowles looked expectantly at Thom.

'Yes?' offered Thom. The correct answer to the question seemed to be yes, rather than no.

'That's the way it appeared. The more so because there weren't any rocks left on the table, they were all in the jar. But then Stephen reached under the table and this time produced a cup of washed gravel that he poured slowly over top of the rocks with his one hand while he agitated the throat of the jar with the other,' Bowles continued.

'And the gravel worked its way down into the spaces between the big rocks.' Thom picked up the gist of Bowles' drift and Stephen Roman's theatrical presentation.

'Of course, so now do you think the mason jar was full?' asked Bowles.

'Probably not,' responded Thom, warily.

'You're hedging your bets,' Bowles smiled. 'I've been warned that you are somewhat less of a printer and often more of a philosopher, but you're right of course, Roman also had a small dish of sand that he sifted carefully into the spaces between the bits of tailings. So now do you think the jar was full?'

'Pretty close,' Thom answered.

'Close is a counter only in horseshoes,' Bowles advised.

'So what else did Stephen Roman have under the table? Water?' asked Thom.

'Water,' confirmed Geoffrey Bowles, 'to top up the mason jar right to the brim. And the moral of the story is?'

'That no matter how busy you may think you are, there's always time to squeeze in another lesson in management theory?' suggested Thom.

'You're being facetious, I recognize that, but no, the point Stephen Roman attempted to illustrate is that you have to put the big rocks into the jar first, or you'll never get a second chance. If Sophie wants to go to Spain, go to Spain,' Bowles advised.

'And Aldebaan?' Thom persisted.

'Don't worry about things you can't control,' Bowles insisted. 'You don't know how to drive a lorry, for example, but you've never yet been hit by a wayward van. Aldebaan is still under sail for all I know, but he may as well be sailing to Byzantium. It could take a while, if he is. Maybe forever. Just get the big rocks into your mason jar first. That's the part Thom Penmaen can control.'

Sally Ann presented the bill for lunch with a small bowl of brown-striped humbugs done up in individual cellophane wrappings. 'Compliments of the management.' She smiled and dipped forward to give Thom an unexpectedly intimate glimpse of her superstructure.

'Try a humbug,' Bowles encouraged Thom, reaching for the bowl himself.

The Main Street of Glendaele Village was lined on either side with giddy throngs, and the bells of All Saints Anglican pealed out the happy news. Thom and Geoffrey Bowles pushed their way with difficulty through the mixed assembly of well-wishers, wannabes and Saturday afternoon shoppers as the wedding procession marshalled itself at the foot of the steps in front of All Saints.

Dirk McTavish, best man, took the lead, easing himself in to the saddle of the biggest 1200cc Harley-Davidson chopper Thom had ever seen. Liam McTavish, the father of the groom, and Liam's brother Derek both clambered up to the cockpit of the Glendaele stage, a replica nineteenth-century stagecoach that might once have plied the Glendaele, Primrose, Ospringe to Guelph run. Liam loosed the reins of a pair of matched Clydesdales while his brother Derek took up the shotgun position and the groom, Sterling McTavish and the lucky Witherspoon girl climbed into the box coach.

Sterling's younger brother Struan brought up the rear of the procession, piloting a restored 1959 Cadillac Eldorado done up with paper flowers, a pair of intertwined horseshoes hung from the rear-view mirror, a set of two-four in cans attached individually to the rear bumper and tail fins that seemed to stretch to Hawthorne. It wasn't a big parade, but it was, most certainly, one of the more elaborate public events that had been staged in Glendaele Village for some time.

'They do have their separate tastes in carriages,' marvelled Thom. '... the McTavishes, that is,' as the Harley coughed and throttled into gear. Thom recognized Henry Ramesbottom, in the throng, interviewing bystanders for the Glendaele *Gazetteer*.

'It would have to be a Harley,' Bowles remarked, 'not a Norton, or a Triumph.'

'Dirk is very much a New World sort,' Thom agreed.

'I fancy the Eldorado myself,' enthused Bowles. 'I don't care for the beer hanging from the bumper, but look at the tail fins, will you?' Bowles attempted a loose translation to the local dialect. 'Will you get a load of the bloody tail fins!'

* * *

'How much is it that you pay out for the Nubtex cloths?' Philippe LeBoubon started in to his annual employment review on the offensive.

The tactic was effective, in a circumspect sort of a way. Thom Penmaen was immediately offended, and defensive. 'The blue ones?' Thom replied, tentatively.

'Ho, ho! There we have it,' crowed LeBoubon. 'Not only do you admit to labour your mechanisms of controlling the costs are inadequate, but you agree also you don't know even the colour of Nubtex cloths being used in the room with the printing press every day of the year!'

'Does it matter?' Thom was genuinely perplexed. 'What colour Nubtex cloths are used by you in the pressroom every day? M. LeBoubon,' Thom added, as an afterthought.

'What is the policy of the Penmaen Lithography Company —' LeBoubon ignored Thom's question and continued the assault from a prepared script '— as to the regards for the suggestions from employees that are saving costs?'

'I'm not sure that I understand what you are talking about,' Sophie interrupted LeBoubon, 'and I'm not sure that I appreciate the tone of this conversation.'

'Ho, ho!' replied LeBoubon. 'There we have it!'

'What,' Sophie interrupted him a second time, 'do we have?'

'The proof,' LeBoubon was beside himself with uncommon glee, 'that middle management is equally incompetent!'

'What?' Sophie exclaimed. 'What middle management? We don't have middle management.'

'Down, Sophie,' Thom advised. 'M. Philippe may or may not be correct, but he does seem to think he has a point, and this *is* employment review, and I don't think we are understanding the point as presented by Philippe LeBoubon.'

Thom did not enjoy formal personnel reviews.

The alternative, on the other hand, was not an option. Any sort of abuse was preferable, in Thom's estimation, to the sort of ad hoc employment-review-by-water-cooler practised previously, whereby any malcontent had only to seed a campaign of whispers and the morale of the shop was wrenched askew for months. 'How much,' Thom turned his attention to LeBoubon, 'do we pay for Nubtex cloths?'

LeBoubon consulted his notes. 'Four cents.'

'Four cents,' Thom repeated. 'Thank you for sharing that pithy bit of intelligence with Sophie and myself.'

Thom's parry was successful in that LeBoubon had not expected to be thanked at that precise point in his presentation. He also wasn't sure what pithy meant. It wasn't in the script. LeBoubon looked down at his notes, paused, and then renewed the attack. 'How many Nubtex cloths do I desecrate myself personally and hurl to the trash in a shift?'

'As many as you need to complete the task at hand,' Thom speculated. 'I am not aware of any rationing programme in effect at the moment on the use, abuse or misuse of Nubtex cloths, and I don't really see that I care!'

'Ho, ho! There we have it!' exulted LeBoubon.

'What do we have this time?' asked Sophie.

'Lack of inventory control!' LeBoubon ticked off a second diamond on his litany of complaints.

Thom did not wish to prolong a discussion of the statistical fate of Nubtex cloths. 'How many times in a month do you oil the yellow nipples on the Heidelberg?' Thom asked, just to divert the assault.

'What do you mean' — Philippe was instantly suspicious —

'how many times do I oil the yellow nipples? There's a chart on the side of the delivery that says all the information about the colours of the nipples.'

'"The red nipples, daily; the yellow nipples, weekly; the green nipples, semi-annually,"' Thom recited from memory. 'I know that. I know what Heidelberg recommends, and I also know that Heidelberg recommends an oil with a viscosity saybolt 650 second at 100°F but that's not my question. I didn't ask if you can read, I asked how many times in a month do you oil the yellow nipples, and the reason I asked is because I notice that the grease gun and the oil gun both happen to be empty as we speak.'

'How would you know,' LeBoubon's eyelids narrowed perceptibly, 'about the grease gun and the oil gun?'

'Because I checked!' Thom replied. 'How else would I know?'

'Ho, ho! There we have it again on sorry display for all in horror!' exclaimed Philippe LeBoubon.

'What is it that we have,' Sophie asked, 'this time?'

'Invasion of employee privacy and self-respect by senior management,' replied LeBoubon self-righteously.

'What the hell are you talking about?' asked Thom.

'You don't try to tell me your criticisms.' LeBoubon punctuated his conviction with a finger in Thom's face that waggled a bit, to and fro. 'You don't play sneak around at the middle of the night in employee toolboxes, that's not your description of the job. Your description of the job,' Philippe continued, 'is to make the food, the clothing and the shelter for your employee and his family, and to make my happiness complete with positive enforcements at all times and I am *not* happy, sufficient, and my wife is *not* happy also, so you have a record of some performance to improve, notwithstanding!'

'Really?' Thom could barely contain his anger.

'I have decided I am not making talk about your oilcans,'

said LeBoubon, concluding that part of the discussion. 'I will be making talk about the savings in the Nubtex cloths.'

'What savings are you talking about?' Sophie was starting to worry that Thom might not be able to contain himself much longer.

'Ecoloclean, Prisco, gum, fountain etch, scratch remover, ... and so on.' LeBoubon momentarily lost his place. 'Thirteen Nubtex cloths a day it used to be the sorry waste but now I wash four and use the ones again tomorrow. Four cents a cloth, times four cloths a day, times five days a week, times fifty weeks a year comes to you owe me forty dollars.' Philippe LeBoubon looked up from Imogene's text, and added, '... for cost savings in employee suggestion planning.'

'A month ago' – Thom commenced the counteroffensive – 'we gave you a five-hundred-dollar bonus to tide you over the impending inconvenience that Sophie and I were about to be distracted with the Aldebaan deal, and we were concerned that your employment review would be delayed as a result, and now you want forty dollars more? What about the five hundred bucks we gave you in August? Since when did you start washing four Nubtex cloths a day anyway? Last week? And who do you think pays you $13.25 an hour to *wash* the damned Nubtex cloths? And who do you think pays for the gas to heat the water you use washing the bloody Nubtex cloths? Eh? What about the detergent? The laundry soap? I can't hear you. Who?'

'Thom!' Sophie leapt into the fray before LeBoubon could land another sucker punch. 'Shut up!' Sophie turned to face LeBoubon directly, 'And you, Mister Philippe, could stand to be a little more generous in your appreciation of the things Thom does for you....'

'Quelle horreur!' exclaimed LeBoubon. 'Name me one thing that senior management does in respect of labour in this printing place! Apart from the August money that doesn't count because Imogene my wife had to buy a dentist which is your fault also that labour doesn't have a dental plan for the health of my family and my offsprings!'

'OK,' Sophie replied, coolly. 'Like how about Thom pays your wages on time, every time, twice a month on the fifteenth and the thirtieth, regardless of whether we're rich or poor, or cash flush or covering for bad debts or accounts past due. Has Thom ever, once, been late with a payroll cheque?' Sophie expected the reasoned moderation of her position might prevail.

Sophie was mistaken.

'That too!' LeBoubon ran a finger rapidly across and down a page of prepared text. 'The employees of this company have made the strategy to change the pay period to each Friday at 3:00 p.m. with an extra fifteen minutes breaking-time to deposit the paycheque to the bank.'

'What?' Thom's lower jaw came unhinged from the tension of the line drawn taut between his lips.

'What matters did Yvette Charbeau tell you at her employing review?' LeBoubon demanded. 'What was the news that Lorrie Wright had to say also to each of management?'

'Not much,' Sophie stepped between the two combatants once more. 'Lorelei and Yvette each said something, in different words, about how much they enjoy working at Penmaen Lithography....'

'That's not the truth,' charged LeBoubon. 'You are making a lying twister of the true matter.'

'Ex-cuse me?' Sophie glared.

'I told them, Yvette and Lorelei Wright, to change their payments to mortgages each week and they are retired at age only fifty-five!' LeBoubon revealed.

'But Lorelei doesn't have a mortgage, Philippe,' Sophie reminded the pressman. 'Lorelei rents a one bedroom.'

'You've been taking a course,' Thom suddenly recognized,

DOMINION LUMBER

'in financial planning. From Glendaele Valley Secondary. At night, right? That's where you got the idea about accelerating your mortgage payments to weekly from monthly, am I right?'

'I have decided,' LeBoubon announced, with a stiffness in his voice that suggested, to Sophie at least, maybe not Thom, that LeBoubon realized he was on thin ice, 'that I am working now only the first four days in the weeks to be coming, and on the fifth day I am doing the studies full-time to be a registered financial planner.'

'Is that a fact?' Thom responded with a restraint that Sophie thought improbable and likely not sustainable. 'A four-day week, weekly payroll, forty dollars a year for laundered Nubtex cloths ... is there anything else you wanted to mention today that could add to make your happiness more complete?'

'Jayne Beauregard has two coats hung on the coat rack inside the front door,' LeBoubon announced.

'Her raincoat and her dry coat. So?' Sophie could not imagine where this new tack might be headed.

'Ho, ho! There are only eight hooks supplied by management for the coats. There are four employees employed full time plus two management printing work here each day, that makes six not including visitations so Jayne Beauregard has to be insisted by you to put both her coats on one hook. Rules are meant to be followed,' LeBoubon intoned, officiously.

'Rules? What rules?' asked Thom. 'What rules are you talking about? I don't remember setting out any corporate policy on the expected use of coat racks!'

'Ho, ho! There we have it!'

Sophie was starting to get a sickening sense of motion inside her small intestine each time LeBoubon tallied 'Ho, ho!' and checked another diamond in his notebook with a flourish. 'What do we have this time?' Sophie asked.

[199]

'Lack of clear written direction in policy from management in the appropriate use of employee coathooks leading to unfair equality in the treatment of workers,' LeBoubon read from his prepared text. 'And the lock to the employee washroom is broken, as such a deliberate humiliation on the part of management to workers with no clothing.'

'Is that it?' Thom rubbed at the psoriasis in his eyebrows with the back of a palm. 'Are you quite finished? Do you think we could just leave the humiliation where it lies and maybe go our separate ways and take the opportunity to consider some of your many suggestions?'

'Not me,' Philippe replied. 'I don't have to consider anything that was said that is true about management. And, on top of the mountain, I will tell you that as soon as you sell to the Misters Aldebaan and Bowles you are fired — *parce que* you don't know about the managing of workers, and I propose to seize the controls!'

'Really?' asked Thom. 'You propose to seize the controls.'

Sophie froze, nervous about what might happen if Thom were to lose his temper.

'And is that it, then, or do you have a last niblet to add to the sorry litany of humiliation and woe?' Thom indulged himself, or so he thought.

'The niblet is that Jayne Beauregard is smoking the cigarettes, sneaking in the employee washroom without a lock and poisoning my lung breath,' LeBoubon added. 'There you have it, your niblet!'

* * *

'Do you make up windows to order?' Thom enquired of Liam McTavish over the counter at Dominion Lumber. 'Storm windows. I doubt that the windows on our shop would be anything close to a standard size, or any kind of a size that has been standard since 1890....'

'I'm not that surprised,' Liam replied. 'How long have you and Sophie lived in that building?'

'In the Overland building? Since 1974. Sophie and I first came to the village in the fall of 1970, but we rented, at first, in the Grundy building next door. We bought the Overland building in 1974,' Thom explained.

'From old Mister Wesley, did you?' prodded Liam.

'That's right,' Thom agreed, 'but I'm surprised you would remember that?'

'As reeve of the Village I generally know who bought what, and maybe from whom, though I might not remember precisely when. In this case I also have a vague recollection that Dominion Lumber may have made up the storms you want replaced, but from what you just said it may have been fifteen years ago at least, and likely longer,' Liam McTavish speculated. 'It's conceivable we did a helluva job, if the storms we made fifteen years ago are still serviceable.'

'You have records on storm windows that go back fifteen years?' Thom was impressed.

'Not the kind of records you'd be thinking of, no,' chuckled Liam. 'But let's go out back to the mill and see if maybe Buck Sawyer or young Chip Aitken don't remember something about making up storms for John Wesley. Have you ever been inside the mill?'

'Just the office on the ground floor,' Thom said, remembering the pin-up of Marilyn Monroe and wondering if it would still be tacked to the wall. Wondering if the pin-up he remembered as Marilyn Monroe was actually a pin-up of Jayne Mansfield in a cashmere sweater. 'Are Buck and young Chip ... related?' asked Thom, briefly considering attempting a witticism about a chip and an old block. He decided against it.

'Buck is young Chip's uncle,' Liam confirmed. 'We're hoping that maybe some day we'll get to the point Chip will be able to keep the mill in operation if Buck Sawyer ever decides to pack it in.'

Marilyn Monroe, in each of her several splendours, was in fact still on the wall behind the pot-bellied stove, but neither Buck Sawyer nor young Chip Aitken were anywhere to be seen. Marilyn was not wearing a cashmere sweater in the photograph. Thom had remembered the pin-up accurately. It was Marilyn Monroe, on the wall. Not Jayne Mansfield.

'We don't operate the machines on the ground floor as often as we once did,' explained McTavish, raising his voice above the low rumbling and gentle belt-slapping sounds of the mill under power. 'There's a sander,' McTavish pointed to a mound of sawdust in a corner, 'built in Galt by MacGregor & Gourlay, maybe about 1870.'

'And it works?' Thom asked, dusting the nameplate, admiring the exquisitely superfluous filigree scrolling on the castings of the machine, which clearly had nothing remotely to do with its intended function.

'It works,' Liam replied, 'when we need it to work. Sometimes in a really cold February we get ourselves into trouble with ice around the turbine. One winter we had to persuade a mother beaver and her three kits to vacate the sluice gate before we could deliver power to the tenoner.'

'Tenoner?' Thom queried. 'That's not a term that I know?'

'I wouldn't know how to operate the thing myself,' Liam shrugged. 'That's Buck Sawyer's thing. One of the things he's supposedly teaching young Chip, we hope! I do know the tenoner is used to make mortise joints, and I'm told there are not too many of these machines left operational in southern Ontario anymore. None in the Credit Valley watershed.'

'I wouldn't doubt it,' Thom agreed, thinking of the inch-and-a-half-wide flange on the flywheel of Penmaen's Smythe National book sewing machine and wondering if that, too, had originally been engineered for belt-drive off hydraulic power.

'The machines upstairs,' Liam continued, raising his voice, pointing to the ceiling, 'the rip saw, the band saw, and the sticker for mouldings, those we use more frequently....'

'How do you manage to disengage the equipment separately from the power train?' Thom interrupted, watching more belts than he could easily count slap against their fittings overhead.

'For instance,' McTavish replied, stepping forward, 'you could slide this one wooden lever to push a belt from the idler pulley to the drive pulley ...' and the McGregor sander with the filigree detail on the nameplate started up slowly and steadily built momentum until it reached a piercing whine at 2,500 rpm.

'Did all of this stuff come from the same McGregor foundry?' asked Thom, reading from the nameplate.

'Some of it, not all of it. A few of the saws were built in Toronto at J.R. Williams. A couple came from Preston, I forget the name of the place.' McTavish scratched at his scalp.

'But none of these foundries still exist?' asked Thom.

'Not that I'd ever really thought much about it, but no, I don't believe they do,' Liam agreed. 'Dominion Lumber, on the other hand, now there's a much longer-term proposition.'

'How do you figure?' Thom was uncertain.

'Argus McNaughton built the floor you are standing on, in 1838. That's not bad, for a rough and tumble piece of joinery. The floor, as you can see, is not exactly spirit level, but after a hundred and fifty years I don't see any part of it that's damp, or rotten. McNaughton did a creditable job as a carpenter, but McNaughton was a venture capitalist at the same time, and a Scot. He raised the money for the mill, and he did provide some minimal level of long-term employment for the Village, but he also extracted his due in water rights out of the local council.'

'Don't tell me, let me guess,' Thom smiled. 'A big number, right? McNaughton would have been looking for a big number?'

'You wouldn't likely guess high enough,' Liam McTavish acknowledged.

'How long?' asked Thom.

'Nine hundred and ninety-nine years,' Liam was almost apologetic.

'Nine hundred ...' Thom started. Then he stopped, 'And this document was signed in what year?'

'1838,' Liam answered. 'The lease for the hydraulic potential of the West Credit River at Glendaele Village is attached to the deed for the planing mill until the lease expires in the year 2837. That's what my father's father bought into when he took an assignment on the property in 1896.'

'And how much did you say that Argus McNaughton paid, originally, for the lease?' asked Thom.

'Not a lot,' admitted McTavish, 'but the fate of the lease on the hydraulic power of the Credit River in the year 2837 is of considerably less interest to me personally than the fate of Dominion Lumber at any time in the next fifty. There's always the big picture, of course, and most entrepreneurs don't think in terms of millennia, but the immediate challenge is whether Derek and I can persuade Dirk and Sterling and Struan to buy into the vision. That's my personal pension plan we're talking about, particularly if Sterling decides to pursue his inclination to stand for alderman in the next municipal election.'

'Are you going to run too, for re-election?' asked Thom.

'My father was reeve of this Village for ten years, and now my son is talking about running for council. On the one hand it might be advisable to stay on as reeve and provide some continuity. Sterling is barely twenty-five, and just recently married. There's a lot he doesn't know.'

'And on the other hand?' asked Thom, to be polite, not that he really cared one way or the other.

'On the other hand the work at council involves a fair commitment of time. I rather doubt that Dirk or his father would necessarily want Sterling and me both elected to council simultaneously. Then there's Struan to consider, who hasn't shown any interest in politics, thank God! but may not be happy tracing special orders on the micro-fiche forever, as a career. There's some family politics involved that will have to be resolved at some point, but we came out to the mill to talk to Buck Sawyer about storm windows. In a way I think you're fortunate that you and Sophie don't have children involved at Penmaen Lithography.'

'I guess,' Thom agreed, less than enthusiastically, thinking about Philippe LeBoubon and the compensation required for the hypothetical future non-use of Nubtex cloths. 'Though I might be persuaded to trade you one malcontent for two strapping sons and future considerations,' Thom added. 'And I might even throw in a George Bell, for a Kirk Gibson.'

Liam McTavish heaved on a counterweight hung from a rafter, and a huge trap door in the ceiling yawned open to a cacophony of woodworking machinery.

★ ★ ★

'I thought you had me convinced that you don't enjoy shopping at Dominion Lumber.' Sophie was confused.

'I said that I don't like the McTavish prices,' Thom corrected Sophie, 'but I do enjoy the convenience of charging expenses to the one account so we don't misplace receipts for petty-cash items or miss out on any input tax credits.'

'Is that all you ever think about, man?' Sophie challenged. 'Input tax credits?'

'If you ain't got nuthin',' Thom started in, but then thought better of making a copyright joke in print. 'I was talking to Liam McTavish about a quote for new storm windows before the winter sets in and we freeze, and I was shopping, for Christ's sake, Sophie, for a 220 volt adapter so your curling-iron will work in Spain. I thought you told me you wanted to go to Spain? So why do you insist on ragging me about tax receipts when I'm just trying to be helpful with curling irons? God knows it's not me that needs the bloody curling iron,' Thom added, running his fingers through his receding hairline.

'I said I wanted to go to Majorca,' Sophie took a deep breath. 'Not Spain. Majorca. To stay at La Residencia.'

'I know that,' Thom took a deeper breath. 'You said that. I heard that. La Residencia, we talked about Majorca. The compromise we accepted is that, since we've only got a week, and seven days isn't enough time to reach Majorca because the connecting flights take the better part of two days at either end, we are flying direct to Malaga. Because it's simple. One flight, eight hours, and we're there. And now courtesy of Dominion Lumber you'll even be able to curl your tresses in Andalusia! Just watch it that your feet aren't wet when you plug this thing in to 220 volts.'

'Is Andalusia a province or a region of Spain? And how do you know that this thing will work?' Sophie asked dubiously, inspecting a fistful of something-or-other quite substantial, with plugs.

'Will it work?' repeated Thom. 'How could you possibly question the cumulative wisdom of four generations of the McTavish clan?'

'Dirk is working at Dominion Lumber now too?' Sophie asked. '*Four* generations, that's what you just said?'

'Not only did Derek McTavish finally get that n'er-do-well son of his connected to the family empire, but now that Sterling's done the right thing by the Witherspoon girl, Sterling's apparently taken to considering public office himself.'

DOMINION LUMBER

'What is it that Dirk does?' Sophie asked innocently, 'at Dominion Lumber? Somehow I can't quite picture Mister Mac the Knife in paint and wallpaper.'

'There's the sixty-four-thousand-dollar question,' Thom replied. 'Though he's probably more comfortable in paint than he would have been on Broadway. Difficult to say just precisely what it is that Dirk contributes to the common good at Dominion Lumber, though he does tell jokes.'

'Jokes? What kind of jokes?'

'Airplane jokes, coincidentally enough,' Thom explained. 'I was standing in a lengthy queue waiting to put your name brand General Electric 220 volt curling-iron adaptor on the Penmaen corporate account when I overheard Dirk telling Sterling a story about a lawyer and a blonde who were seated next to each other on an overnight flight from Vancouver to Pearson. The lawyer leaned towards the blonde and asked if she would like to play a fun game.'

'I do not think I like the sound of this joke,' said Sophie.

'Easy, girl, I'm telling you.' Thom tried to reassure his wife. 'The blond lady wins out in the end.'

Sophie was not to be convinced.

'"The blonde is tired," this is the way Dirk tells the story,' Thom explained. 'So she declines and rolls over to the window to sleep. The lawyer persists and tries to convince the blonde that the game is ever so easy and a lot of fun to boot.'

'Why is the woman blond?' Sophie wanted to know.

'It's a story, OK? I'm trying to tell you this story the way I heard Dirk McTavish tell it. The woman was blond, that's what Dirk said,' Thom stood his ground. 'The lawyer explains "I ask you a question, and if you don't know the answer, you pay me five bucks. And vice versa." Again, the blonde declines and tries to get some sleep. The lawyer says, "Okay, what about if you don't know the answer you pay me five bucks, and if I don't know the answer, I pay you fifty

[207]

bucks?" Fifty bucks. This catches the blonde's attention and, figuring that there will be no end to the harassment unless she plays, agrees to the game.'

'I can't believe you would stand there in a queue listening to this stupid story,' Sophie challenged. 'Why didn't you just do the right thing, and leave?'

'Because I was holding your curling-iron adapter in my hand,' Thom explained, 'and I hadn't paid for the damn thing. The lawyer asks the first question. "What's the distance from the earth to the moon?" The blonde doesn't say a word, reaches in to her purse, pulls out a five-dollar bill and hands it to the lawyer.'

'I don't think I like this story,' Sophie reiterated.

'Don't jump to conclusions!' Thom continued. 'Now it's the blonde's turn. She asks the lawyer, "What goes up a staircase with three legs, and comes down with four?" The lawyer doesn't know. He thinks it must be some kind of a trick question, and he considers it. In the interim the blonde falls asleep. An hour later the captain announces the aircraft is approaching Thunder Bay. The lawyer gives up, and taps the blonde on the shoulder. He hands her a fifty-dollar bill. The blonde accepts the money and turns back to the window. The lawyer, who is now out of pocket forty-five bucks, touches the blonde again on the shoulder and asks, "So what *is* the answer?"'

'I'm waiting,' Sophie informed.

'The blonde reaches into her purse, hands the lawyer an engraved picture of a belted kingfisher, and goes back to sleep.'

'This is supposed to be amusing in some way?' Sophie inquired.

'I promised you the blonde won,' Thom insisted.

Chapter Eight
S. M. Eleña de Compostela

'I don't,' Thom put his palm to his left buttock and looked up sheepishly, at Sophie, rubbing at the sleep in her eyes as they each watched an Iberian Airline baggage carousel pirouette on empty in the very early Malaga morning, 'have my wallet.'

'*I* don't,' Sophie repeated, backed up half a step, then continued in a measured tone, 'believe that this could possibly be happening to me. Your wallet, for Christ's sake, Thom, I really do not understand how you manage to do these things.'

'This isn't,' Thom took umbrage at the clinical precision of his wife's diction, 'actually happening to you. It's my wallet that I lost, not your purse, and thank the good Lord Jesus for that small mercy. Whatever the hell it is that may or may not be happening this morning, in the rain, in Spain, this is happening to me, not you. You're not involved, Sophie, in any way.'

'In any way. Really? Is that a fact? This is my vision, my dream, my damn vacation, and you don't think that I am involved. In any way!' Sophie charged. 'As a wife? Or as a woman? Or a lover? Which? Pick one. Where is it that you come upon these impossibly dopey ideas? And where did you leave your wallet, then, Thom? If you don't mind the intrusion of my asking?'

'On the plane,' Thom speculated. 'I hope.' But he wasn't certain. 'I remember I still had the wallet in my pocket in Toronto when you asked for cash to buy yourself sunglasses in the duty-free. I can't believe you spent a hundred dollars on a pair of designer sunglasses,' Thom railed.

Sophie rolled her eyeballs in their sockets.

'I had no idea that sunglasses could possibly cost a hundred dollars retail, never mind on special.' Thom's limp attempt at a diversion trailed off.

'And just how is it you propose to talk your way back on to the aircraft?' Sophie ignored Thom's clumsy attempt to change the subject, the pitch of her voice rising as she began to grasp the potential for complexities inherent in the misfortune. 'Given that we've already cleared Spanish immigration? And you don't have your wallet? That's what you just said, Thom? No wallet. No money, no credit cards, no health insurance, no driver's licence, none of that stuff, that's what you just said?'

'I really do not think that I am in need of more of your insightful tactical analysis just right at the present,' Thom said stiffly, 'and don't forget that I've still got my passport. It's not like I lost my identity, just my wallet. I probably left it on the plane.'

'And so what do you suggest I am supposed to do while I wait?' Sophie kicked at a baggage cart in frustration. 'While you attempt to recover the missing bits of your identity, in Malaga, of all unlikely places!' Sophie stopped for air. 'I *really*, Thom Penmaen, cannot believe that this is happening to me.' Sophie was tired. She felt chilled. Her body clock was set to 3 a.m., Eastern Daylight Saving Time, back in Toronto. Sophie had intended to check in to the Hotel Melia Torremolinos at the earliest possible minute and sleep through as much of the Spanish afternoon as possible until dinner. But alas, the best-laid plans ... The mice, the men, and all that. Particularly the men. One in particular.

'Get the bags,' Thom advised, and handed Sophie two gaily coloured ticket stubs.

'And then what?' Sophie demanded, clutching at the stubs. 'And then what, Mr Penmaen? Could you answer that? Just one simple little question?'

'I don't know, OK?' Thom replied, testily. 'Completely and honestly, right at the present moment, I do not know.' His voice receded through a pair of frosted glass doors.

'Hola!' cried out a voice.

Thom whirled to face the muzzle of a Kalashnikov assault rifle shaking visibly in the hands of a wild-eyed teenager wearing the poison pea-green trappings of the Guardia Civil.

Trouble, thought Thom, a bead of early morning sweat pushing its way through the premature creases on his forehead. 'Do you speak English?' Thom inquired, doubting very much that would be the case. The barrel of the rifle rocked from side to side three inches in either direction, then up and then down an inch and a half, but not predictably, in English or Spanish, up or down, east or west.

Thom Penmaen had no prior history of cholesterol problems, excess blood pressure or heart murmurs. Cool, Thom cautioned himself, be cool, feeling his pulse quicken and the sweat push through his brow and watching the gunsight on the end of the rifle barrel gesticulate spastically.

'Habla usted español?' the young gunman demanded, from a distance of maybe twenty yards across the deserted immigration concourse, his eyes, if anything, blacker and wilder as he closed the gap. The gunman began to shift his weight uncomfortably from one foot to the other, and back, almost as if the rifle were a bit much for him to manage, shuffling from side to side in a strange kind of choreography that might have been as humorous as it was certainly ungainly if it weren't for the working end of the Kalashnikov and the fact that the steps of the shuffle were apparently aggressive.

Twenty yards narrowed to fifteen.

Thom's gaze swept the floor of the deserted sala d'inmigración, looking for what kind of assistance he couldn't quite imagine, his blood pressure rising, his heart pounding against the confines of a ribcage that seemed, suddenly, not quite large enough for the organ under pressure. Through a plate-glass window facing out onto the tarmac Thom could distinguish, but only barely, through the early morning fog, the shape of an Iberian Airline DC 10 in the process of refuelling.

Fog, thought Thom, in Spain? I didn't know there was bloody fog in Spain. Rain, maybe, on the plain, in Spain. There was a song. About the rain, in Spain, but not bloody fog. Then Thom's attention refocused on the one agitated, armed, and extremely nervous teenager now no more than a metre in front of his nostrils.

'Habla español?' the cadet fairly screamed at Thom from a distance of fifteen centimetres.

Thom felt the hairs on the back of his neck bristle against the starch in his collar. 'Do you speak English?' Thom countered, for want of anything better to say. He tried to appear annoyed. Displeased, but not upset. A measured response, preferably a metric response, Thom decided, rather than imperial.

The cold steel of the Kalashnikov under his chin was amply sufficient to direct Thom's attention to a small anteroom off the main immigration lounge that looked as if it might be labelled the 'interrogation' room, but Thom's Spanish was limited, and he was likely mistaken in his pessimistic attempt at a translation of the signage.

In the anteroom there was a desk, and behind the desk there was an official wearing the number of stripes Thom assumed might designate a sergeant, but whom the cadet with the Kalashnikov addressed deferentially as 'Capitán'.

'Do you,' Thom could take a hint, seeking the higher ground, 'el Capitán, happen to speak any English?'

'Español?' the portly sergeant replied, grimly.

'Por favor,' Thom tried frantically to think of a way to

convey the true nature of his plight in sign language. Thom could, he thought, pull his pants pockets inside out – but such a ploy risked misinterpretation. Many, misinterpretations. Thom did not wish to suggest to the Guardia Civil, even in hieroglyphics, that he was impecunious, or destitute.

Thirty minutes later, the business of the interrogation apparently complete, the sergeant who fancied himself el 'Capitán' led a small platoon of Thom, the Guardia Civil and a translator with severely limited capabilities in the diction of Canadians from Toronto out of the immigration hall in the terminal building and into the uncertainty of the fog, then marched the little party towards a parked 1940s-vintage military jeep on which the words UNITED STATES ARMY were clearly legible under the most recent ineffectual attempt at a paint job.

The sergeant took the wheel in person and directed Thom to the seat beside his corpulence. The two young soldiers positioned themselves gingerly on top of the jump seat in the back. Rifles cradled. Muzzles in the air.

God only knows, Thom ruminated, what this must look like from inside the terminal building, though in the fog there was no immediate danger of the jeep being seen by anyone not within twenty yards of the knob on the sergeant's stick shift.

The fog had thickened in the past half hour to the point where Thom could no longer distinguish the shape of the aircraft until the jeep lurched to a stop, quite literally, at the foot of a boarding ramp. The two junior guardsmen jumped from the rumble seat and took up rehearsed positions at either side of the ramp, rifles held at the ready in what Thom gathered might be standard procedure for the escort of suspected Algerian terrorists out of sovereign Spain.

Thom took a deep breath, stepped from the jeep and approached the honour guard.

Thom thought of the Alcazaba, of Jennifer Dickson and

Barbary pirates, and giggled nervously in spite of himself. Thom did not feel comfortable with heights, or ladders. His arms, stretched horizontally to the tips of his fingernails, barely grazed the banisters on either side of the boarding ramp. A DC-10 is a large aircraft. Thom took the metal steps tentatively, one at a time, careful to land a first step solidly before attempting a second. The muscles in his legs quivered, from fright more than exertion, and his biceps ached from the strain of reaching for the lateral support of the banisters.

At the top there was a landing where Thom paused just long enough to notice the insignia of a monkey, with wings, painted on the fuselage by the door.

'Hola!' the captain of the aircraft called out to Thom from the cockpit.

Thom marvelled, despite the immediacy of his predicament, at the intricate complexity of the flight deck of a McDonnell Douglas DC-10, and marvelled as well at the familiarity of the Birkstone leather wallet the Spanish air Capitán held out triumphantly towards him.

'You are no longer in Canada, Mr Penmaen,' the air Capitán advised in mid-Atlantic English.

'I recognize that, sir,' Thom started to apologize for the inconvenience he had caused already but the Spanish Capitán cut him short with a dismissive gesture. A perfunctory apology was clearly not going to suffice, in this cockpit.

Thom focused on the stickpin the Iberian Air Capitán wore in the middle of his necktie engraved with the same image of the monkey with wings Thom had seen painted on the fuselage of the aircraft by the door. The monkey continued speaking. 'The captain of my cleaning staff wishes me to inform you that this wallet contained eight hundred and eighty-six dollars and some change when it was handed to him by one of his many trusted subordinates, and one credit card.'

'Yes sir. Thank you, sir,' Thom replied, wondering if he

S. M. ELENA DE COMPOSTELA

would be asked to recite the number printed on the credit card as proof of ownership. A number which Thom did not have committed to memory.

'And a scarab,' the pilot continued, 'strangely enough. You are a man of good fortune, Mr Penmaen, and much vision, to carry such a thing as a scarab in your wallet. If it weren't for the fog and the delay this morning, this aircraft, and your wallet with it, would both be halfway to Madrid. Spain is a Third-World country, Mr Penmaen.'

Thom was having some difficulty following the thread of this logic.

'If you had misplaced your wallet, for example, in the Kansas City heartland of the United States of America, do you really think in your own mind the wallet would still contain eight hundred and eighty-six dollars in cash when you recovered possession?' the Spanish pilot asked, mischievously. 'Or even eighty-six cents?'

'I do not,' Thom agreed. 'Sir!'

Thom resisted the temptation to salute the stick-pin monkey.

'Neither do I, Mr Penmaen,' the pilot concluded the interview in the cockpit. 'Neither do I.'

★ ★ ★

'I don't like the looks of that dog,' Sophie warned, pointing some distance up the beach at a huge shaggy Great Dane and some other sort of a long-haired mongrel cross standing by the water's edge.

The fog for the most part had lifted by mid-morning, but check-in at the Hotel Melia Torremolinos was apparently not permissible before 2:00 p.m. local time and there were to be no extraordinary permissions, not even in the face of weary protestations from female turistas coming off the redeye flight from Toronto, in Canada.

'It's OK,' Thom reassured his Sophie. 'You see a big dog, but I do not think you see a problem. The werewolf's mistress seems to have a whistle or something. She's calling to the dog, see?' Thom squinted into the distance. 'And she's got a leash.'

'Well, there you go,' Sophie observed, whistling to herself, nodding in the direction of the woman who bent over to attach the dog's chain to its collar.

It was apparent in profile that the woman with the dog was not wearing a blouse, or anything much of any sort of textile above her waist. 'How does she compare?'

'Compare?' Thom took pains to be grammatically precise and gender neutral in his response.

'To your sweetie Gayle Wicket.' Sophie feigned surprise. 'I thought you told me Wicket gave you an eyeful in the summer? Or was it two? One for each?' Sophie opened her pupils wide and raised her palms in mock horror.

'Please do not utter the name of that lunatic in public,' Thom admonished. 'It's bad luck. We're having enough trouble on this trip as it is. The señora with the wolf is older than Wicket. The señora's boobs, at one time, were bigger. Now they hang lower, though I wouldn't have thought it possible. The boobs. But they do.' Thom was as twitchy with this line of questioning as he had been with the Guardia Civil.

'Are you excited?' asked Sophie.

'Am I ... what? Could you explain just precisely what you mean by a comment like that?' Thom equivocated.

'Sure,' Sophie replied. 'Do you have an erection? You've already had quite a night of it on the plane trying to pretend you weren't ogling the Spanish stewardesses in their elbow-length leather gloves, and the heels. If heels are so damn wonderful, why don't men wear them?'

'I,' Thom exhaled. 'That is. I mean, that is, I dunno. Maybe some do? I really don't think that ...'

'You do, don't you?' Sophie glared at her husband. 'Have a

hard-on, looking at that old hag on the beach,' Sophie insisted. 'Big boobs do it to you every time, even ancient boobs. You can't even control your own body functions. Are you sure you don't need a pee? A little whiz?'

'I don't. No. I wouldn't say, or at least, I wouldn't want to admit ... ha, ha, you know.' Thom fiddled for words.

The shoreline of the Mediterranean at Torremolinos was a sorry pastiche of the wine-dark sea Sophie remembered fondly from her university study of Homer. The air smelled sharply of untreated sewage and the remains of rotting fish. The fog had lifted, but not cleared.

The cries of the gulls were as raucous as the gulls at Hanlan's Point in Toronto, but no more exotic than that. The sand was dun-grey and littered with garbage and the tumbledown shacks of beach vendors, nothing remotely similar to the miles of manicured white silicate Sophie remembered from winter vacations to Ixtapa, and Puerto Escondido.

'Hold still.' Thom strode into Sophie's reverie and flicked with his finger at a wasp that had settled on her shoulder.

'What was it?' asked Sophie. 'Don't pick at me. I don't like to be picked at.'

'A wasp,' replied Thom. 'Nasty-looking creature. You didn't get stung, did you? And look, now you've got a mark or something on your forehead,' Thom added, offering Sophie a tissue from his pocket.

'You would have heard from me long before now if I had been stung, believe me, Mr Penmaen,' Sophie assured her husband. 'Did I hear you talking again on the phone to Geoffrey Bowles the other day?' Sophie asked, as they resumed walking the beach, eyes down and careful to avoid the dozens of skittish sand crabs underfoot. 'I hope?'

'Bowles phoned. Thank God. At last. It's been a while and I didn't want us to be phoning him or Bowles might get to thinking we're too eager. Desperate even, to sell. Then the price spirals down the toilet.'

'And? Did Bowles mention anything about the financial statements you sent him? Or the inventory analysis? It's been weeks now,' Sophie complained. 'Not just "a while". Weeks.'

'I wish,' Thom agreed. 'I busted my butt pulling the bulk of that stuff together for Bowles to review.'

'It's probably the stupid flow-chart you sketched,' Sophie speculated. 'You really could not leave it alone, could you?'

'What? You mean "The Rain in Spain"? It was a joke. Funny. A lighthearted but insightful overview of our corporate cashflow,' Thom replied. 'I don't think it was stupid. I wouldn't agree that it was stupid.'

'It was flip,' insisted Sophie. 'Bowles probably thinks you're disrespectful, that you're not taking his offer seriously.'

'Not so,' Thom disagreed. 'Bowles was serious. We talked about the buildings. That's one of your big bugaboos, right? Pegaesean has no use for either of the properties. We anticipated that, but I do think Bowles himself is sympathetic to your concern that we don't want to risk living above a licensed speakeasy at some point in the not distant future....'

'I doubt that,' Sophie interjected. 'I don't think Geoffrey Bowles is sympathetic to my concerns and I don't think he understood a word I said that night in the summer at the Horseshoe Inn. I think Bowles was talking to you, rather than listening to me. It's you that Aldebaan wants, you're the entrepreneur, not me.'

'Whatever,' Thom agreed to be agreeable, ignoring Sophie's complaint. 'Best thing from Bowles' point of view would be if maybe we just sell the buildings privately and then we all know their true market value but the sticky wicket, of course, is what happens if we commit to Pegaesean and then try to unload the buildings and they don't sell?'

'Pray tell.'

S. M. ELENA DE COMPOSTELA

'I gather from talking on the phone to Bowles that he's leaning towards providing you with some sort of a guaranteed minimum in case we don't attract a reasonable offer, but what that guarantee might look like, we don't know,' Thom replied.

'So how are you, and Geoffrey Bowles, going to puzzle it out then?' Sophie was unsure, between the two men, whom she trusted less with her precarious financial future.

'Bowles was talking about a couple of ways of looking at commercial property,' Thom explained. 'The simplest one, from my point of view, the one that I understand best, is the one Bowles calls direct comparison, but the problem there is that there haven't been any similar buildings on the Main Street of Glendaele Village that have sold recently, so what are you going to compare? And to what? Witherspoon's Dairy is the same vintage, but I don't think the price old Fred Witherspoon paid in 1947 is going to help us much.'

'What about the Holmewood?' Sophie brightened at her own idea. 'I thought your buddy Dirk McTavish got himself out of the liquor business not that many months ago.'

'My buddy?' Thom didn't quite catch the snide allusion.

'You seemed pretty chummy when you were printing those stag tickets for his cousin's wedding,' Sophie replied. 'Tacky as they were.'

'Oh yeah, right, the stag tickets that I never did get paid for,' Thom reminded Sophie, 'by my good bubba. I mentioned the Holmewood sale to Bowles. The problem with the Holmewood is that the hotel is more than double the 1,500 square feet of either of your buildings and it's got parking for fifty cars. There's a lot more land. It is zoned commercial, though, and it's on the Main Street, so it might be helpful if we knew what Dirk got for the Holmewood and divided the number by the number of square feet in the hotel and multiplied the result by the number of square feet we've got to sell, but then you'd have to figure that our buildings are probably in better shape, at least superficially, and smaller buildings usually sell for more per square foot than bigger buildings, that's what Bowles said. But this is getting complicated. Too complicated.'

'And it doesn't sound like a particularly compelling, or conclusive argument.' Sophie was frequently amazed that Thom could talk knowledgeably to the likes of Geoffrey Bowles on subjects he knew precisely nothing about, and yet couldn't be trusted to keep a wallet in the pocket of his trousers. Sophie bent to collect a conch shell from the beach and held it to her ear.

'What's the number?' Thom asked.

'What number?' Sophie looked puzzled.

'Inside the shell,' Thom joked.

'I'm listening to the sea,' Sophie protested. 'What makes you think I'm all that interested in Geoffrey Bowles's theories of property evaluation?'

'Because you asked?' Thom replied. 'But I'm not so sure that your method might not be equally useful. Pick a number.'

'Yeah, right,' Sophie acknowledged, rather less than enthusiastically. 'You said Bowles had a couple of ways of evaluating property? I've heard the one. And?'

'He talked a bit about replacement cost,' Thom continued. 'As far as I can fathom it the idea is you start by assuming the properties are vacant lots and you put a value per square foot on the land....'

'How?' interrupted Sophie.

'Iroquois land is worth more than Cree land,' Thom answered, 'or Chippewa, because it's closer to the City and the Six Nations can defend it better.'

'Seriously,' Sophie replied.

'There have been some lots sold, recently, in the Village. More lots, for sure, than commercial buildings on the Main Street. The trick to figuring replacement cost is you have to be careful to compare apples and apples and even at that you've got to compare McIntosh with McIntosh and not McIntosh with Granny Smith or Red Delicious and the strip of land along the millpond behind Mrs Grundy's building is worth a lot less per square foot than the two lots that are high enough above the millpond to build on. This gets complicated too,' Thom admitted.

And tedious, Sophie thought. She was tired. Her eyes burned. The aftereffects of the Gravol were making her dizzy and they still had to survive past lunch before the hotel would consider check-in.

'And then you put a value on the construction cost of replacing,' Thom droned on, 'each individual component of each of the properties ... like maybe you get a local contractor like Tom Longfellow or even young Chip Aitken at Dominion Lumber to give you a price on putting a floor and a ceiling in a basement and that's maybe no more than twenty-five bucks a square foot, but to finish the drywall in a storefront would cost easily double that, which is maybe what a modest but functional apartment might be worth...'

'Like in the rental building? That's what you would consider "modest but functional",' Sophie found it easier to grasp the specific rather than the theoretical.

'That's what I think Geoffrey Bowles means by "modest but functional",' Thom corrected his wife. 'Then there's our place, with the wainscoting and the skylight and the bay window looking out over the water at the back. The embellishments add to the replacement cost, maybe eighty dollars a square foot, all in.'

'Which leads us of course to the pregnant question of who it is who puts the numbers on each of these separate categories,' Sophie noted. 'You think that Geoffrey Bowles, or Aldebaan, would necessarily swallow a sheaf of hypothetical quotes we traded Tom Longfellow in exchange for a case of two-four?'

'I don't, quite frankly,' Thom agreed. 'I don't think either one of them would buy it, and I wouldn't fault them for that. I think the third approach is the one that's going to end up being the most useful to us in dealing with Aldebaan.'

A lunch of prawns on the terrace at the pizzeria, tapas bar and grill 'Pizzaro' was disrupted by a commotion at an adjacent table.

'What's this?' asked a young American sailor, in uniform, pointing a finger aggressively at his wineglass.

'Rioja,' the proprietor, presumably Pizzaro himself, answered tentatively, uncertain as to the nature of the complaint.

'I didn't ask you where the red stuff comes from, you monkey,' the sailor complained, not completely coherently. 'This wine is warm!'

'You want the wine warmed?' Pizzaro was apparently accustomed to teenage American naval personnel making idiotic requests in loud voices. Pizzaro may also have been play-acting at stupidity.

'No, no, no, you big ape, not warmed, the wine is already too hot,' the sailor replied. 'I want ice, ice. ICE, you comprende, señor? To make the wine cold.'

The sailor's buddy emitted from the pit of his stomach a noise that Thom identified in his mind as a guffaw, and remembered guffaws from incessant summer reruns of the Andy Griffith show on television in the 1960s. Mayberry, that was the name of the place. Thom wondered if maybe the sailor with the gastrointestinal problem hailed from Mayberry, or thereabouts.

'You want to turn this wine, Rioja, perfectly palatable red wine, you wish me to turn this wine, into water?' Pizzaro could hardly believe his ears.

'Terrifying, isn't it?' Thom remarked to Sophie, nodding

in the direction of the United States Navy, 'to think that a kid from Nebraska could have his finger on the trigger of a nuclear missile.'

'How do you figure the kid's from Nebraska?' Sophie had had enough of her husband's cocky non sequiturs for one day. Particularly *this* day, of all days.

'See the label on his jersey?' asked Thom. 'USS OMAHA?'

'That's the name of a boat, you dolt, not the name of his hometown,' Sophie replied. 'And the USS OMAHA is just as likely to be a tugboat as it is a warship. Maybe more likely.'

'A tugboat? In the United States Navy? I don't think so, but look at the acne on his face. Do you really think he's all of eighteen? His zits, for Christ's sake, would cause a diplomatic incident if more than two of them were to erupt simultaneously. Be careful,' Thom cautioned, 'it could happen any second.'

'Thom!' warned Sophie. 'Maybe you could be just a little teeny bit more respectful to foreign cultures? The United States Navy being one of them. Like maybe this kid from Nebraska is distantly related to Warren Buffet?'

'Berkshire Hathaway? That Warren Buffet?' Thom considered the prospect. 'You think this cowboy with the complexion problem owns a hundred thousand shares of Coca-Cola? Doubt it. He may, on the other hand, be one of their better customers, I'll grant you that.'

'Thom!' Sophie made a theatrical presentation out of adjusting her brand-new hundred-buck discount-special Ban-Sol sunglasses.

'OK, OK, OK, I get the picture,' Thom acquiesced, reluctantly. 'I'll drop it.'

Pizzaro himself delivered a tumbler of ice to the American navy and relative peace was restored to the terrace overlooking the harbour at Torremolinos.

'The third option,' Sophie resumed the discussion of property valuation. 'What was the third option Bowles mentioned?'

'We can't work it so great for the building we live in, but you do know the kind of rent you're getting for the flat next door?' Thom began.

'Six hundred and seventy-five dollars,' Sophie replied, 'to the dime.'

'And you know how much you collect each month for the storefront?'

'Eight hundred and fifty dollars. But if we could ever evict the music store and rent to some kind of a business that actually generated more than ten dollars an hour for banjo lessons,' Sophie speculated, 'I bet we could goose the take to $950, maybe a thousand.'

'And there's the little bit of rent you get for the off-street parking, and the $1,300 a year the Witherspoons pay to park their trailer on the corner of the lot behind the spruce trees ... these are all real, arm's-length, true-market-value kinds of numbers....'

'What about the basement in the rental building?' Sophie interrupted.

'OK,' Thom agreed, 'that one isn't quite so solid a number. At the moment Penmaen Lithography pays a nominal, what?'

'Three hundred dollars a month,' Sophie advised.

'OK, $300 a month for the basement and that's not a real number but it can't be that far off, and all the other numbers *are* real, *and* we know what we paid out in hydro....'

'... much too much!' Sophie exclaimed.

'Too much, I agree with you. For maybe the first time this morning in Spain I agree totally with what you are telling me. The rental building would be worth a helluva lot more than it is if we could get rid of the baseboard heaters and replace them with some kind of a gas appliance, but at the moment the building doesn't have gas. We know what we paid out in hydro, municipal taxes, insurance and maintenance, we know these numbers, right?' Thom prodded.

'Not off the top of my head, I don't,' Sophie replied, 'No, of course not.'

'I don't, either, off the top of my head,' Thom admitted. 'But I checked a few of them, after I talked to Bowles.'

'And?' Sophie asked, impatiently.

'It's not as bad as I might have thought....'

'Nothing ever is,' Sophie interjected, 'as bad as you think it's going to be. Your horoscope isn't usually as bad as you think it's going to be, and even this holiday isn't going to be as bad as you think it's going to be, though some of us might want to keep a closer grip on our personal effects.'

'Sophie!'

'OK, OK, OK,' Sophie replied, mimicking her husband. 'You walked into it. I couldn't resist, OK? Lighten up.'

'I don't remember the exact numbers but you've got something like $25,000 a year in income and only $7,000 in expenses, so you're pocketing $18,000 a year without the mortgage, that part's pretty clear. This next bit I don't understand myself quite so great but Bowles claims a reasonable sort of a value for the rental property would be the net income exclusive of mortgage payments divided by .08....'

'Why .08?' Sophie asked. 'Why not .09, or .07? Why not .10, just to keep it in round numbers?'

'I know.' Thom acknowledged the legitimacy of Sophie's uncertainty. 'And I don't have a clue why it's .08. I think it's a ratio the banks use to measure the value of an investment but I dunno,' Thom admitted. 'The part I do understand is that you're supposed to divide your net income from a rental property by .08 and if you do that you discover that your rental property on the Main Street, for example, is worth $225,000.'

'What did we pay for it?' Sophie asked.

'A hundred and fifty-four thousand and change. It might have been $154,900. I don't remember either, and I haven't had time to look,' Thom answered.

'So this means that, let's just say we sell the rental property to Aldebaan for $225,000, then we make a profit of $70,000?' Sophie asked.

'Not really, and remember that's before taxes unless Grant Robinson figures a tricky way to make them disappear, but we would pocket something,' Thom agreed.

'And our home? The building that we live in?' Sophie asked.

'We know the rental building measures 1,900 square feet, and we know our own building is 1,500. If we figure the rental building is worth $225,000, then our own building is worth $178,000 just by running the math as a straight percentage.'

'Which we bought for $39,000,' Sophie did remember that number.

'True thing, but that was 1974,' Thom reminded his wife. 'Which is about as useful a number as knowing what old Fred Witherspoon paid for the Dairy in 1947. If we had bought the Grundy building in 1970 when we first moved to Glendaele, we would have got it for $18,000 and we'd be wealthy by now!'

'But the building didn't have indoor plumbing, in 1970,' Sophie recalled.

'That may have been one of the more persuasive reasons we didn't buy it in 1970,' Thom agreed.

'Did you know,' Thom asked Sophie, reading from a travel brochure in the lobby of the Hotel Melia Torremolinos, 'that there's a piece of Spain in North Africa?'

'The Canaries?' Sophie replied.

'No, no, not the Canaries. Well, yes, I mean of course the Canaries, but that's not what I meant,' Thom continued. 'There's a little place called Ceuta. I'd never heard of it before.

Directly south of Gibraltar. That appears to be Spanish, on this map, not part of Morocco.'

'So?'

'So why don't we go there? You said you were looking for something to do for a day trip,' Thom explained. 'There's a tour bus from Torremolinos that stops in Gibraltar for lunch. That might be OK, there's no way we'd need a visa for the British Commonwealth. Do the see-sights, feed the Barbary apes, and then later the tour includes a crossing on the hydrofoil from Terifa to Ceuta. We could say we'd been to Africa, if only for an afternoon. Does that not sound romantic or what?'

'I thought we had agreed.' Sophie sighed. 'We did agree, I'm sure we agreed, that you wanted to tour the Alhambra palace in Granada. Remember Jennifer Dickson's exhibition? We talked about this, we agreed.'

'I remember, I remember. "The Moor's Last Sigh." See? I even remember the name of the show,' Thom advised. 'It's just that I happened to notice this tour described in a brochure I picked up in the lobby while you were fencing with the desk clerk, and the idea occurred that we've already been to Europe, and it's not likely that we'll get within half a day of Africa again anytime soon. Seize the moment, that's what I was thinking. It's not like I'm suggesting a camel train to Timbuktu, just an afternoon at a bistro in Ceuta. You're the one who's always accusing me of being too caught up in my own little world ... this is a continent, for the price of a ferry ticket, that I'm suggesting we add to your wealth of life experiences. Where's your sense of adventure, woman?'

'You're thinking of Casablanca,' Sophie speculated. 'Morocco. Bogie and Bacall, but you are dreaming in Technicolor if you think you're going to get me on a boat before the Gravol has worn off completely. We are going,' Sophie insisted, 'on a tour bus, not a boat, and we are not going to North Africa. We are going to Granada, Thursday, for a day trip. To see the see-sights.' Sophie concluded the discussion with uncharacteristic finality.

* * *

The bus tour to Granada was already well into the mountains when the motor coach stopped at a wayside station for a sticky bun, mid-morning, and orientation. 'Free information', as it was billed.

'Did you notice the roadsign we passed a few miles back?' Thom asked Sophie, backing away from the precipitous edge of an unexpectedly impressive scenic *mirador*, an overlook.

'El Suspiro del Moro?' Sophie replied.

'It's almost as if some of this landscape were familiar. Like we've seen it before.'

'It doesn't look anything like Kansas,' Sophie observed, looking several hundred feet down into a parched river valley forested sparsely with scrub brush and abandoned olive trees.

'Kansas?' Thom wrinkled his forehead.

'Kansas,' Sophie confirmed, and pursed her lips.

'That's a weird thing to say,' noted Thom, thinking about the insignia of the monkey on the Spanish airline pilot's stickpin. 'The pilot in Malaga said something about Kansas when he handed over my wallet, but I think he was using Kansas City as a contemporary metaphor for the nineteenth-century lawlessness of Tombstone, Arizona.'

'What?' Sophie had not the foggiest of ideas what her husband might be talking about.

'Nothing. A joke, OK?' Thom replied. 'Actually, in retrospect, I think the Spanish airline captain was trying to give me a hard time.'

'Today of all days we are having the rare privileges,' the tour guide hostess began her dissemination of free information, 'of visiting at one of the most remarkable wonders in all of the world, at the site of the Alhambra Palace and the

S. M. ELENA DE COMPOSTELA

Gardens of the Generalife planted by the architect whose name itself is being lost in the sands of time.' Santa Maria Eleña de Compostela took an obvious pride in her employment and in her heritage, and dressed for the part in an emerald-green shift cut in the traditional Andalusian style, though Sophie thought her use of castanets as a means of marshalling attention was a bit excessively folkloric to be quaint. 'When the tour bus together with our skilled Capitán have been reaching Granada City itself in the Alcaiceria district we are first paying our respects at the tomb of Ferdinand of Aragón and Isabella of Castile, conquerors of Granada and of the Moors in Spain and patrons of that very same Christopher Columbus who invented America....'

'That is not,' Thom said, chuckling in spite of himself as he marvelled at the novelty of an unvarnished Spanish view of the second millennium, 'a text she found at the Dallas School Book Depository, but I'll bet Rebeca Labellarte would allow herself to be persuaded.'

'In the City of Granada itself,' Maria Eleña continued, 'the home of the poet, Federico García Lorca, there are many small alleys, streets and narrow passageways for a tourist in which who is becoming lost. And in the Sacromonte district as well there are even the caves with the gypsies whose services the Tour Group Torremolinos does not commend to the use of tourists, but if this misfortune visits do not despair, but ask of any taxi driver on the street who will stop to deliver you to the Bar La Paloma where in all last resorts you will be saved at our arrival for tapas at two after the noon.'

'There you have it,' Thom enthused, smacking his right fist into the palm of his left hand. 'Not only do we get to see one of the most remarkable wonders in all of the world this very morning, but Redemption itself is at hand, at the Paloma. And to think I tried to talk you into Africa!'

'I think I'm going to melt,' Sophie announced, adjusting her sunglasses to the glare off the flagstones outside the Puerta de la Justicia.

'The Palace of the Alhambra is the single most peopled site for the pleasure of tourists in all of Western Europe,' Santa Maria Eleña de Compostela intoned reverentially, positioning herself directly beneath the alabaster keystone described by Washington Irving in his *Tales of the Alhambra* published in New England in the early part of the nineteenth century. 'More visited by peoples than the Vatican in Rome itself, and so it is we share with you the misfortune this very morning that we are hopelessly waiting at this entrance gate until the crowds themselves have thinned inside the Plaza de los Aljibes close by the Torre Quebrada, which as you are about to know yourself was damaged in the earthquake of 1522.'

'Do you know,' asked a voice from the back of the tour group, 'what the temperature is in this courtyard, Miss, ah, Miss Eleña?'

'Granada under the Romans –' Santa Maria Eleña was not easily to be swayed from her text '– had not been achieving the high status accorded, how do you say that in English, accorded? Yes, accorded by its neighbours in the mountains, Seville and Córdoba. But you must know what is true and happened at this place in 1246 when Jaén fell to the Christian hordes and the Arab Ibn el-Ahmar was being forced to move his capital to Granada City itself where he became a start for the dynasty of Nasrite families who built the palace of beauty beyond description beyond this very gate.' Santa Maria Eleña de Compostela made a sweeping motion with her right arm.

'Excuse me, Miss, ah, Miss Eleña?'

'Muslim refugees flocked to Granada,' Santa Maria continued, to all appearances oblivious both to the heat and the increasing discomfort of the more vulnerable of her clients, 'in the thirteenth century where the population was swelling to two hundred thousand – over four times and then more the size of London City itself in England at the time of the Black Death plague. The Alhambra Palace of the Nasrite kings is for many peoples the sophistication of culture which was inventing itself at the very time when the English in Burgundy were burning Joan of Arc at the stake. Fourteen thirty, to be precise.'

'Excuse me, Miss, ah, Miss Eleña?' the disembodied voice at the back of the group was losing volume, and timbre.

'At the moment, yes ...' Maria Eleña turned to confront her supplicant. 'We are indeed very fortunate that the time is not yet noon twelve and the sirocco wind from the sands of Morocco is not hard blowing. I am thinking the temperature here is nothing more than thirty-five degrees,' Maria replied.

'In Fahrenheit?' the tourist in distress was obviously not German.

'I am not knowing that same answer, señor, in the Fahrenheit degrees. Warm, but not hot. For many peoples,' Eleña resumed, 'the Alhambra Palace of the Nasrite kings is serving them also as some kind of a footbridge for psychic peoples walking in truth between the minds of the Orient and the Western peoples.'

'What would you call hot, if this isn't hot?' A second disembodied voice, a woman, took up the refrain.

'At forty-five degrees if we are standing in this place by the Puerta de la Justicia, we will be exceedingly hot,' Santa Maria acknowledged, frustrated by her apparent failure to engage the group in a studied consideration of history rather than the weather.

'Hot?' Sophie wiped at her forehead, unfamiliar with the Celsius scale in that register. 'If this is a mere thirty-five degrees, at forty-five degrees I would be a puddle on the flagstones.'

'Inside the gates of the Alhambra as well,' Maria Eleña

reiterated, as the tour group broiled in the sun reflected off the stone, 'there are many passageways in which for a tourist becoming first disoriented, and then losing their touch with the world, but do not despair!'

'Do you lose many tourists, Miss Eleña?' the male disembodied voice spoke a third time.

'The Tour Group Torremolinos of course is accepting no responsibility in any way for the unfortunate loss of tourists, but there have been others known to be overtaken by the wonders of the palace they are about to see with their own eyes that they are finding themselves, in the end, lost,' Maria Eleña acknowledged, 'and for this reason as well we are advising that Redemption can be found at the Bar La Paloma, in two hours' time after the noon, for tapas.'

'What does "Paloma" mean?' Sophie whispered to Thom. 'Do you know?' In the valley of the River Darro, in the middle distance, a donkey brayed.

'Pigeon?' Thom was guessing, he didn't really know. 'Did you bring the dictionary?'

'You're sure it doesn't mean "dove"?' Sophie persisted. 'I remember a song that Joan Baez recorded. I'm sure it had something to do with a dove.'

'Pigeon, dove, six of one, half dozen of the other. Some days you're the pigeon, other days you're the statue,' Thom replied sardonically as the gates to the Puerta de la Justicia swung aside and Santa Maria Eleña de Compostela reminded the group a third time of the name of the restaurant where Redemption was to be had with tapas at two o'clock.

'There's a woman after your own heart,' Sophie observed to Thom, 'if in fact you have one.'

'Really,' Thom inquired. 'You really think she could give me a heart?'

'Jerk. Are you paying attention to anything other than her figure? She smiles at you, she's looking at you. She wants you to understand the speech she's supposed to deliver. You look, to her, like someone who might actually have the brains to understand what she's talking about and you look at her like you're deaf and dumb!'

'No, actually,' Thom admitted. 'I'm not. That's not what I meant. I mean I'm paying attention to her castanets and I'm hot as hell and I'm starting to think I should have gone heavier on the underarm deodorant this morning. Double dose, either armpit. Why does Santa Maria Eleña de Compostela look, to you, like a woman after my heart?' asked Thom. 'Prithee, enlighten me!'

'Tourists get lost, but the Tour Group Torremolinos is accepting no responsibility,' Sophie explained. 'Sounds like your Druckfehlerteufel has been blindfolding *turistas* in the Garden of the Generalife.'

'It is indeed fortunate,' Eleña de Compostela commented, raising her voice above the noise of the rabble passing under the keystone set above the Puerta de la Justicia, 'that we will have no opportunities in this short a tour to visit at the Palace of Charles the Fifth, a silly man who funds gave to both Hernán Cortez and Francisco Pizarro and conquered America, but squandered the gold and lost an empire.' At that point her voice was lost in the hubbub and the press through the archway to escape the heat and the sun.

It was in the Court of the Lions, just at the moment Eleña de Compostela set about explaining that the word harem in fact has nothing to do with sexual promiscuity, that Thom suddenly, apropos of nothing, came up with a number.

'If we're going to sell to Aldebaan,' Thom began.

'We were talking about Aldebaan?' Sophie cut him short. 'I don't recall talking about Aldebaan, or Pegaesean, or Geoffrey Bowles either today, for a refreshing change of subject matter. I do seem to remember, on the other hand, that I am supposed

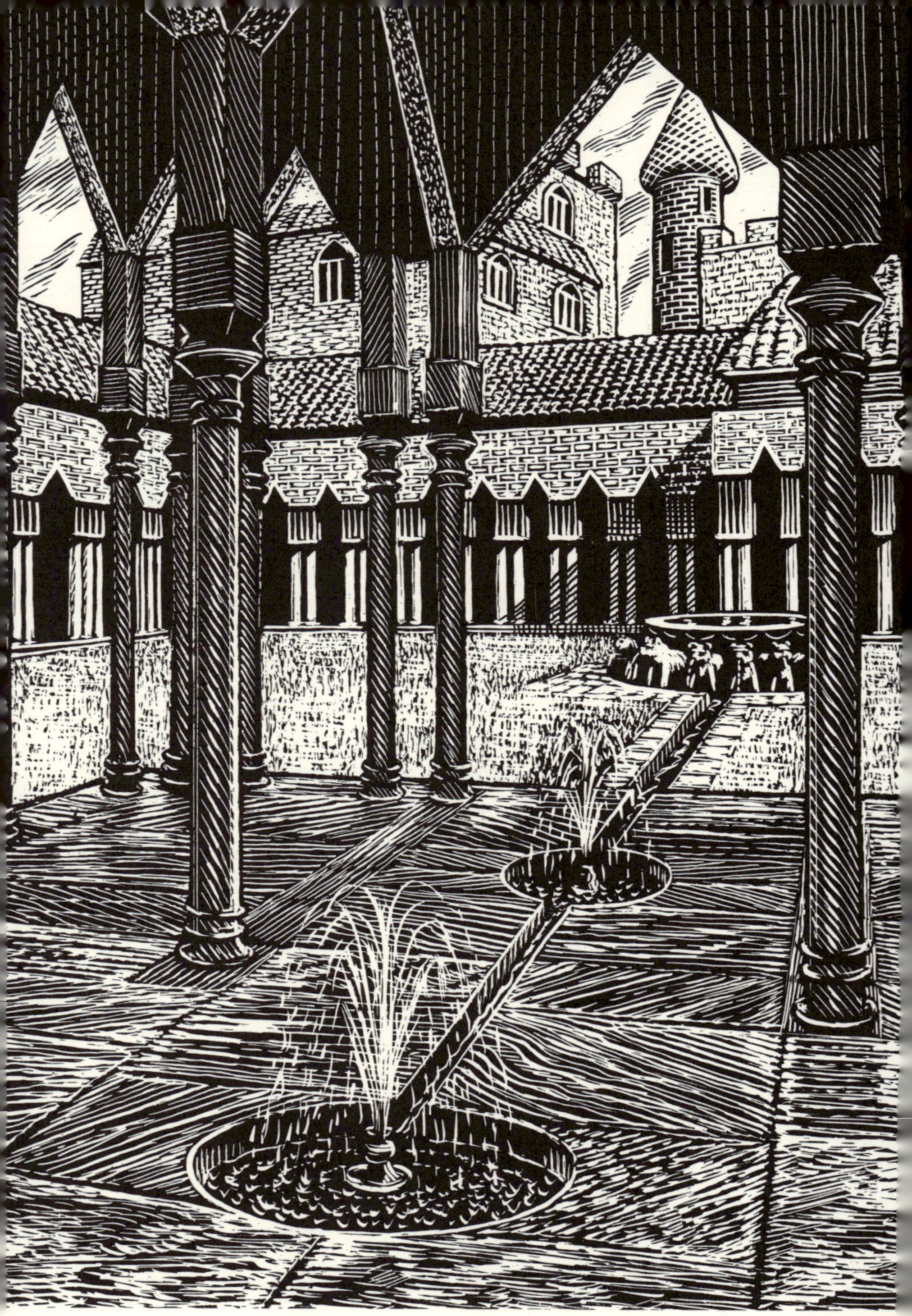

S. M. ELENA DE COMPOSTELA

to be trying to enjoy an abbreviated vacation with my husband, some of us more successfully than the other of us.'

'Yeah, right. We weren't talking about Aldebaan. I was *thinking* about Aldebaan,' Thom explained, quietly, talking under Eleña de Compostela's history of the treachery of the last of the Nasrite Kings associated with the Hall of the Abencerrajes, 'and what I was thinking is that just so long as we're under no particular obligation to sell....'

'Who ever said we ever were,' Sophie adjusted her sunglasses, then flicked at her hair, 'under any obligation to sell?'

'No one,' Thom agreed. 'That's just the point. My point. We aren't under any particular obligation to sell, so why do we have to fret and fuss about what is reasonable and what is not reasonable for an asking price. We don't, right? Have to fret? Duane Eddy has to fret, Les Paul has to fret. We don't have to fret. We don't give a damn. Right? So it just occurred to me. I want a million dollars.' Thom peered through the dozens of columns in the Court of the Lions towards the central fountain.

'You're crazy,' Sophie replied. 'You are absolutely crazy, Thom Penmaen. You're out of your mind. A *million* dollars? On the basis of what? The two buildings, the business and your beloved printing machines all put together amount to, what? Five hundred thousand, *may*be. That's what you told me. And those are your numbers. Not the bank's, not Bowles's, and not Aldebaan's. So how do you figure you're going to ask for double that and not end up looking anything other than utterly foolish? Honestly, Thom, you drink too much beer, you can't be trusted to keep a wallet in your pants, and you embarrass me when you spout idiotic ideas like that, some times more than other times. Paladin, as you will doubtless recall, only got a thousand, and that was on television.'

'The coffee at the truck stop in the mountains was stiff,' Thom agreed, 'but not spiked. It wasn't me who invented

Aldebaan, or Pegaesean, and I don't recall wiring San Francisco for a management consultant, because the management of Penmaen Lithography can't afford bloody management consultants. If I wanted a consultant, I'd hire somebody who knew something useful, like how to run a Heidelberg so I could get rid of that pompadour Philippe LeBoubon, but I can't afford that particular luxury either. A thousand bucks was a lot of money, in 1870. Now it isn't. I can't afford the services of Paladin, and I can't get rid of LeBoubon but I want a million bucks for Penmaen because I want a million bucks. That's the number, that simple.'

'You're crazy,' Sophie repeated. 'You are out of your mind. A million bucks? You're dreaming, man, in Technicolor, and you've been watching too much Walt Disney. You'll never get it.'

'OK fine, no problem. No *problemo*,' Thom pontificated, slowing his delivery. 'Then we don't sell. We graciously decide to decline. That's it. Over. Done. Checkmate. No deal.'

'For Christ's sake, Thom Penmaen, what's gotten in to you? And the word in Spanish is problema, not problemo.'

'You remember the sitcom, *The Millionaire?*' Thom asked.

'We talked about that in the summer. *The Millionaire*? I remember. Michael Anthony,' Sophie replied.

'Yeah, right,' Thom smiled. 'We talked about it. Michael Anthony and John Beresford Tipton. I watched that programme on a twelve-inch black-and-white fuzzy kind of a TV screen in the rec room of the basement in Montreal in the late fifties. With rabbit ears for an antenna. A million dollars was a lot of money, on television, in the late fifties. That's what I want from Aldebaan. And that's why I want it. It's a trade-off, don't you see? That's the deal. I'll part with my dream, my company, even the Heidelberg, but what I bloody get in return is respect from my father, dammit, that's the bottom line. And respect, to my father's generation, is a number that has six zeros in it, and two commas.'

'What can we afford,' asked Sophie, 'to give the employees at Christmas?'

'Christmas!' exclaimed Thom. 'It's 35 degrees Celsius out there in the shade. Whatever got you thinking about Christmas?'

'I don't like it when you get greedy,' Sophie replied. 'You should think more about others.'

'Greedy? Who's greedy?' Thom protested.

'You just got finished telling me you want a million dollars from Aldebaan,' Sophie recalled.

'That's not greed, that's my just deserts,' Thom insisted. 'And I do wish you wouldn't call Christmas bonuses, Christmas bonuses. Profit sharing is not a bonus.'

'What's the difference?' asked Sophie.

'Plenty!' replied Thom. 'Christmas happens regularly right after winter solstice, year in and year out. Profits, on the other hand, are not quite so predictable.'

'Your profits seem predictable enough,' Sophie charged, 'to me.'

'What's that supposed to mean?' Thom asked.

'You diddle the books.'

'I do not diddle the books. How could I possibly diddle the books with Grant Robinson doing the accounting?'

'Last spring you told me to devalue all the Heidelberg parts in inventory. To zero.'

'Yeah, because otherwise we were going to show a bit too much profit,' admitted Thom.

'So?'

'So putting a bit aside for a rainy day is not diddling the books,' Thom insisted. 'Try returning the Heidelberg parts to Heidelberg and see what you get for them. The Heidelberg parts were over-valued in inventory.'

'Call it profit-sharing, then, if you must. Call it anything you want to call it, just so long as I have a signed cheque to hand out to each employee on December 22nd.'

'Twenty-second? I thought we agreed we were working until the 23rd?' asked Thom. 'What if we don't make any profit?'

'Christmas Eve is Saturday. No one wants to work on the 23rd,' Sophie replied.

'You're already giving the employees the week off between Christmas and New Year's, and you're already paying them for the extra week's holiday on top of the vacation and now you want to extend it to the 22nd!' Thom exclaimed. 'No wonder we're not making any profit.'

'Twenty-third, not the 22nd. Don't exaggerate,' Sophie chided. 'No one likes to work the day before Christmas, but they do like to get a cheque. And I want to be able to distribute *generous* cheques this year. I don't care about profits, or losses, but I don't want LeBoubon or Jayne deciding we're niggardly. You have to treat people the way you'd like to be treated yourself.'

'I'd like to be paid for a week off between Christmas and New Year's,' Thom suggested.

'Oh, shut up,' Sophie replied.

'Where is everyone?' Sophie asked, emerging at last from a tacky souvenir shop after what seemed to Thom an interminable delay.

'The Tour Group Torremolinos?' Thom asked for clarification. 'Or Santa Maria Eleña and her castanets?'

'Both. Either. Where did everyone go?' asked Sophie, taking off her sunglasses, looking puzzled.

'That way,' Thom pointed to a cobblestoned alley leading away from one monolithic façade of the Palace of Charles the Fifth. 'Eleña said they were headed to the Gardens of the

S. M. ELENA DE COMPOSTELA

Generalife. What took you so long?'

'Never mind what took me so long. It's personal. Do I ask you for a report on what you do when you visit the men's room? No. Why didn't you ask the group to wait?' Sophie glared.

'Why didn't I ... what? Yeah, right, no problema there at all. With my limited command of Spanish you expect me to explain discreetly to three dozen turistas and Santa Maria Eleña that my wife is having difficulty with her bowels? I don't think so! Why didn't you hear the damn castanets? You're the one who's always accusing me of being deaf,' Thom protested.

'Leave it,' Sophie came to a fork in the alley. 'Which way?'

Thom paused, looking for a sign, or an arrow.

'We're lost, aren't we?' Sophie decided.

'We're not lost, we're just trying to locate the entrance to the Generalife, which I seem to remember reading somewhere is planted on the side of the Hill of the Sun, on higher ground than the Alhambra, so all's we do is keep walking up and we'll find it. Up is up, and down is down. We'll get there, sooner, maybe later, and once I navigate us close enough, you will hear with your own ears the ubiquitous sound of the castanets of Santa Maria Eleña de Compostela and then all your dreams will come true!'

'Idiot!' Sophie replied. 'Which way?'

'Up,' Thom shrugged.

The Gardens of the Generalife were more extensive and elaborate than Thom had anticipated. Avenues of towering cypress were lined on every side with rivulets of water that appeared and then reappeared, at times animated, other times emptying themselves quietly into the stillness of reflecting pools.

One mirador led immediately to the next or to yet another pavilion or a central fountain or an astonishingly intricate parterre planted in oranges, carpeted in myrtle and edged with boxwood pruned to complex geometric forms.

Roses in profusion competed with jasmine for olfactory dominance and as one fountain began to closely resemble the last, the intricacy of each clepsydra served to remind Thom of the passage of time, and the thought occurred that the cacophony of gentle water sounds mingled with the delighted cries of excited children was effectively masking the sound of Santa Maria Eleña's castanets.

'We're lost, aren't you?' Sophie repeated.

'We are not lost,' Thom insisted. 'I am not lost. You are not lost and we are not lost. Even they,' he added, pointing to group of apparently disoriented and agitated Japanese, 'are not lost.'

'What was the name of the restaurant we're supposed to meet at for tapas?' Sophie persisted.

'La Paloma,' Thom replied, 'but we don't need a taxi, because, as you will have already noticed, there aren't any roads in this garden. We do need to find a gate in the wall, and when we find the gate we will also find the Tour Group Torremolinos, Santa Maria Eleña, her castanets and the one motor coach with the fearless coachman that is about to deliver us to La Paloma for free. Redemption is at hand, and we are *not* going to pay extra for the favour, *por favor!*' Thom completed his rant.

'Which way?' asked Sophie.

Chapter Nine

Hessen Atlantic

'Congratulations!' announced a distant, garbled, and heavily accented mechanical voice.

Sophie looked up at Thom.

'Tape.' He shook his head, negatively. 'Yakushin is either not at home or he's on the other line.'

'Can you leave a message?' Jayne Beauregard whispered. 'Maybe he's in the middle of something. Shovelling snow in his driveway or something?'

Thom straightened his index finger and reared an eyebrow to quiet Jayne. Then he spoke directly into the machine. 'Hi. Alex? This is Thom Penmaen, the printer, calling from Glendaele Village. It's been a while, but I'm hoping you'll remember we worked on a Pixel installation together, about four years ago. The ground fault? The coloured pencils? I'm told you're retired now, but I wondered ... that is ... we seem to have been clobbered by some kind of power event that vaporized a six-thousand-dollar transformer, fried a sizeable Tycor power filter and scrambled a film processor downstream from the Tycor. The one queer thing is that the reflection lamps in the Klimsch camera are toast and yet the fluorescent back-lighting doesn't seem affected in the least.

'I remember you recommended we install some sort of a sophisticated third-level power filtration on our three-phase service some years ago. And I wish in retrospect that I had done just that, of course, but I must confess I've forgotten the specifics of your proposal. Do you accept private consulting work, now that you're done with the workaday world?' Thom couldn't think of much else to say, into the tape. 'Give me a call at 519 837-3686.'

'Well?' Sophie looked at Thom.

'Well, what?' Thom was not forthcoming.

'Can he help us?' Jayne asked.

Thom shrugged. 'Congratulations!' he reiterated, looking from Jayne to Sophie. 'You have reached 383-7666. Consign your message to the machine and I will make a consideration of your plight. This is the voice of Strelnikov speaking.'

'The guy gives me the creeps,' Jayne added.

'Yakushin gives you the creeps, so what?' Thom replied. 'Spiders give you the creeps. Snakes give you the creeps. Yakushin isn't a viper, and he isn't a black widow and he isn't Strelnikov either! Yakushin knows how to fix stuff, and right at the moment we have a lot of charred stuff that needs fixing! Four years ago we hired some yahoo who charged us a fortune in genuine United States pesos for the loan of a Dranetz meter that gave us a tickertape that demonstrated explicitly just how bad the feed from the Glendaele PUC was, at the time. But what am I supposed to do with such a tape, if the Glendaele PUC doesn't deign to address the issue? The creepy Yakushin slithers in with a set of Crayola pencils and reconstructs a schematic of the wiring inside the building that demonstrates there's a leak in the isolated ground, so we plug it. Same junk coming down the pike for juice, but now we've got a steel ground rod sunk eight feet into the Laurentian Shield to redirect the junk. Isolated ground. Yakushin doesn't do high-tech horse manure. He fixes stuff. With coloured pencils. You have a better suggestion?'

'He doesn't wear underarm deodorant,' Jayne sniffed.

'Yakushin is malodorous, I agree with you,' Thom agreed.

'Jayne is right, Thom,' Sophie interrupted. 'Yakushin is weird, you can't deny it. Scary, even. The way he looks at a person.'

'Yakushin asked me a question once, four years ago,' Thom was thinking out loud. 'I didn't understand what he was saying. I asked him to repeat it, and he refused. But of course he refused. I'm just beginning to understand that Yakushin probably wasn't speaking English.'

'Yakushin does speak German,' Sophie confirmed, 'as I remember.'

'I know that. And I also know what German sounds like to the ear, though I can't make sense of it much beyond *der Rauch von der Pfeife in der Abendsonnenschein*,' admitted Thom.

'Pfft. What the hell is that supposed to mean?' scoffed Jayne.

'Not that Hell is exothermic or endothermic.' Thom was strangely distracted. 'It's a line from a poem by Rilke I used to be able to translate in my flaming youth, before I ruined my lungs with pipe tobacco. Yakushin wasn't speaking German.'

'Estonian?' Sophie interrupted.

'Estonian, yeah, maybe. You always said you thought Yakushin was from one of the Baltic states. Maybe Estonia, maybe Latvia. Could be. And I'll grant you that I'm not fluent in either Latvian or Estonian, but I don't think that's what he was speaking either,' Thom concluded. 'It was Russian.'

'What is this? Some sort of rehash of a John le Carré spy thriller?' Jayne Beauregard sneered derisively. '*The Spy Who Came in from the Cold?*'

'"They're about the only ones left who still believe in it all,"' Thom quoted in response to Jayne's challenge, '"the Canadians." Yakushin used to train glider pilots, at the Buttonville Soaring Academy.' Thom started to defend his rationale.

'Gliders?' Sophie was surprised. 'I knew that Yakushin spoke German but I didn't know that he was a pilot.'

'Yakushin told me once, in English, that he learned to fly

gliders in the forties. Of course it never occurred to me to ask him *where* he learned to fly gliders in the forties, and it also never occurred to me to ask him if he learned to fly gliders in the early forties or the late forties, but now that I think of it he did mention that he was in Germany during the war,' Thom continued.

'His accent is *sehr gut*,' Sophie confirmed, which added a shred of legitimacy to Thom's thesis. Jayne Beauregard was buying none of it.

'Oh for Christ ...! Get realistic. What are the pair of you cuckoos planning to do about the inconvenience that Penmaen Lithography does not have an operational darkroom?' asked Jayne. 'I've been taking calls, from Wastrel Editions who would like to remind you the Canada Council deadline for receipt of finished books is December 15!'

'Did Wastrel ever finish paying for the reprint of *Ibo*?' Thom countered. 'Yakushin has a degree in something, maybe electrical engineering, from someplace, maybe the University of Riga, and we know he graduated in the late thirties and we know that he was a young man when he gravitated to Russia, looking for work. Am I doing OK so far?' Thom paused, looking at Jayne.

Jayne admired the sheen on her manicure.

'Thom?' inquired Sophie.

'Yeah, I know, it's a bit of a stretch. But I also know that this Yakushin character was working at A.V. Roe in the early fifties on the most advanced jet fighter of its day in the entire world, and I'm just trying to figure how we get an electrical engineer from Riga in the late thirties somehow or other into Russia. Out of Russia. Into Germany. Out of Germany and into Canada in the early fifties. To work on the aeronautics of the Avro Arrow. This guy,' Thom paused, 'was trained to fly glider planes in Soviet Russia. And that's how he managed to slip *very* quietly one night into Nazi Germany in the early forties.'

'But how did Yakushin get to Canada from Germany after the war?' Sophie was confused.

'Oh, come on!' Jayne was incredulous. 'Sophie, you can't be serious? You believe this cock-and-bull story?'

'Yakushin isn't his real name. Yakushin is a minor character in Dostoevsky, or something. Yakushin is Alexei's *nom de guerre*. Yakushin is a spy.' Thom added slowly, as if he were trying to convince himself, 'Yakushin is KGB.'

'Piss off!' Jayne could not restrain herself. 'More likely Pasternak, than Dostoevsky. *Dr Zhivago*, maybe. Ilya Yakushin was the Man from UNCLE, wasn't he? Or was that Han Solo?' Jayne confronted Thom. 'You actually expect me to believe that we have uncovered a Soviet espionage agent operating in Glendaele Village? Real-ly?' Her pitch rose on the second-last syllable.

'Retired,' Thom corrected Jayne. 'Yakushin's cover surname is Alexei, not Ilya. And it's Yakushin, not Kuryakin, and it wasn't Han Solo, it was Napoleon Solo. Robert Vaughn did a cameo on an early episode of *The Millionaire*. Yakushin speaks fluent Russian, as well as German. Yes, I believe it,' Thom confirmed, 'but I don't ask you to believe, or disbelieve, anything. I'm not selling subscriptions, I'm not canvassing for the CAW, and I'm not pressuring you to take the pledge.'

'You are nuts! Crazy!' Jayne was fairly screaming into Thom's face.

'Yakushin speaks Russian,' Thom continued, 'and Yakushin thinks, for some strange reason, that I do too. That's what he was asking me. That's why Yakushin wouldn't repeat the question when he asked it, four years ago. That also explains why we got exemplary service when we encountered power problems with the Pixel installation. Yakushin couldn't care squat about Penmaen Lithography other than that he thinks Penmaen Lithography is deep cover,' Thom paused. 'Yakushin is KGB, and Yakushin thinks I am, too.'

'I always suspected you were out of your mind.' Jayne struggled to keep her response coherent, 'but I never realized until this very minute that you are certifiable. Are you sure you wouldn't feel more comfortable in subsidized housing in Penetanguishene? Perhaps in a suite with padded walls?'

'You think I think I'm Jimy Williams?' Thom took up Jayne's lead. 'Or do you think I'm George Bell?'

'Maybe Yogi Berra,' Jayne fired back. 'You make about as much sense.'

'It ain't over till it's over.' Thom grinned.

* * *

'So what does the intrepid Alexei Yakushin have to say today?' Jayne asked Thom, some days later. 'About the Klimsch?'

'Intrepid?' Thom furled his eyebrows.

Jayne Beauregard adjusted the strap of her brassière.

'Yakushin exchanged the ignition transformer from the backlighting with the reflection lamps. We can make film in the morning, we're back in business. If Wastrel phones again, tell them to chill out. In the longer term Yakushin thinks maybe he can rewind the defective transformer by hand while we're closed over Christmas if we can't get parts from the States, but he also thinks we've lost a lot of money so maybe we have to pursue the insurance option,' Thom replied. 'I've made some notes.'

Jayne accepted the sheaf of handwritten chicken scratch with some disdain. Jayne Beauregard did not enjoy typing on a terminal any more, or less, than she once enjoyed typing on an IBM Selectric, and she did not appreciate Thom Penmaen presuming to take advantage of her word-processing expertise as if she were some tadpole in the typing pool. Jayne started to peck at keys, reluctantly rather than diligently:

To Whom It May Concern: Pursuant to the Material Loss

suffered at Penmaen Lithography in Glendaele Village on Tuesday, 6 December. Please be advised, as follows,

- Glendaele PUC (the local utility) supplies a nominal 220V 3-wire, 3-phase high-leg Delta service with no neutral. This service is very uncommon in Wellington County, and has been characterized as antiquated, possibly obsolete since the mid-1940s.
- On Monday, 5 December, power delivery was interrupted for several hours in the morning while hydro effected repairs, ostensibly to a transformer on a pole by the Cross Street dam.
- On Tuesday, 6 December, Penmaen suffered a power incident which has subsequently been characterized as 'single-phasing' sometime between 12:00 noon and 1 pm.
- This same event burned two electric motors at Witherspoon's Dairy (downstream on the power grid), and damaged a compressor at Glendaele Jug Milk (upstream), all within the same hour. Witherspoon's Dairy will admit to the incident, but not publicly. The owners of Glendaele Jug Milk are recent arrivals in the village and reluctant to admit to anything.
- The extent of the damage at Penmaen Lithographers, which is still not yet completely repaired, follows.

YEAR   COST   DESCRIPTION

1981 $3,030   NuArc Platemaker FT26V2UP
                 Serial #223L80-22 (23x26)
The platemaker blew two fuses the next time it was powered up. This is not common, & led us to suspect the power board (which has given us problems in the past) may have been damaged. So far this seems not to be the case.

1989 $18,978 Klimsch Super Vertical
                 Graphic Arts camera, C215000YY
Extensive diagnostics by Alexei Yakushin (P. Eng., ret.) has verified that one (of two) ignition transformers is partially cooked. This machine is currently 80 per cent operational and we have

[247]

ordered a replacement part from Chicago for $355.97. If and when the transformer arrives, we still face the expense of installation.

1989 $3,500   Sola (constant voltage transformer,
                to protect camera)
This transformer melted. It has been replaced ($5,375.68, receipt attached). The damaged equipment is currently with Frank Watt (local electrician) for diagnostics.

1989 $1,688   Tycor Power Filter
                (surge protection for Klimsch)
Totally disabled. Returned to manufacturer in Alberta who repaired it, gratis. We paid UPS shipping both ways. This thing weighs forty pounds. The freight was costly.

1992 $9,403   Screen LD-220-QT 91240-1361
                Film Processor
Extensive (eight hours) diagnostics by Alexei Yakushin give us reason to suspect the CPU board. Replacement part ($1,586.54, receipt attached) has arrived but is not yet installed. This machine is currently 80 per cent operational, bypassing the CPU board with an analog thermometer cannibalized from a waterbed.

'You really think you're going to get a dime out of an insurance claim?' Jayne asked, placing the typed document theatrically on Thom's desk.

'I'm not sure I'm making a claim,' Thom replied. 'Sophie started off by asking the local agent for an opinion as to whether damage caused by an incident of single-phasing might be covered under our policy. Maybe yes. Maybe no. So then the adjustor speculates that none of our equipment is covered because a lot of it is over ten years old, and then I hear that the business interruption rider maybe doesn't apply because it wasn't big enough of an interruption, and now I'm talking to some yahoo who thinks our policy just maybe excludes anything that plugs into a plug. So maybe I am starting to wonder just what it is that our coverage does include.'

'Fire?' asked Jayne.

'You might think so, and I certainly would have thought as much until very recently, but it ain't necessarily the case,' Thom reported. 'Sophie had a visitor, the other weekend, an old flame she hasn't seen since high school days at Oakville Trafalgar. I was out, lucky for me. Sophie lit one of those fake Yule logs you buy at Dominion Lumber and offered the guy a Witherspoon's eggnog and Bacardi. Season's greetings.'

'We were talking about fire insurance,' Jayne re-examined the nail polish on her right hand in some detail.

'The fire got crackling, then the study got warm, then the chimney started to roar, and wheeze and snort, and belch and Sophie panicked and called the Glendaele Fire Brigade and who do you suppose led the charge of half a dozen burly guys in hip-waders bearing broad-axes up the stairs to the study?'

'The insurance cowboy?' Jayne didn't get it. Thom, in her considered opinion, knew about as much about the delicate art of flirtation as a novitiate. She flicked at a ducktail.

'Are you kidding? No, of course not! Dirk McTavish!' exclaimed Thom.

Jayne closed her one eye and squinted through the other.

'Dirk McTavish led the assault yelling and hooting at Sophie to get the paper wrapping off the Yuletide log and out of the house because burning fake logs in a woodstove apparently nullifies your insurance policy. Good old Mac the Knife couldn't really have cared less if the building and the shop burned to the ground just so long as Dominion Lumber doesn't get cited in an insurance claim,' Thom explained. 'That's an advantage of living in a small town. The thieves cover for one another.'

★ ★ ★

Jayne Beauregard lit a cigarette. That started it. Right away Philippe LeBoubon was on her case, in her face and, emboldened by a second complimentary digestif after the Penmaen staff Christmas dinner, suddenly eighteen inches closer to her imported French lip gloss than Jayne would once have considered charming.

'So! There it is, then it's true,' Philippe paused, expectantly, staring into Jayne's flared nostrils.

Jayne drew on her Matinee Light, waited for effect, exhaled deliberately, cocked her head a bit to her better side in what Jayne had been assured by any number of men was a passable imitation of Marlene Dietrich at a desirable age, and regarded M. Philippe LeBoubon.

Je regarde, she thought, a curious and undoubtedly dreary individual, but then quickly thought better of it.

Jayne was more than a bit inebriated herself. A quaint joke *en français* might not go over at all well. Jayne recomposed her riposte into English. 'What is it then, that you think is true, M. Philippe?' she asked, drumming the nails of her one free hand on the glass of an adjacent light-table.

'What I am thinking,' Philippe answered, distracted by Jayne's gentle tapping, 'is what Yvette and Lorrie said about you in the summer. Last.'

'That someone said about *moi?*' Jayne could not resist. 'In the heat of the summer? I'm sure I don't remember, anything. Nothing,' she confirmed. 'I must have forgotten, so what of it?'

'That you smoke cigarettes!'

'My dear M. Philippe,' Jayne began, and then paused to roll a slicked ducktail theatrically off her right temple. She straightened her face and fixed LeBoubon with a weary look. Then paused again as if to gauge the effectiveness of the gesture. Jayne wondered what Cleopatra had really thought of Marc Antony. Probably not a great deal. 'I never said that I didn't,' she began, 'smoke.'

'You did. You did too!' Philippe insisted, his face contorted with the righteousness of his allegation.

'Did not!' Jayne spat back, then smoothed the mascara above her right eyebrow with a tissue. The nails of her free hand resumed their tapping.

'Yvette said in the summer that you were smoking cigarettes in the washroom. Yvette said she could smell the sulphur matches before you flushed them down the toilet and poisoned my lung breath and you were saying that you didn't even smoke! Liar. You are a liar —' Philippe struggled to unleash the wrath of an avenging angel, but he was stopped well short of Armageddon by Jayne's quick rejoinder.

'— Yvette's nose may well be bigger than the constraints of her rare and somewhat limited imagination, and *your* imagination, M. Philippe LeBoubon, may be less radiant than Yvette's left nostril....'

'But you said you didn't smoke.' Philippe could not, or would not, let it go.

'I did not, M. Philippe, say that I did not smoke. As I recall I made it abundantly clear at the time that I do not smoke on the job because I choose not to smoke on the job, but I do not, at the present, consider myself to be on the job, so at the present I believe that it is perfectly acceptable that I indulge in some fun. And having fun, M. Philippe, is something that I do!' Jayne Beauregard punctuated the close of her spiel with a puff of Matinee Light directed full at Philippe's face.

Yvette Charbeau waded into the cocktail banter wearing the same poison-green party dress in which she once had hoped to graduate from high school in Kirkland Lake.

'What happened with Yakushin and the camera, in the end?' she asked Thom, awkwardly. Yvette was still not comfortable talking to management.

'The adjustor discovered a subordinate clause in the policy

that says liability for damage caused by electrical arcing is limited to events that originate no more than 150 feet from the fuse panel. Lucky for him the transformer on Cross Street is 153 feet from the pressroom door.'

'What's that got to do with Yakushin?' Yvette was confused. Ten years had passed since Yvette had left high school, and then some, and she had never yet been favoured with an occasion to wear a green satin party dress but she also never once abandoned the idea that maybe, just maybe, someday she would graduate from something. In the meantime nine months' employment at Penmaen Lithography would have to suffice as cause for celebration.

The dress was strapless and a bit tight in the hips, and Yvette hoped ('*mon dieu tabernac*, for sure') that she didn't accidentally drop anything that evening in case she bent over quickly and split the thing stem to stern. The dress itself smelled a bit of mothballs, and the hem was probably half a foot shorter than the latest styles illustrated in the Sears shop-at-home catalogue, but Yvette didn't care much about hem-lengths and the dress did have the one obvious advantage from her reckoning in that it was snug at the top too.

'Yakushin is our only hope,' Thom explained. 'Alexei was here last Sunday, talking to Franklin Watt about power filtration. The printing machines aren't like computers, it's not as if you're trying to clean up the bad power so much as just shut it down, but fast. Yakushin brought with him a three-phase voltage monitor, a couple of industrial-size fuses and a big black hunk of used electromagnet that obviously had been cut roughly out of a previous installation.'

Thom's skill at storytelling attracted the interest of Jayne Beauregard, who had been drinking Sleeman's Pale Ale steadily all evening.

'There were bits of wire, lugs and frayed cable hanging off the thing in all directions,' Thom elaborated. 'Watt asked

Yakushin where he found it and Yakushin said he couldn't remember exactly, but he thought maybe Eastern Europe. From Romania perhaps, or the Ukraine. Franklin Watt was fondling the thing, rolling it over in his two hands, it's pretty heavy, and not listening closely when Yakushin casually mentioned Chernobyl.' Thom snickered.

'I hardly thinks that's an amusement,' Jayne sniffed.

'Yakushin's accent is difficult to follow. For the two or three seconds it took before Watt figured out that he'd been had,' Thom insisted. 'It was pretty funny.'

'Got a light?' Yvette asked Jayne, bending ever so slightly at the waist to give Jayne the fullest possible view of the sort of cleavage Jayne herself could only covet.

'Bitch,' Jayne answered, shrugging at her cowl-necked sweater to expose an extra inch or two of her most arabesque black bra strap.

Philippe LeBoubon brushed his hand lightly across the silken fabric stretched taut between Yvette's twin cheeks.

'Oooh,' Yvette teased him. 'Was that an accident? Or were you looking for something, Philippe?'

LeBoubon flustered easily, and blushed. He tried to pretend that he didn't know what Yvette was talking about. Philippe did not make a great job of it.

'Are you *sure* you don't want to try that again?' Yvette teased Philippe, wiggling her dress a little in the face of his obvious discomfort.

'The two of youse are each *dis*gusting,' Jayne Beauregard decided, drunkenly. 'The both of youse. And I,' her voice tailed off uncertainly as if she wasn't quite sure of what it was she intended to say.... 'And I,' Jayne hit upon a strategy, triumphantly, 'am going to have a pee!'

The telephone rang, several times. Little Lorrie Wright

answered and called across the room to Philippe. 'It's your son, Tomas,' she said. 'Tomas says to tell you that Gérard is afraid of lightning.'

Lightning. Sophie thought the excuse was a bit flimsy, as she looked out the window and watched a few flurries of snow drift down through the light from the streetlamps onto the Main Street.

LeBoubon prepared quickly for his departure.

Almost as if he had been expecting the call. Thom was thinking unChristian thoughts as Sophie handed LeBoubon the envelope with his Christmas cheer. Or maybe the call had been scripted? LeBoubon snatched at the bonus with one hand and handed Sophie something in return.

'Bon soir, Philippe,' Sophie added.

Good riddance, thought Thom.

'Did you hear the one about the little old lady and the Bank of Canada?' Jayne asked Sophie on her return from the business of her recent triumph. Jayne scanned the office. 'What happened to the ever charming M. Philippe LeBoubon?'

'Ah, no. I don't think so,' Sophie answered, more to humour her employee than for any prurient interest in one of Jayne's tales from the Holmewood. 'His son phoned. Tomas said his brother is afraid of lightning. Philippe left. Where did you hear this story then, Jayne?' Sophie reached out to touch her shoulder.

'Don' remember,' Jayne replied, and weaved, and Sophie was starting to think maybe Jayne wasn't coherent enough to carry a plot.

'The lady, the little old lady insisted to speak at the bank guy to open an account because it's a lot of muney!' Jayne tittered.

'Are you sure you're OK, Jayne?' cautioned Thom, who wasn't completely sober himself.

'OK. I'm OK,' Jayne answered, steadying herself. 'I drink beer. I'm OK. You drink beer. You're OK. So the bank guy ask how much she got on her to put it in. The little old lady.'

'You are pissed,' Lorrie Wright sneered. 'Euchred.'

'How much money did the old lady have to deposit?' Thom frowned at Lorrie Wright.

'Sixty-five thousands of bucks! In little bills. The little lady.'

'Where did the little old lady get the $65,000, Jayne?' Thom rolled his eyeballs at Sophie who was about to offer a service of freshly brewed Jamaican high mountain coffee as a means of drawing the evening to an early close.

'That's what the bank guy wants to know. "Where ya gets the muney?"' Jayne nodded. '"Where ya gets the muney?" he ask her and she tells him "I makes bets,"' Jayne swayed on her feet, righted herself like a gyroscope, and plunged forward. '"Bets?" he ask, "What kinda bets you makes?" and right away she betchim twenty-five thousands of bucks his balls are squares. Ha!' Jayne Beauregard hoisted another bottle of the local brew to her lips, and sucked.

'The little old lady wagered the bank manager twenty-five thousand dollars that his balls were square,' Thom repeated, to clarify the central plot device of the anecdote.

'She betchim the little old lady twenty-five thousands his balls are squares, yup.' Jayne drained another slug of Sleeman's Pale Ale. 'Squares. Like the brownies at Witherspoon's. Squares. You know squares?'

'And did the bank manager accept the wager?' Sophie asked, awkwardly.

'Yup, and he says that's a stoopid, and then the little lady asks she bring 'em lawyers and stuff as witness, and he says it. 'Hokay,' Jayne hiccuped.

'So what happened the next day?' Thom was hoping for an early denouement.

'Never mind the morrow. First thing is the night the banker guy is some scared shits about twenty-five thousands and he drops his and he goes full to a mirror and he rolls them around and has a good look, ha! Then the little lady shows up next day with her law guy and the law guy says fair's square and we gotta see what they look to pay up and the bank guy drops 'em and the little lady checks 'em out couple times for records and the law guy is banging his head against the wall.' Jayne paused for air and just one more sip of Sleeman's.

'The little old lady's lawyer is banging *his* head against the wall?' Thom asked for clarification.

'Yah, fer sur.' Jayne's eyes were wide with astonishment as well as alcohol. 'The little lady betchim the law guy too, up on the side. Fifty thousands of bucks up on the side she gets the bank guy by the short hairs, ha! Fifty up. Twenty-five down. Good deal, and the balls for free!'

'The party,' Sophie intervened, 'is over. Say goodnight, Jayne.'

★ ★ ★

'A goose?' Thom repeated, with discernible unease at the prospect. 'Whatever gave you the notion that I eat goose?' Thom asked, pushing his chair back from the dinner table.

'It's traditional,' Sophie replied.

'It is *not* traditional,' Thom insisted. 'It's *Christmas* for Christ's sake. At Christmas at home we ate turkey. With cranberry sauce, sage stuffing, roast potatoes and gravy. Brown gravy, as I recall. What did LeBoubon have to say, in his Christmas card?' Thom may well have stood rightly accused of a limited taste for gourmet foods, but he could articulate what little taste he did have with a certain clarity.

'In Canada you eat turkey. In Königswinter at Christmas when I was a girl I remember my *Oma* always talked about roasting a goose,' Sophie continued, thumbing through the musty pages of an heirloom cookbook, 'with red cabbage and boiled potatoes. And butter. Sometimes sauerkraut, but *nein* ... red cabbage was always the more traditional, more festive!'

'A goose?' Thom could not quite get his tongue wrapped around the idea of an alternative notion of Christmas fowl. 'You would actually consider swallowing one of those things we feed breadcrumbs on the millpond at spring break up?'

'Things? What things?'

'The *geese!*' Thom exclaimed, reaching for an open bottle of Pelee Island red. 'What did LeBoubon have to say in his Christmas card?'

'Those are *Canada* geese, you turkey,' Sophie sighed, 'on the millpond. I'm not talking about *Canada* geese, I'm talking about Christmas geese. Different bird altogether,' Sophie added, with the confidence of a practised amateur ornithologist. 'How does this sound? ... "Prick the skin in numerous places, especially around the throat and wings to allow the fat to drain. Knead the skin gently with the juice of a lemon, a little salt and some pepper. Dust the cavities ..."'

'Let me see that recipe,' Thom insisted, reaching for the cookbook. '"... care must be taken to draw off *all* the excess of fat, and this is easier to be said than to be achieved."' Thom recited, '"Pour out all of the pan drippings and allow to stand at room temperature until the fat has ample time to surface, then skim off as much of the paler fluid as possible. Refrigerate the balance and skim a second time, then add cubed ice to the brown essence and allow the suspended globules of goose fat to affix themselves to the ice." This doesn't sound to you like I won't like this?' Thom asked ironically, his voice rising a note. 'Not at all?'

'*Beleidige Leberwurst!*' Sophie chided, then added '*mein Schatz*', reaching for the cookbook.

'And just what is *that* supposed to mean?' Thom demanded, holding Sophie's heirloom cookbook deliberately half a foot beyond arm's reach.

'It means you sound like a sausage,' Sophie replied, reaching again for the cookbook, 'with its butt out of order. And you're drinking too much wine. How many glasses is it that you've had already tonight?'

'Listen to this, it gets worse,' Thom continued to read from the next page. '"*Schmalz*. Goose fat. Place the solid yellow fat reamed from inside of the carcass in a cast skillet together with the clear liquid accumulated during roasting. Heat slowly until the solid fat liquefies. Add a quartered onion and one small apple, unpeeled. Cook gently until the onion is soft, but not brown. Remove the apple and strain the liquid through a fine mesh sieve. Refrigerate. When firm the *Schmalz* may be spread on dark rye bread in place of butter." Uuugh!' The sensitivity of Thom's delicate palate recoiled in horror. 'What did LeBoubon say in his Christmas card?'

'It wasn't a Christmas card,' Sophie replied.

'You handed him the envelope with his Christmas bonus last night at the party. He handed you a card, in an envelope, I saw it. What did it say?' Thom insisted.

'It wasn't a Christmas card,' Sophie explained, reluctantly. 'He resigned.'

'He resigned effective when?' Thom was incredulous. 'What do you mean he resigned?'

'LeBoubon quit. He's giving you ten days' notice, and he's not coming back in the New Year. How can I explain it to you any more clearly?' asked Sophie.

'You handed the prick an envelope with a seven-hundred-dollar Christmas bonus in it, he took the bonus and quit? Two days before Christmas?' Thom could not believe his ears.

'I didn't want to tell ...' Sophie started, but Thom interrupted.

'Is the bank open Boxing Day? Can we get a stop payment on that cheque?'

'We're not putting a stop payment on that cheque,' Sophie advised.

'Why the hell not?' asked Thom. 'A bonus is an incentive to spur an employee to greater efforts in the future —'

'It wouldn't be right,' Sophie interrupted.

'What do you mean it wouldn't be right?' Thom would not let it go.

'I want to do things right,' Sophie insisted. 'Just because LeBoubon happens to be a jerk doesn't necessarily mean you have to be a jerk too.'

'Jerk?!'

'Give it a break now,' Sophie continued. 'I'm not exactly warm and there isn't any kindling left to light the woodstove. Why don't you give the goose a rest, take your little hatchet outside and do something useful? And don't drink any more wine!' Sophie added.

Thom was breathing hard. The mechanical cuckoo clock in the study announced the top of the hour. Six o'clock. The CBC evening news started up on the radio.

'Oh, and Thom?'

'What now? I don't even have the kindling cut yet.'

'I'm just about done decorating the tree, but I couldn't reach to put the bird at the top.'

'Which bird?' Thom called impatiently from the study, looking at a box of Christmas ornaments.

'The cardinal, the fancy one with the little golden beak, and don't be so crabby all the time. It's Christmas, for God's sake, man, lighten up!'

The stairwell was dimly lit. At the foot of the first flight Thom was startled to come suddenly cheek to jowl with the spectre of Gayle Wicket, her bulbous nose pressed flat against the glass outside the shop door. The shock of seeing a wart on Wicket's face at close range knocked Thom momentarily off his stride on the last step. His arm reached for support and clipped an edge of Paul Fournier's lithograph, which clattered noisily against the wall. Thom tripped, and staggered, and simultaneously broke the fall of the lithograph before the glass in the frame had a chance to shatter. Goddamn poltergeist, he cursed.

'Thom?' Sophie enquired anxiously from the second floor.

'Nothing,' replied Thom. 'I'm all right. It's nothing,' he added, glaring at Gayle Wicket who had retreated not more than a foot from the window and jauntily tossed a fur boa back over her shoulder.

In profile, Wicket appeared to have done herself up in an elaborate masquerade costume Thom assumed was intended to depict one of the archangels. Gabriel, perhaps, to Wicket's mind. Lucifer, in Thom's. Wicket the Gabriel extracted a leather-bound musical score from the recesses of her robes and began to sing the Hallelujah chorus from Handel's *Messiah*, off-key.

Jesus Christ, thought Thom, as he straightened the lithograph of Fournier's hanging dead crow. Season's greetings.

The pressroom was equally dark, but not totally black. There was a glow reflected back through a window off a fresh snowfall as Thom skirted the Baumfolder and the Heidelberg and approached the back door.

Outside, the snow was still falling, but ever so gently. Thick flakes. To the west the sky had cleared. Sirius would normally be a star of the first magnitude not far from the three stars in Orion's belt, but tonight it was close enough to the horizon that it shone with the brightness of a lesser planet.

Thom chose a round of black willow from the tool shed and set about the business of splitting kindling. The willow was detritus left over from the maelstrom in June, but the wood was still not dry to the touch. Thom set himself to the task at his feet, mindful of the distance between his left thumb and the dull blade of the hatchet.

Thom did not hear well, particularly in the upper registers. A host of heavenly cherubim could have passed down the alley from the Main Street and reached the millpond unheralded. Thom most certainly did not hear the electric whine of a radio-controlled vehicle in the alley.

The whine stopped.

'Excuse me,' said a voice that Thom either chose to ignore or didn't hear.

'Sir?' the voice added, insistently.

Thom looked up from the chopping to face a boy, maybe eight years old, maybe ten, standing in the snow at the top of the ramp, looking down. A distance of a dozen feet, maybe not quite. The boy was wearing a blue T-shirt, and short pants — Thom would remember that for a long time, thinking about what had happened, because he recalled noticing the boy's knees and thinking that was odd because there was snow in the air, and looking up again Thom saw there was starlight behind the boy's hair that looked not unlike a fuzzy kind of a halo. It wasn't cold, particularly, not more than a degree or two below freezing. Thom was comfortable in a sweater, but he was working at the chopping and the child was wearing nothing heavier than a T-shirt and short pants. No socks, and the child was not wearing shoes.

'Excuse me, sir,' the child said. 'For the noise I mean. I've just received new treads for my Rover and I wanted to test them straight away. On snow. If you don't mind?'

'No problem,' Thom muttered, wondering what the child was talking about and watching his fingers as the hatchet hived another split of kindling off the chosen stump. Thom was breathing heavily. When he looked up again, the boy was not there.

Thom climbed the half-dozen paces to the top of the ramp and looked down into the snow. The ground was riddled with dozens of tracks that were very likely cut by some sort of radio-controlled something or other, but there weren't any footprints, which was odd because Thom distinctly remembered that the child was not wearing shoes.

Thom was puzzled, and his right arm felt numb.

There was snow. And there were tracks in the snow.

But there was no boy.

And there were no footprints.

That was the thing. Not that the child was strange, though the child was surely better mannered than any child Thom had ever met previously in Glendaele Village and that in itself might be considered a departure from the ordinary. And something about the child's diction was peculiar, as if the boy's English were being translated mechanically from some alien tongue just seconds before the words spilled from his lips, but the thing about it was that there were no footprints.

Thom retraced his steps slowly, past the Baumfolder and up the stairs to the second floor, carrying a dull hatchet and half a box of split kindling that felt a good twenty pounds heavier than it looked. There was feeling, in his arm, but the limb tingled.

Sophie was sitting by the Christmas tree, reading a newspaper. 'Did you notice,' she began, and then left off just as abruptly. 'Good God, Thom, you look like you've seen a ghost!' She was jesting, of course, but Thom did not look well at all, and Sophie was correct in her assessment that his face had taken on the pallid sheen of a cadaver.

'I,' Thom struggled to push oxygen through his larynx but the attempt surfaced as an incomprehensible gurgle. His right hand began to twitch, and then tremble.

Thom stood, as if rooted to a spot at the top of the staircase, leaning on the banister. He put down the box of wood, slowly, and straightened, but his hand was shaking visibly and there were little beads of sweat forming just below his hairline. 'I don't actually feel all that great,' Thom admitted. 'I think I better sit down for a bit.'

Sophie took hold of Thom's hand, which was shaking uncontrollably, and forcefully, and led him to the sofa. His skin temperature was chill to the touch and there was water under his eyelids.

'Talk to me. Say something,' Sophie was starting to register concern. 'What happened out there?'

'Nothing. I'm OK. I drink beer,' Thom tried to make light of the situation. 'Do you drink beer?'

'That isn't funny,' Sophie replied. 'Not funny at all.'

'Wicket startled me. She was peering in the front door, and then she backed off a bit and started singing the *Messiah*, of all bloody things,' Thom explained. 'She was wearing a costume. Angel wings.' Thom's voice trailed off. His breathing was laboured and Sophie could see the pressure of the blood pumping through the veins in his neck. 'And there was. In the alley. A boy.' Thom started talking again but his voice was thin and his eyes glazed as if he were *thinking* about saying something more than actually saying it.

'A what?' Sophie was incredulous. 'It's snowing out there!'

'It is snowing, yes.' Thom began to evaluate Sophie's realistic assessment of the situation. 'And there was a child, a boy, and he said something. I didn't hear him, or the car, at first, but then he spoke and I looked up and there he was....' Thom's voice drifted like a ventriloquist's across the room.

'There was a boy ...' Sophie repeated slowly. 'There was a boy, Thom, and what did the boy say to you?'

'The boy,' Thom stopped. 'The boy said: "Excuse me, sir."

The boy said, "I hope I'm not disturbing you, with my Rover." I looked up.' Thom's voice dropped lower and his gaze fixed on the empty woodstove. 'The boy was wearing short pants and a T-shirt. The boy was standing at the top of the ramp holding his Rover in the one hand and some sort of radio gizmo with a long antenna in the other....'

'And?' Sophie could not begin to plumb the nature or the depth of Thom's discomfort, or of her own. Sophie thought she was afraid, but she wasn't sure why she was afraid.

'... then the boy wasn't there,' Thom finished.

'The boy wasn't there?' Sophie was confused, that was it. She was confused, maybe, more than fearful.

'The boy,' Thom continued, 'was barefoot. The boy was wearing short pants and a T-shirt. I remember I could see his knees, and he wasn't wearing any shoes. I walked up the ramp, and I looked down at the snow, and there weren't any footprints. That's the problem. It's like the boy was never there.'

* * *

Three days later, Christmas and the last of the turkey salad was done. Thom opened the *Globe and Mail* at breakfast and there it was, the second article on page 2 of the Business Section.

ALDEBAAN, HESSEN, SET TO JOIN FORCES
IN ELABORATE STOCK EXCHANGE

One-time stockbroker Galen Nicholas Aldebaan, long noted for the filigree complexity of his deal-making, announced late last week that he is joining forces with the managers at Hessen Atlantic in an exchange of paper that will diminish neither party's faculty for obfuscation.

'Heads up,' Thom exclaimed. 'Here it comes.'

'What?' asked Sophie. 'Now what are you nattering about? Ever since the shop closed before Christmas you make even less sense than usual, which isn't, if you must know, a great deal to begin with. Are you quite certain you feel all right?'

'I'm talking about what is past, what is pissing and maybe even a little bit about what is yet to come,' Thom intoned. He re-read the first paragraph of the piece aloud for Sophie's benefit, then continued.

Mr Aldebaan holds a controlling stake in the Toronto-based Pegaesean Corporation Ltd., a merchant banker that just this past summer puzzled Bay Street with the unexpected purchase of Duckworth & Osborne, Labellarte, the distinguished but profit-challenged literary publishing house. Hessen Atlantic is controlled by the brothers Mandrake, heirs to the Oceanic fortune, whose role at Hessen has been likened to that of royalty – inasmuch as they enjoy unlimited power, so long as they choose never to exercise it in contravention of the advice of their managers, who manipulate the strings of influence.

'Uh, oh. I wonder what that does to D&OL,' Sophie interjected.

'Hessen is into mining, bauxite in Brazil, forest products, financial services and beer,' explained Thom. 'I would imagine that William Duckworth is going to have a time of it trying to convince the lords and ladies at Hessen that literary publishing in Canada cannot reasonably be expected to contribute much to their average return on investment of 30 per cent a year. Ha! Thirty per cent? Duckworth is going to be pressed to within a centimetre of his kidneys to explain why he can't do better than 3 percent,' Thom replied. 'Six months, I'll bet, and Duckworth's neck swings from a yardarm overlooking Bay and Richmond.'

Stripped of a wealth of its intricacies, the deal gives Aldebaan a seat on the board of Hessen, and the chair of its executive committee. He also receives one million newly minted common shares – a one percent voting interest with a market value of about $28 million, in return for which, Hessen takes a 50 percent voting interest in Aldebaan's private holding company Maple Leaf Investment which owns the controlling block of Pegaesean class B special voting stock. Hessen also gets all of the non-voting preferred shares of Maple Leaf Investment with a par value of $28 million.

Hessen president Jake Wellcock committed his firm ...

'Jake Wellcock!' Thom interrupted his own reading. 'Remember him?'

'Ah, no,' Sophie admitted. 'Should I? Wellcock?'

'At school. Remember we used to watch the Blues play hockey at Varsity Arena on Friday nights?'

'Vaguely. It was twenty years ago.'

'Jake Wellcock played defence for the University of Toronto Blues. He was good, too,' Thom admitted. 'Wellcock could play hockey.'

'And you think this is the same guy?'

'I'm not thinking, I'm sure it's the same guy. But listen to this ...' Thom continued.

Hessen Atlantic president Jake Wellcock committed his firm to an early evaluation of the Pegaesean maze of shareholdings.

'We're going to go in and we're going to write a business plan for every piece. Separately. We may, or we may not make changes in the coming year.'

Speculation on the street suggests this latest boondoggle may have been triggered by boardroom tension at Pegaesean operating subsidiary Springfield, Incorporated and by personal animosity between Springfield co-founder Oliver Blakeley and Hessen Atlantic president Jake Wellcock.

'Apart from Blakeley, and Springfield, he's talking about D&OL, isn't he? Wellcock is talking in code about Will Duckworth and Rebeca Labellarte,' Sophie speculated.

'Maybe,' Thom answered. 'Maybe even probably, but the good news is that Wellcock is *not* talking about Thom and Sophie Penmaen!'

'Of course not! What would Hessen Atlantic want with a piddling little printing company in Glendaele Village? Honestly, Thom, sometimes you suffer these delusions of grandeur that lead me to question whether you're quite firmly attached to the planet.'

'Yada, yada, yada, but the thing is,' Thom replied, 'if I were Will Duckworth this morning, and I had just sat down to read the *Globe* and contemplate the immediate future of this monument I'd built to my own magnificence, I'll bet I'd rather be Thom Penmaen, from Glendaele Village, and I'll also bet I'd wish I'd never heard of Geoffrey Bowles, Pegaesean or Galen Nicholas Aldebaan.'

'For Galen,' Wellcock explained, in response to a question from an analyst, 'what he gets is diversification into the Hessen group of companies – real estate, natural resources, personal entertainment, that sort of thing. Not that I'm suggesting Galen needs help, of course, I just mean the management depth of Hessen Atlantic. We think we can help him. We also think he can help us.'

★ ★ ★

'Is that Geoffrey Bowles?' Thom spoke into the receiver.

'Speaking.'

'This is Thom Penmaen. Penmaen Lithography. You remember me? Thom the printer, from Glendaele Village?'

'Thom! One of half a dozen key people I've been trying desperately to avoid for weeks. How are you?'

'Still in business. Beyond that, I'm not so sure. You tell me.

Do you have a minute? Do you have an hour? Did you read the *Globe* this morning?' asked Thom.

'I did.'

'And?'

'And I don't really know what to tell you because I don't know much beyond what you've doubtless read already. "Hessen president Jake Wellcock committed his firm to an evaluation of the Pegaesean maze of interlocking shareholdings",' Geoffrey Bowles quoted from the *Globe*. 'What is that supposed to mean? I wouldn't have a clue. I've got a call in to Aldebaan but he's either at his place in Bermuda or he's on his yacht somewhere between Hamilton Harbour and the Bay of Fundy and all I know for sure at this point is that Nicholas came to me in October, just after Thanksgiving, and said to hold fire because there might be a dinger of a deal going down....'

'You've known about this thing since Thanksgiving? And it never occurred to you to give us a call? Cut us into the loop? Something? Nothing?' Thom raised his voice.

'No. No. No. I didn't know anything, not really. Aldebaan just told me to back off, that everything was on hold. Nothing more than that. Of course I couldn't phone, because I didn't have anything to tell you,' Bowles squirmed.

'The *Globe* says that Aldebaan gets the chair of the executive committee at Hessen,' Thom continued.

'I read that, that's what the report said, yes.' Bowles was not giving anything away for free.

'So the part that I don't understand is why does Aldebaan all of a sudden decide he wants a job?' asked Thom.

'Good question. Maybe he's bored, I really couldn't begin to speculate,' admitted Bowles.

'A job. Aldebaan decides out of the blue he wants a job, of all unlikely things, and that's it. The deal's off. And now it's over?' Thom could not quite accept that the clarification he was seeking was also the one thing he didn't want to hear.

'I'll know better when Aldebaan returns my call, *if* Aldebaan returns my call, but for the moment it looks to me like the shark just got swallowed by a whale!' Bowles concluded the exchange.

Thom cradled the receiver and turned to face Sophie.

'It's over?' she asked. 'That's what he said, right? Thom? Talk to me.'

'Bowles said he doesn't really know. It seems that way. Bowles is out in left field, and Aldebaan is either in Bermuda or he's on his yacht somewhere in the Gulf Stream trolling for mackerel,' Thom answered. 'It looks to Bowles like the shark just got swallowed by a whale.'

'A whale? What about Majorca? Our hopes? Our dreams?' Sophie was incredulous. 'Now we're right back where we started.'

'Not really,' Thom replied. 'Baseball season is over. Kirk Gibson won it for the Dodgers but Orel Hershiser was named Series MVP. Duckworth was right. Good pitching beats good hitting two times out of three.'

'So, smartass,' Sophie continued, after a long pause. 'What are we supposed to do now?'

BOB HOUSSER

Grant Robinson was born and educated in Guelph, Ontario, where he earned his degree in Chartered Accounting (CA) in 1976. A year in Bermuda under the auspices of Morris and Kempe convinced Grant and his doubles partner, Sheila, that Wellington County was actually a better place to raise a family than they had realized, just as the young couple's one attempt to grow forty acres of corn convinced them of the utter necessity of crop insurance.

Grant Robinson is a partner in Robinson Management Consultants Ltd., a consulting group focused on the facilitated development and succession of family-owned businesses. Grant is active within the community and was awarded a Fellowship of the Ontario Institute of Chartered Accountants (FCA) in 1991. He has two children, Jason and Danielle. *Great Expectations* is his first book-length publication.